American History Through Literature

JOHN RANDOLPH

American History Through Literature

Paul Finkelman
Series Editor

FREEDOM ROAD
Howard Fast
Introduction by Eric Foner

JOHN RANDOLPH
Henry Adams
Introduction by Robert McColley

THE LIFE OF WASHINGTON
Mason L. Weems
Introduction by Peter S. Onuf

JOHN RANDOLPH

a biography by

HENRY ADAMS

A new edition with
primary documents
and introduction
by ROBERT
McCOLLEY

M.E. Sharpe
Armonk, New York
London, England

Library of Congress Cataloging-in-Publication Data

Adams, Henry, 1838–1918.
John Randolph / Henry Adams :
a new edition with primary documents and introduction by Robert McColley.
p.   cm. — (American history through literature)
Includes bibliographical references and index.
ISBN 1-56324-652-X (alk. paper). — ISBN 1-56324-653-8 (pbk. : alk. paper)
1. Randolph, John, 1773–1833.
2. United States—Politics and government—1783–1865.
3. Legislators—United States—Biography.
4. United States. Congress. House—Biography.
I. McColley, Robert.
II. Title.
III. Series.
E302.6.R2A64   1996
328.73′092—dc20
[B]
95-33361
CIP

Printed in the United States of America

The paper used in this publication meets the minimum requirements of
American National Standard for Information Sciences—
Permanence of Paper for Printed Library Materials,
ANSI Z 39.48-1984.

MV (c)   10   9   8   7   6   5   4   3   2   1
MV (p)   10   9   8   7   6   5   4   3   2   1

Contents

JOHN RANDOLPH
by Henry Adams

Foreword

Novelists, poets, and essayists often use history to illuminate their understanding of human interaction. At times these works also illuminate our history. They also help us better understand how people in different times and places thought about their own world. Popular novels are themselves artifacts of history.

This series is designed to bring back into print works of literature—in the broadest sense of the term—that illuminate our understanding of U.S. history. Each book is introduced by a major scholar, who places the book in a context, and also offers some guidance to reading the book as "history." The editor will show us where the author of the book has been in error, as well as where the author is accurate. Each reprinted work also includes a few documents to illustrate the historical setting of the work itself.

Books in this series will primarily fall into three categories. First, we will reprint works of "historical fiction"—books that are essentially works of history in a fictional setting. Rather than simply fiction about the past, each will be first-rate history presented through the voices of fictional characters, or through fictional presentations of real characters in ways that do not distort the historical record. Second, we will reprint works of fiction, poetry, and other forms of literature that are primary sources of the era in which they were written. Finally, we will republish nonfiction such as autobiographies, reminiscences, essays, and journalistic exposés, and even works of history that also fall into the general category of literature.

PAUL FINKELMAN

ix

Acknowledgments

Thanks are due Paul Finkelman and Michael Weber, who encouraged me to prepare this new edition of Henry Adams's *John Randolph*. Paul has subsequently offered several valuable suggestions for making the introduction more coherent. At M.E. Sharpe, Peter Coveney and Eileen Gaffney have facilitated the completion of the project, and Susan Burke has edited out several errors and further smoothed the prose. I should also thank my early mentors, who bear some responsibility for my becoming a professional historian: Arthur M. Schlesinger, Jr., who introduced me to several important themes in American history during my undergraduate years, and later suggested that I write about Adams's *Randolph;* and Kenneth M. Stampp, who directed my doctoral studies at California, Berkeley, and encouraged my studies of the South in the early national period. None of the above are responsible in any way for the further eccentricities I have introduced in this edition of a singular American's biography of another singular American.

ROBERT MCCOLLEY

Introduction

Historians of the United States during the era from 1801 to 1829—from the inauguration of President Thomas Jefferson to the inauguration of President Andrew Jackson—have especially quoted two political characters, each immensely talented for his stringent, acerbic, satiric, and, more often than not, critically cutting comments. On the one hand we have John Quincy Adams (1767–1848); stern, laborious, plainspoken, disciplined, and always the servant of both his own tightly harnessed ambition and an increasingly expansive view of the possibilities of American civilization. John Quincy Adams's sense of propriety prevented his entering into the public record the trenchant views, "written with a pen dipped in acid," that make his *Diary* (published after his death by his descendants) such fascinating reading.

The other wonderfully incisive critic of the era was John Randolph of Roanoke (1773–1833), who sooner or later turned against every president from John Adams to Andrew Jackson. Most history students today have forgotten that Randolph coined the term "War Hawks" for the young congressmen, led by Henry Clay, who took over the House of Representatives in 1811 and pressured James Madison toward his war message in June, 1812; Randolph also ridiculed these birds for their constant song, "Canada, Canada, Canada." Years later he pushed even the easygoing but proud Henry Clay too far by describing him as a "being, so brilliant yet so corrupt, which, like a rotten mackerel by moonlight, shined and stunk." Randolph further denounced the political alliance of then-Secretary of State Clay with President John Quincy Adams as "the coalition of Blifil and Black George . . . the combination, unheard of till then, of the Puritan with the blackleg." For the unforgettable dead-fish metaphor and the telling comparison with two unsavory characters in Henry Fielding's *Tom Jones,* Clay challenged Ran-

1

dolph to a duel (Adams, *Randolph* pp. 188–89). As Henry Adams notes (p. 188), the two exchanged fire on April 8, 1826. Both of Clay's shots narrowly missed Randolph at hip level; Randolph's first missed Clay below the knee, and his second went harmlessly into the air. Adams does not report that Randolph had confided before the duel that under no circumstances could he aim to kill Clay, upon whom a wife and children depended, nor does he cite the judgment of Thomas Hart Benton, no stranger to such affairs, but present as a peace-maker: "It was about the last high-toned duel that I have witnessed, and among the highest toned I have ever witnessed, and so happily conducted to a fortunate issue,—a result due to the noble character of the seconds as well as to the generous and heroic spirit of the principals" (*Thirty Years' View* [New York, 1854], vol. 1, p. 77).

These, and the great majority of Randolph's famous sayings, originated in public speeches, invariably as momentary flashes of inspiration—some would say diabolical possession—and therefore instantly noted, widely quoted, and often distorted by the press and word of mouth. A regular and stylish correspondent, Randolph was rarely as outspoken in private letters as he was in public, a strange reversal for a man of his or any era. As Henry Adams forcefully relates, Randolph broke with President Thomas Jefferson in the congressional sessions of 1805–1806, and was never again the member of any working majority in national politics. His function was to find fault with virtually every major initiative pursued by presidential administrations and congressional majorities for the rest of his life. Old John Adams and young John Quincy Adams were Randolph's lifelong foes. He referred to them as "the American House of Stuart"; in the then-familiar Whig-Republican view of politics, the Stuarts signified the repellent doctrine of monarchy by divine right. Furthermore, Randolph perceived that John Quincy was both abler and more dangerous than his father: "the cub is a greater bear than the old one." If ever the House of Adams had an inveterate and implacable enemy, it was the reactionary Virginian, John Randolph. One is somewhat surprised, therefore, that in 1881 John T. Morse Jr., editor of Houghton Mifflin's American Statesmen Series, chose Henry Adams to contribute a biography of John Randolph. Would Henry Adams bend over backwards to be fair and kind to his family's old nemesis? Hardly.

Any honest critic of Henry Adams's 1882 biography of

John Randolph of Roanoke must argue paradoxically that the book is both immensely valuable and shamefully bad at the same time. Nor will it do to seek some moderated position between these extremes; the book is a rare specimen of a historical biography written with brilliant style and powerful thought, which nevertheless pervasively, even systematically, distorts and misrepresents people and events. It is not simply that, unlike most biographers, Henry Adams begins with a strong animus against his subject, and then hammers it home for most of two hundred pages. So robust and reckless is his spite that he makes no effort at all to conceal it; the book in an odd way is honest in its spite. But Adams especially overuses the *argumentum ad hominem;* that is, he invariably imputes the worst possible motives for his subject's (or perhaps one should say his victim's) every action and attitude, whether good or bad. The observant reader will further note that hardly any other characters are permitted to stand forth as admirable in this extraordinary volume; major characters, especially Presidents Jefferson, Madison, and Monroe, are left relatively defenseless, and minor ones such as the Smiths of Maryland and the Clintons of New York are attacked as savagely by Adams as anyone was ever attacked by Randolph of Roanoke. See, for example, p. 142, where Adams mentions "De Witt Clinton, most selfish, unscrupulous, and unsafe of democrats." Adams judges Randolph and everyone else under austere and abstract standards of political behavior—honesty, honor, integrity, and complete freedom from personal interest—which he assumes his reader shares, yet he rarely informs us of the specific ways in which these lesser characters have failed to measure up.

Nor indeed does Adams specifically indict John Randolph with political or financial wrongdoing until, in the latter part of the book, he justly condemns his protagonist for making the defense of slavery the center of his conservative politics. Indeed, with respect to the long agitation over the Yazoo land question, Adams explains both the issue itself and its constitutional significance, and gives more credit and credibility to the states' rights position taken by Randolph than to the nationalistic one supported by Madison and blessed by Chief Justice John Marshall in the case of *Fletcher v. Peck* (1811). From Randolph's first public embarrassment, in failing to convict and remove Associate Justice Samuel Chase from the Supreme Court, through his strict constructionist's opposition to the chartering of John C. Calhoun's Second Bank of the United

States, Henry Adams is continually in the strange attitude of finding considerable merit in Randolph's positions, yet condemning him for taking those positions for bad or frivolous reasons.

Henry Adams is also at fault for omitting facts about Randolph's personal life and character that would balance if not soften the picture of misanthropy and gloom so deftly painted here. Fortunately, John Randolph has had his ample share of sympathetic biographers, most notably Virginians Hugh Garland in 1850 and William Cabell Bruce in 1922. Later this introduction will consider some of the more attractive characteristics of Randolph of Roanoke that his fellow Virginians discuss in rich detail.

Now, however, one must defend the judgment that Adams's *Randolph* is, with all its faults, an exceptionally important and compelling study. The distilled bitterness of four generations of political Adamses itself must surely have contributed to the author's viewing the early years of the Republic, as he viewed the United States in the Gilded Age, with apprehension bordering on alarm. He begins, disarmingly, by endorsing the principles of the Jeffersonians, perfected as arch foes of his great-grandfather in the last years of the eighteenth century. The nation was then distracted by the Quasi-War with France and the exaggeratedly characterized "Federalist Reign of Terror." Arbitrarily but convincingly, Adams identifies the original Jeffersonian insistence on both strict construction and states' rights with honesty, economy, and the preservation of individual liberties under the Constitution of 1787. He then demonstrates, convincingly enough here, and with relentless detail in his later nine-volume work, that as soon as the Jeffersonian Republicans took office, they began to trample not merely on the Federalist minority, but on their own principles. Even Randolph's brief years as part of a successful and effective majority are rendered as moral dust by Adams. In that happy time, virtually coincident with Jefferson's first term in office, Randolph supported virtually every measure of the administration, including, in Henry Adams's provocative view, the constitutional enormity of the Louisiana Purchase.

During Jefferson's second term, Randolph went into full opposition as the administration abandoned whatever pretense remained of maintaining what Randolph called the Principles of '98. Under the guise of their constitutional authority to regulate trade and foreign relations, the Jeffersonians passed a draconian law, the Embargo, which made it a crime for citizens to sell their goods to foreign buyers, and, more astonishing still, made it a crime for Americans to sail their ships in international waters. It is important to see that both Henry Adams and John Randolph knew the administration had just complaints with Britain and France. Those imperial antagonists had caused a crisis by their attacks on neutral traders. What both protested was the fatally easy assumption by any party in power that it might twist, bend, or stretch the Constitution of the United States to justify any course of action that might seem useful at the time. Henry Adams did not exactly use Lord Acton's famous dictum, but he certainly meant it: "Power corrupts, and absolute power corrupts absolutely."

Important as this insight and analysis by Henry Adams was, perhaps its related sequel was still more illuminating and alarming. When Randolph of Roanoke returned to Congress after the War of 1812, he found an administration more bent than ever on consolidation and, as it seemed to him, unconstitutional assumptions of powers by the federal government. But most of all, Randolph discerned a rising tide of feeling in the northern states for gradually eliminating slavery by restricting its expansion, and promoting schemes for gradual emancipation and colonization. Henry Adams drives the point home over and over again: Randolph taught the "slave power" to use the once pristine doctrines of strict construction and states' rights as instruments for defending slavery, thereby hopelessly corrupting and perverting those doctrines.

More precisely still, Adams left the writers and interpreters of United States history with an unforgettable scene in their minds: John Randolph, prematurely aged, incurably diseased, and always skirting the boundaries of reason, haranguing an empty Senate chamber where, nevertheless, the powerfully dogmatic thinker from South Carolina, John C. Calhoun, vice president of the United States and president of the Senate, listened attentively. Randolph there (in Henry Adams's haunting picture) converted Calhoun from ardent nationalist to premier defender of his own state, the Old South, and its Peculiar Institution.

Obviously, the slaveholders of the Old South would have found—indeed, did find—other minds to prove and other voices to proclaim their exalted ideas of the sanctity of human property and the obligation of all the United States to protect that property forever. Indeed, Calhoun was certainly responding to pressure from his own constituents more than to inspiration from John Randolph when he composed his epoch-making South Carolina Exposition in response to the Tariff of Abominations of 1828. Nevertheless, the record is tolerably clear that the South's earliest, most insistent, and most uncompromising voice in defense of slavery was Randolph's.

Adams hints, but does not say outright, that a "slave power" had already existed, self-consciously, as one of the groups responsible for the election of Jefferson, Madison, and Monroe, and for their bold if not reckless expansionist policies. He does explicitly credit the "slave power" with defeating John Quincy Adams and Henry Clay in the elections of 1828 and 1832, thereby placing Andrew Jackson and John C. Calhoun in the same group. They were, indeed, slaveholders, but they also fell out so fully during Jackson's first four years in office that the two became even greater enemies than Jackson and Clay, or Jackson and John Quincy Adams had been. If President Jackson talked more boldly than he acted in the Nullification Crisis of 1832–33, he nevertheless acted boldly enough to drive the dying Randolph into opposition yet again. Furthermore, when Randolph was no longer on the scene to comment, President Jackson pointedly declined to use his influence in behalf of annexing Texas, hardly the behavior of a self-conscious representative of the "slave power"! But this distinction qualifies without reversing Adams's major theme: that representatives of the slaveholding states became increasingly self-conscious in defending slavery from 1819 onward, and John Randolph was their prophet.

Some readers might be puzzled that this introduction has raised so little complaint about the highly negative views projected by both the biographer and his subject of United States history from 1801 to 1833 and beyond. Were not Thomas Jefferson, James Madison, and James Monroe all distinguished Founding Fathers? And, despite the failure of his four-year presidency to achieve his own grand objects, had not John Quincy Adams been an effective and patriotic diplomat as well as, so many have argued, our greatest secretary of state? Did not the United States, during John Randolph's life, grow triumphantly, spreading its republican institutions from the Atlantic to the Mississippi and beyond? Were not its faults (slavery, and the driving of Native Americans from their ancestral lands) only typical of mankind through the ages, while its virtues promised a degree of freedom, equality, and prosperity previously unheard of? And, however we might wish in retrospect that the Founding Fathers had somehow found the wisdom and courage to add the emancipating of all African Americans to their great accomplishments, was it not an altogether different set of actors who caused the nation's foremost and unparalleled catastrophe, the Civil War?

The questions are, of course, rhetorical: one cannot expect a balanced, mainstream view of Jeffersonian America in Adams's *Randolph*. But one may get something quite valuable because all too rare in United States history: a serious and informed negative view of our historical development. Such a view can hardly be true in the sense that a matter-of-fact statement can be true—for example, that the construction of railroad and telegraph networks transformed the way Americans did business in the nineteenth century. But from the first great national history by George Bancroft down to the special-interest histories and herstories of the 1990s, most American historical writing has been dominated by celebration, apology, and advocacy. As greatly and deeply as Henry Adams disliked John Randolph of Roanoke, he had, almost in spite of himself, a deep bond of sympathy. Both were morally and culturally cut off from the booster-dominated, progressive, materialistic mainstream of United States culture. American aristocrats by birth, education, and wealth, both were insiders turned outsiders.

Henry Brooks Adams (1838–1918) represented, along with his three brothers, the fourth generation of a family uniquely persistent both for its successes and failures in American politics and culture. Educated at Harvard and in Germany, he served in his twenties as secretary to his father, Charles Francis Adams, U.S. ambassador to Great Britain during the American Civil War. Unable to remain in federal service and prominent in the liberal Republican opposition to President Grant in 1872, Henry Adams settled for a time in Boston and Cambridge, where he introduced the graduate study of history at Harvard and edited the *North American Review*. He then moved with his wife, Marian, to Washington, D.C., to pursue his research and writing while also maintaining an intellectual and political salon at the seat of national power. A pioneer in teaching and writing the history of the United States according to the then-highest standards of European "scientific history," his most notable achievement in this field was his enormously detailed, nine-volume *History of the United States during the Jefferson and Madison Administrations* (1889–91). His most enduring and frequently read books were his last ones: *Mont-*

Saint-Michel and Chartres (1904), a meditation on medieval history, and the partly confessional, heavily ironic *Education of Henry Adams* (privately printed, 1907). In 1919, the year after Henry Adams died, a younger brother, Brooks Adams, published two late, strange essays by Henry on the meaning of history, *The Degradation of the Democratic Dogma*, with a long introduction by Brooks.

Personal tragedy and a sort of alienation from American life overwhelmed Adams in his later years; in retrospect, one can perhaps see a sort of uncanny foreshadowing of the pessimism of those years in the unrelieved gloom of his *John Randolph.* The personal tragedy was the suicide of Marian Adams in 1885; childless and a widower, Henry Adams never remarried, and spent many of the next twenty years traveling around the world. More than his ancestors or his brothers, he also took up the quarrel of the Adams family with the United States, history in general, and the universe. Yet at the time Henry Adams wrote *Randolph* and saw it through the press (1881–82), his life was and had been, by any reasonable standards, a brilliant success.

Brooks Adams squarely addressed the issue that Henry Adams treated obliquely in his *John Randolph:* in the free, open, and well-advertised election of 1828, the people of the United States chose an irascible, semi-educated frontier lawyer and military hero in preference to the candidate who was, demonstrably, more experienced and more informed with respect to the life, arts, and policies of nations than any American president before or since. The choice of Jackson over John Quincy Adams was alone enough to disprove the virtue of democracy. And yet the Adams family continued to play a major part in the nation's democratic politics.

To some degree Henry Adams's writings on the early national period are a running defense of the positions John Quincy Adams took, from his youthful support of his father in the 1790s through his largely failed presidency, which ended March 4, 1829. That defense of John Quincy Adams was considerably easier in *John Randolph* than in the nine-volume *History,* where the enormous scale of his treatment required minute inspection of the issues and the positions on them taken by particular statesmen. Briefly, the problem was this: recalled from a diplomatic sinecure in Germany by his father after the Federalists had lost the election of 1800, John Quincy Adams soon returned to Congress as one of two Federalist senators from Massachusetts. In 1807–8, however, he disagreed with both the other senator, Timothy Pickering, and the Massachusetts legislature by supporting President Jefferson's Embargo, and resigned his seat. In effect, John Quincy Adams switched parties, and was soon rewarded with a series of diplomatic appointments far more important than Washington and Adams had given him in his fledgling years. He was one of five United States diplomats to negotiate the Treaty of Ghent, which ended the War of 1812. On the one hand, Henry Adams could and did make a strong if low-keyed case for the political course followed by his illustrious grandfather; on the other, he nevertheless strongly disapproved of most of Jefferson and Madison's actions. Furthermore, he disapproved still more strongly of the increasingly conservative Federalists of New England who, in addition to opposing Jefferson's actions, particularly hated John Quincy Adams for deserting them.

It is a tribute to the skill of Henry Adams, and of course to the brilliant self-justification of John Quincy Adams in his inimitable *Diary,* that Henry could succeed as well as he did in making the policies of Jefferson and Madison seem so often shortsighted and ill-judged, while John Quincy's support of them seemed statesmanlike and judicious. In the biography of John Randolph, however, Henry Adams finessed most of the problem by simply omitting the political history of the years 1811–12, depriving his readers of Randolph's principled, consistent, and eloquent (as it seems to this writer) opposition to the nation's drift toward war, and then the declaration of war itself. Henry Adams passes over all this laconically with a single sentence: "In 1813, however, his [Randolph's] opposition to the war with England proved too heavy a weight to carry, and Mr. [John W., son-in-law of Thomas Jefferson] Eppes, after a sharp contest, defeated him, while the 'Richmond Enquirer' denounced him as 'a nuisance and a curse' " (p. 164). Somewhat to redress Henry Adams's neglect of the matter, this volume includes substantial excerpts from one of Randolph's speeches opposing preparations for the War of 1812. As for Randolph's view of John Quincy Adams, we have already noted that the two were contemporaries, born within six years of each other, and were in almost continuous opposition, often of a highly heated kind, for thirty-five years.

At this point it is appropriate to notice several things about John Randolph either omitted altogether or only briefly mentioned in Henry Adams's biography. It is probably more acceptable now than in 1882 to define those personal and family tragedies that blighted Randolph's life. One of these was a family scandal for which John Randolph bore no primary responsibility. The characters immediately involved, and the only ones who knew precisely what had happened, were John Randolph's older brother, Richard, his wife, Judith, and her sixteen-year-old sister, Nancy. Judith and Nancy were also born Randolphs (Nancy's baptismal name was Ann Cary Randolph); their brother, Thomas Mann Randolph, Jr., married Thomas Jefferson's daughter Martha. In the winter and spring of 1792–93 the rumor spread throughout Virginia that Richard, until then notable for his robust vigor of mind and body, fine marriage, and prosperity, had carried on an affair with his sister-in-law Nancy, that she had given birth to their child while the family had been visiting friends, and that Richard and Nancy, with Judith's assistance, had killed the infant and concealed the corpse. In a bold move to end the rumors, but also perhaps to prevent future criminal prosecution, Richard Randolph hired several of the best lawyers in the state, including Patrick Henry and John Marshall, to prepare a brief for himself, and then requested the Cumberland County Court to hold a hearing to see whether there was cause for an indictment. The hearing resulted in a judgment that no such cause existed; in many retellings of this story, the process has been represented as a criminal trial that resulted in Richard's acquittal. John Marshall summarized the evidence for and against Richard, Judith, and Nancy in notes that argue for their complete innocence; these notes may be read in Charles T. Cullen and Herbert A. Johnson, eds., *The Papers of John Marshall* (Chapel Hill: University of North Carolina Press, 1977), vol. 2, pp. 168–78.

Letters written in 1814 by John Randolph and Nancy's rebuttal of January 1815 leave no doubt whatever that Nancy had in fact delivered a child. She contended that the infant had been stillborn; she further claimed that the infant's father was Theodorick Randolph, John and Richard's youngest brother, to whom she had become engaged and therefore already regarded as her husband. Unfortunately Theodorick had died in February 1793. Although John Randolph had assisted in preparing the family's defense in 1793, he vigorously stated his belief that Theodorick had been too weak and ill to sire a child in the last months of his life, that Nancy had given birth to a viable child, had murdered it, and had taken advantage of Richard's gallantry to protect her from the consequences of her crime. In the end, there seems agreement only that Nancy gave birth either to a dead child, or to one promptly murdered, and that either Theodorick or Richard had been its father. However successful Richard, Nancy, and Judith were in establishing their legal innocence, the judicial ruling did not stop the swirling rumors of adultery, incest, and infanticide.

Richard Randolph died in 1796. John Randolph then assumed the management of his late brother's estates as well as his own and served as the patriarch of Richard's plantation, Bizarre, where he had settled in 1794, while helping Judith raise her children. This situation lasted until 1811, when Randolph became estranged from his sister-in-law and moved to an isolated existence on his plantation, called Roanoke. By that time he had also broken relations with his stepfather, the eminent jurist St. George Tucker.

Randolph's other tragedy was physical. Possibly as the result of severe illness, he never fully developed secondary male characteristics. His voice was a robust soprano, he appeared beardless, and, at the time of his death (so the tradition has it), he was sterile. Enemies occasionally ridiculed him for his effeminate appearance; his most famous retort, though possibly apocryphal, is certainly in the man's style: "You pride yourself upon an animal faculty, in respect to which the negro is your equal and the jackass infinitely your superior." One student of Randolph's early life, William E. Stokes, Jr., has suggested that Randolph may have contracted syphilis in his youth; so far as we know his later medical history, punctuated by frequent and severe illnesses, as well as violent changes of mood and spells of irrationality, the hypothesis deserves serious consideration. Randolph seemed fond and appreciative of women as friends and relatives, but he never married. Evidently Randolph's anguish at being unable to marry and sire children was aggravated by the deaths of both his full brothers (half-brothers, sons of St. George Tucker, survived, but of course they were Tuckers, not Randolphs). Finally, Richard's sons, raised as if his own, also died young and without issue, in 1813 and 1815.

Randolph's personal as well as his political fortunes seemed dashed beyond repair by the time the War of 1812 had come to an end. The scandal that had apparently doomed his brother Richard especially haunted Randolph's later years and caused a shocking episode involving Nancy Randolph in 1814. In

1808 she had escaped from the shadowy existence to which the scandal had doomed her by becoming first housekeeper and then wife of Gouverneur Morris of New York, who was quite literally lord of a manor. The occasion for the episode was the Morrises' receiving and caring for young Tudor Randolph, Judith's son and therefore both Nancy's and John Randolph's nephew. Instead of appreciating the care given his nephew, John Randolph seemed determined to dredge up scandals old and new, even suggesting that Nancy had murdered Richard with poison in 1796 and had carried on illicit affairs since marrying Gouverneur Morris. These allegations he communicated directly to Morris as well as to Nancy, obviously undertaking to wreck their marriage. In this he completely failed, and, unfortunately for his reputation, left a long letter which, with Nancy's spirited reply, may be read in Bruce's biography, as it was read by many citizens to whom Nancy sent copies.

For the next few years, however, John Randolph was tolerably healthy and, for him, cheerful. Henry Adams, in one of his least attractive moments, scoffs at Randolph's religious conversion, which belongs to the same years as the surprising resurrection of his career in Congress, 1815–19. One can in some degree sympathize with the skeptical biographer's impatience with the self-dramatizing piety of Randolph's most intensely religious phase. But it is important to know what sort of Christian he became. Mainstream United States history does not say much about the Protestant Episcopal Church, derived from, yet legally distinct from, the Church of England, and knowledge of today's Episcopal Church may be somewhat misleading. The Episcopal Church in Virginia, from 1815 to 1833, very much partook of the movement known as the Second Great Awakening. Far less concerned with elaborate and historically informed liturgy than today's Episcopal Church, it was evangelical in outreach, and as centrally concerned as any revivalist denomination with the experience of salvation through the atoning grace of the crucified Christ. And John Randolph's religious letters, however bathetic, make that abundantly clear. At the same time it was surely no accident that Randolph chose the church of his ancestors and a church which, however independent of English rule and republican in politics since 1776, still maintained cordial ties to its Anglican parent. Furthermore, all Episcopal services were set forth in a *Book of Common Prayer* whose words, though largely arranged from Biblical texts, were nevertheless translated and arranged to teach peace, good order, responsible behavior, and respect for authority. Randolph's conversion was surely genuine, yet it was also of a piece with his growing nostalgia for an imagined Anglo-American golden age of order and deference.

In joining the church, John Randolph had the benefit of sustained and cordial encouragement from two remarkable contemporaries, Francis Scott Key of Maryland and the Reverend William Meade, later bishop of Virginia. He also had the unflagging friendship for the last twenty-five years of his life of Dr. John Brockenbrough of Richmond, who abandoned the practice of medicine in 1812 to become president of the Bank of Virginia. Though on poor terms with his closest surviving relatives, Randolph took considerable interest in other relatives and friends, with some of whom he maintained wholesome and extensive correspondence. His life, for the whole period 1815–33, was therefore hardly the period of bitter isolation that Henry Adams portrays—in this matter taking the self-pity of Randolph's letters and speeches far too literally. Perhaps the strangest aspect of Randolph's later life, at least at first sight, was the warm personal and political friendships he enjoyed with old Federalists, especially Harmanus Bleecker of New York and Josiah Quincy of Massachusetts. Taken altogether, John Randolph was not the traditional rustic planter his extensive tobacco plantations and cultivated self-image indicated; his all but continuous terms in Congress, frequent visits with friends and relatives, and trips to England betrayed a fondness for urbane, haute-bourgeois society. Not accidents, then, but part of his settled pattern of existence were these friendships with learned and cosmopolitan men and their wives, highly placed in the worlds of business, law, politics, charity, and religion.

Henry Adams ended his biography of John Randolph with a splendid flourish of spite which has the merit of being transparent except in one case, the matter of Randolph's last will and testament. Adams wrote, with reference to the series of trials that delayed the freeing of Randolph's slaves for thirteen years: "It is, perhaps, difficult to draw any precise line between eccentricity and insanity, but it is still more difficult to understand how the jury could possibly have held the will of 1821, which emancipated his slaves, to be a saner document than that of 1832, which did not" (p. 199).

This was inexcusable in any writer, but especially in one who had taught young Harvard men how to be good historians.

John Randolph knew that he was dying in Philadelphia in May 1833, and he knew the laws of Virginia were very strict about last-minute changes in wills. He therefore summoned a group of responsible citizens as witnesses, to whom he carefully and repeatedly declared it his final will to free all his slaves, and sell enough land and other assets to settle them on lands in the free state of Ohio. Henry Adams therefore misstated the problem: How could the courts of Virginia have delayed for so long the execution of the last wishes of a perfectly lucid man who had made those wishes perfectly clear to a room full of credible and disinterested witnesses, none of whom could benefit in any way from the distribution of his estate? Adams also ignored the testimony of Randolph's closest friends, a highly respectable group, that he was indeed insane in January 1832, when he drew up a will that sold or bequeathed his slaves. Probably the recent Nat Turner rebellion in Virginia influenced Randolph's thinking, whether rational or not.

Paradoxical to the end, Randolph of Roanoke emancipated four hundred slaves and did so in the most responsible way, making as full a provision as possible for their future prosperity rather than turning them loose on an unsympathetic world. Such behavior was rare in Jeffersonian and antebellum Virginia; certainly Thomas Jefferson and James Madison accomplished no such wholesale emancipations. In his private life, then, Randolph cordially associated himself with the colonizers and even moderate abolitionists who sought a gradual but early end to slavery in the United States, and even received a posthumous tribute from the abolitionist poet John Greenleaf Whittier.

One final observation, not on Randolph but on Henry Adams and his own eccentricities: The strict construction and states' rights view of the U.S. Constitution was not peculiar to Virginia, and Virginia considered in its entirety was never wholly dedicated to it. George Washington and John Marshall were just as good Virginians as Thomas Jefferson. More to the point, Jefferson did not wait until his presidency to adopt broad national views; he had held them, in varying degrees, from his first and memorable term in the Continental Congress, 1775–76, through his diplomatic career in Paris, and his four years as secretary of state. The later 1780s found him advocating the construction of a United States Navy and the development of an interstate system of canals. Though critical of certain details in the Constitution of 1787, during his five-year term as minister to France he must be counted as one of the nationalists who advocated greatly strengthening the federal government. But more particularly, James Madison was never merely Jefferson's henchman; he assuredly deserved his unofficial title, "Father of the Constitution," and never thereafter held the view that individual states retained their primordial sovereignty and the right of secession. Even in 1798–99 Madison was careful to avoid Jefferson's bold doctrine of nullification. The Virginia of the early Republic was itself a society far from monolithic, in spite of the great interest in tobacco and slaves.

The initially brilliant administration led by President Thomas Jefferson, Secretary of State James Madison, and Secretary of the Treasury Albert Gallatin had *not* won the election of 1800 on the old anti-Federalist principles of state sovereignty or even on the idea that the Federalist financial program, including the Bank of the United States, had hopelessly violated the Constitution of 1787. A large portion of the Jeffersonian vote in 1800 was from partisans who still believed the French republic to be fighting the cause of liberty; whatever else its admirers saw in that nation, they could not conceivably have seen decentralization, local rights, and strict construction! Indeed, whether or not Thomas Jefferson had made any informal promises to break the deadlock in the House of Representatives in order to secure his election to the presidency, he continued Hamilton's Bank of the United States throughout his two terms, and Secretary of the Treasury Albert Gallatin both expanded its operations and urged its recharter in 1811. The doctrines of nullification and interposition devised by Jefferson and Madison in response to the Federalist Alien and Sedition Acts of 1798 were much more in the nature of short-term expedient measures, partly designed to head off unnecessarily violent actions by their friends, than to permanently cripple the federal government.

But even if Jefferson, Madison, and their followers had been permanently wed to the proposition, characteristically phrased by Jefferson, "That government is best which governs least," their advocacy would not make it true. We of the United States struggle today, have always struggled, and will no doubt continue to struggle with questions of where government should and should not act, how best to distribute power among local, state, and national government, and when elected officials are or are not carrying out the popular will, or acting within the bounds of the Constitution. An inadequate constitution such as the Articles of Confederation can thwart a nation, but there is no guarantee that a perfect constitution, if such there be, can guarantee good government, which depends on honest, dedicated, and well-informed agents. Henry Adams surely knew these axioms; one must therefore conclude that the very respect he paid to the strict construction and states' rights views of the Jeffersonians in opposition was in part ironic. Had not the Adamses of the third and fourth generations thrown themselves into the defense of the Union, during the crisis of 1861–65?

John Randolph's Old Republican doctrines were suited to naysaying, to opposition, to protest; they might serve to prevent the federal government from doing harm, but they might also serve to defend and protect local abuses and prevent national benefits as well. For better and for worse, John Randolph of Roanoke was, with the possible exception of John Taylor of Caroline, their greatest lifelong exponent. But it will not do to pigeonhole this strange man too precisely. When he declared, "You may no more deprive a state of part of her sovereignty than you can deprive a lady of part of her chastity," he was playing as much on the sexual anxieties of his age as on its political anxieties. And when, on being asked by his friend Josiah Quincy to name the greatest orator he had encountered, he answered, "A slave. She was a mother, and her rostrum was the auction block." This was not the language of an apologist for slavery.

Robert McColley

Suggestions for Further Reading

The story of Henry Adams writing *John Randolph* appears in rich detail in the second of Ernest Samuels's three-volume biography, *Henry Adams: the Middle Years* (Cambridge: Harvard University Press, 1958). Especially illuminating among the many discussions of Adams as a writer of history are William H. Jordy, *Henry Adams, Scientific Historian* (New Haven, CT: Yale University Press, 1952), and Earl N. Harbert, *The Force So Much Closer Home: Henry Adams and the Adams Family* (New York: New York University Press, 1977). Harbert has also collected *Henry Adams: A Reference Guide* (New York: New York University Press, 1978).

William Cabell Bruce's *John Randolph of Roanoke* (New York: Putnam's, 1922; 2 vols.) remains in a class all its own as a complete biography; its two volumes total 1,465 pages! Robert Dawidoff, in *The Education of John Randolph* (New York: Norton, 1979), has taken the trouble to recreate Randolph's reading, and relate his impromptu speeches and self-characterization to their literary and political sources, chiefly in England. This, and his suggestive psychologizing, make the book indispensable. Russell Kirk, *John Randolph of Roanoke* (Indianapolis, IN: Liberty Press, 1978; 2d ed.) makes a case for Randolph as an important conservative thinker. Whether or not one is convinced, he succeeds in giving a fairer and fuller picture of Randolph's thought than anyone since the copious W. C. Bruce. Furthermore, Kirk's second edition contains over three hundred pages of letters and speeches. Kenneth Shorey, ed., *Collected Letters of John Randolph of Roanoke to Dr. John Brockenbrough, 1812–1833* (New Brunswick, NJ, and Oxford: Transaction Books, 1988), offers in print the longest and most revealing of Randolph's series of letters.

Norman K. Risjord, *The Old Republicans: Southern Conservatism in the Age of Jefferson* (New York and London: Columbia University Press, 1965), places John Randolph more firmly within the political traditions of Virginia, making him seem much less isolated than he appears in Henry Adams's biography.

⫷ I ⫸

Youth

"WILLIAM RANDOLPH, gentleman, of Turkey Island," born in 1650, was a native of Warwickshire in England, as his tombstone declares. Of his ancestry nothing is certainly known. The cause and the time of his coming to Virginia have been forgotten. The Henrico records show that in 1678 he was clerk of Henrico County, a man of substance, and married already to Mary Isham; that in 1685 he was "Captain William Randolph" and Justice of the Peace; that in 1706 he conveyed to son Henry "land called by the name of Curles, with Longfield," being all that land at "Curles" lately belonging to Nathaniel Bacon, Jr.; that in 1709 "Col. William Randolph of Turkey Island" made his will, which mentioned seven sons and two daughters; and finally that in 1711 he died.

Turkey Island, just above the junction of the James and Appomattox rivers, lies in a region which has sharply attracted the attention of men. In 1675 Nathaniel Bacon lived near by at his plantation called Curles, and in that year Bacon's famous rebellion gave bloody associations to the place. About one hundred years afterwards Benedict Arnold, then a general in the British service, made a destructive raid up the James River which drew all eyes to the spot. Neither of these disturbances, historical as they are, made the region nearly so famous as it became on June 30, 1862, when fifty thousand northern troops, beaten, weary, and disorganized, converged at Malvern Hill and Turkey Island bridge, and the next day fought a battle which saved their army, and perhaps their cause, without a thought or a care for the dust of forgotten Randolphs on which two armies were trampling in the cradle of their race.

19

William Randolph of Turkey Island was not the first Randolph who came to Virginia, or the only one who was there in 1678, but he was the most successful, when success was the proof of energy and thrift. He provided well for his nine children, and henceforth their descendants swarmed like bees in the Virginian hive. The fifth son, Richard, who lived at Curles, Nathaniel Bacon's confiscated plantation, and who married Jane Bolling, a great-great-granddaughter of John Rolfe and Pocahontas, disposed by will, in 1742, of forty thousand acres of the choicest lands on the James, Appomattox, and Roanoke rivers, including Matoax, about two miles west of Petersburg, and Bizarre, a plantation some ninety miles further up the Appomattox River. John, the youngest son of this Richard of Curles, born in 1742, married in 1769 Frances Bland, daughter of a neighbor who lived at Cawsons, on a promontory near the mouth of the Appomattox, looking north up the James River to Turkey Island. Here on June 2, 1773, their youngest child, John, was born.

In these last days of colonial history, the Randolphs were numerous and powerful, a family such as no one in Virginia would wish to offend; and if they were proud of their position and importance, who could fairly blame them? There was even a Randolph of Wilton, another of Chatsworth, as though they meant to rival Pembrokes and Devonshires. There was a knight in the family, old Sir John, sixth son of William of Turkey Island, and father of Peyton Randolph, who was afterwards president of the American Congress. There was a historian, perhaps the best the State has yet produced, old William Stith. There were many members of the Council and the House of Burgesses, an innumerable list of blood relations and a score of allied families, among the rest that of Jefferson. Finally, the King's Attorney-General was at this time a Randolph, and took part with the crown against the colony. The world upon which the latest Randolph baby opened his eyes was, so far as his horizon stretched, a world of cousins, a colonial aristocracy all his own, supported by tobacco plantations and Negro labor, by colonial patronage and royal favor, or, to do it justice, by audacity, vigor, and mind.

This small cheerful world, which was in its way a

remarkable phenomenon, and produced the greatest list of great names ever known this side of the ocean, was about to suffer a wreck the more fatal and hopeless because no skill could avert it, and the dissolution was so quiet and subtle that no one could protect himself or secure his children. The boy was born at the moment when the first shock was at hand. His father died in 1775; his mother, in 1778, married Mr. St. George Tucker of Bermuda, and meanwhile the country had plunged into a war which in a single moment cut that connection with England on which the old Virginian society depended for its tastes, fashions, theories, and above all for its aristocratic status in politics and law. The Declaration of Independence proclaimed that America was no longer to be English, but American; that is to say, democratic and popular in all its parts,—a fact equivalent to a sentence of death upon old Virginian society, and foreboding dissolution to the Randolphs with the rest, until they should learn to master the new conditions of American life. For passing through such a maelstrom a century was not too short an allowance of time, yet this small Randolph boy, not a strong creature at best, was born just as the downward plunge began, and every moment made the outlook drearier and more awful.

On January 3, 1781, he was at Matoax with his mother, who only five days before had been confined. Suddenly it was said that the British were coming. They soon appeared, under the command of Brigadier-General Benedict Arnold, and scared Virginia from Yorktown to the mountains. They hunted the Governor like a tired fox, and ran him out of his famous mountain fastness at Monticello, breaking up his government and mortifying him, until Mr. Jefferson at last refused to reassume the office, and passed his trust over to a stronger hand. St. George Tucker at Matoax thought it time to seek safer quarters, and hurried his wife, with her little baby, afterwards the well-known Judge Henry St. George Tucker, away to Bizarre, ninety miles up the Appomattox.

Here he left her and went to fight Cornwallis at Guilford. Henceforward the little Randolphs ran wild at Bizarre. Schools there were none, and stern discipline was never a part of Virginian education. Mrs. Tucker, their mother, was an affectionate and excellent woman; Mr. Tucker a kind and admirable stepfather; as for the boy John Randolph, it is said that he had a warm and amiable disposition, although the only well-authenticated fact recorded about his infancy is that before his fifth year he was known to swoon in a mere fit of temper, and could with difficulty be restored. The life of boyhood in Virginia was not well fitted for teaching self-control or mental discipline, qualities which John Randolph never gained; but in return for these the Virginian found other advantages which made up for the loss of methodical training. Many a Virginian lad, especially on such a remote plantation as Bizarre, lived in a boy's paradise of indulgence, fished and shot, rode like a young monkey, and had his memory crammed with the genealogy of every well-bred horse in the State, grew up among dogs and Negroes, master equally of both, and knew all about the prices of wheat, tobacco, and slaves. He might pick up much that was high and noble from his elders and betters, or much that was bad and brutal from his inferiors; might, as he grew older, back his favorite bird at a cocking-main, or haunt stables and race-courses, or look on, with as much interest as an English nobleman felt at a prize-ring, when, after the race was over, there occurred an old-fashioned rough-and-tumble fight, where the champions fixed their thumbs in each other's eye-sockets and bit off each other's noses and ears; he might, even more easily than in England, get habits of drinking as freely as he talked, and of talking as freely as the utmost license of the English language would allow. The climate was genial, the soil generous, the life easy, the temptations strong. Everything encouraged individuality, and if by accident any mind had a natural bent towards what was coarse or brutal, there was little to prevent it from following its instinct.

There was, however, another side to Virginian life, which helped to civilize young savages,—the domestic and family relation; the influence of father and mother, of women, of such reading as the country-house offered, of music, dancing, and the table. John Randolph was born and bred among gentlefolk. Mr. Tucker had refinement, and his wife, along with many other excellent qualities, had two very feminine instincts,—family pride and religion. To inoculate the imagination of her son with notions of family pride was an easy task, and to show him how to support the dignity of his name was a natural one. "Never part with your land," was her solemn injunction, which he did not forget; "keep your land, and your land will keep you." This was the English theory, and Randolph acted on it through life, although it was becoming more and more evident, with every passing year, that the best thing to be done with Virginian land, at the ruling prices, was to part with it. His passion for land became at last sheer avarice, a quality so rare in Virginia as to be a virtue, and he went on accumulating plantation after plantation without paying his debts, while the land, worth very little at best, was steadily becoming as worthless as the leaves which every autumn shook from its forests. Not an acre of the forty thousand which his grandfather bequeathed now belongs to a Randolph, but the Randolphs or any one else might have bought back the whole of it for a song at any time within half a century.

Thus the boy took life awry from the start; he sucked poison with his mother's milk. Not so easy a task, however, was it for her to teach him her other strong instinct; for, although he seems really to have loved his mother as much as he loved any one, he was perverse in childhood as in manhood, and that his mother should try to make him religious seems to have been reason enough for his becoming a vehement deist. At what age he took this bent is nowhere said; perhaps a little later, when he went for a few months to school at Williamsburg, the focus of Virginian deism. At Bizarre he seems rather to have turned towards story-books, and works that appealed to his imagination; the kind of reading he would be apt to find in the cupboards of Virginian houses, and such as a boy with fits of moodiness and a lively imagination would be likely to select. Thus he is said to have read, before his eleventh year, the Arabian Nights, Shakespeare, Homer, Don Quixote, Gil Blas, Plutarch's Lives, Robinson Crusoe, Gulliver, Tom Jones. The chances are a thousand to one that to this list may be added Peregrine Pickle, the Newgate Calendar, Moll Flanders, and Roderick Random. Whether Paradise Lost or Sir Charles Grandison and Pamela were soon added to the number, we are not told; but it is quite safe to say that, among these old, fascinating volumes, then found in every Virginian country-place, as in every English one, Randolph never learned to love two books which made the library of every New England farmhouse, where the freer literature would have been thought sinful and heathenish. If he ever read, he must have disliked the Pilgrim's Progress or the Saint's Rest; he would have recoiled from every form of Puritanism and detested every affectation of sanctity.

The kind of literary diet on which the boy thus fed was not the healthiest or best for a nature like his; but it made the literary education of many a man who passed through life looked on by his fellows as well read with no wider range than this and as Randolph had a quick memory he used to the utmost what he had thus gained. His cleverest illustrations were taken from Shakespeare and Fielding. In other literature he was well versed, according to the standards of the day: he read his Gibbon, Hume, and Burke; knew English history, and was at home in the English peerage; but it was to Shakespeare and Fielding that his imagination naturally turned, and in this, as in other things, he was a true Virginian, a son of the soil and the time.

As he grew a few years older, and looked about him on the world in which he was to play a part, he saw little but a repetition of his own surroundings. When the Revolutionary War closed, in 1783, he was ten years old, and during the next five years he tried to pick up an education. America was then a small, straggling, exhausted country, without a government, a nationality, a capital, or even a town of thirty thousand inhabitants; a country which had not the means of supplying such an education as the young man wanted, however earnestly he tried for it. His advantages were wholly social, and it is not to be denied that they were great. He had an immense family connection, which gave him confidence and a sense of power; from his birth surrounded by a society in itself an education, he was accustomed to the best that Virginia had, and Virginia had much that was best on the continent. He saw about him that Virginian gentry which was the child of English squirarchy, and reproduced the high breeding of Bolingbroke and Sir Charles Grandison side by side with the coarseness of Swift and Squire Western. The contrasts were curious, in this provincial aristocracy, between old-fashioned courtesy and culture and the roughness of plantation habits. Extreme eccentricity might end in producing a man of a new type as brutal at heart as the roughest cub that ran loose among the negro cabins of a tobacco plantation, violent, tyrannical, vicious, cruel, and licentious in language as in morals, while at the same time trained to habits of good society, and sincerely feeling that exaggerated deference which it was usual to affect towards ladies; he might be well read, fond of intelligent conversation, consumed by ambition, or devoured by self-esteem, with manners grave, deferential, mild, and charming when at their best, and intolerable when the spirit of arrogance seized him. Nowhere could be found a school of more genial and simpler courtesy than that which produced the great men and women of Virginia, but it had its dangers and affectations; it was often provinical and sometimes coarse.

John Randolph, the embodiment of these contrasts and peculiarities, was an eccentric type recognized and understood by Virginians. To a New England man, on the contrary, the type was unintelligible and monstrous. The New Englander had his own code of bad manners, and was less tolerant than the Virginian of whatever varied from it. As the character of Don Quixote was to Cervantes clearly a natural and possible product of Spanish character, so to the people of Virginia John Randolph was a representative man, with qualities exaggerated but genuine; and even these exaggerations struck a chord of popular sympathy; his very weaknesses were caricatures of Virginia failings; his genius was in some degree a caricature of Viginian genius; and plus the boy grew up to manhood, as pure a Virginian Quixote as ever an American Cervantes could have conceived.

In the summer of 1781 he had a few months' schooling, and afterwards was again at school, about one year, at Williamsburg, till the spring of 1784, when his parents took him on a visit to Bermuda, the home of his stepfather's family. In the autumn of 1787 he was sent to Princeton, where he passed a few months; the next year, being now fifteen, he went for a short time to Columbia College, in New York. This was all the schooling he ever had, and, excepting perhaps a little Latin, it is not easy to say what he learned. "I am an ignorant

man, sir," was his own statement. So he was, and so, for
that matter, are the most learned: but Randolph's true
ignorance was not want of book-learning; he had quite
as much knowledge of that kind as he could profitably
use in America, and his mind was naturally an active
one, could he only have put it in sympathy with the
movement of his country. At this time of life, when
the ebullition of youth was still violent, he was curiously
torn by the struggle between conservative and radical
instincts. He read Voltaire, Rousseau, Hume, Gibbon,
and was as deistical in his opinions as any of them.
The Christian religion was hateful to him, as it was to
Tom Paine; he loved everything hostile to it. "Very early
in life," he wrote thirty years afterwards, "I imbibed an
absurd prejudice in favor of Mahometanism and its
votaries. The crescent had a talismanic effect on my
imagination, and I rejoiced in all its triumphs over the
cross (which I despised), as I mourned over its defeats;
and Mahomet II. himself did not more exult than I did
when the crescent was planted on the dome of St. Sophia,
and the cathedral of the Constantines was converted into
a Turkish mosque." This was radical enough to suit
Paine or Saint Just, but it was the mere intellectual fashion of the day, as over-vehement and unhealthy as its
counterpart, the religious spasms of his later life. His
mind was always controlled by his feelings; its antipathies were stronger than its sympathy; it was restless
and uneasy, prone to contradiction and attached to par-
adox. In such a character there is nothing very new, for
at least nine men out of ten, whose intelligence is above
the average, have felt the same instincts: the impulse
to contradict is as familiar as dyspepsia or nervous
excitability; the passion for referring every comparison
to one's self is a primitive quality of mind by no means
confined to women and children; but what was to be
expected when such a temperament, exaggerated and un-
restrained, full of self-contradictions and stimulated by
acute reasoning powers, remarkable audacity and quickness, violent and vindictive temper, and a morbid constitution, was planted in a Virginian, a slave-owner, a
Randolph, just when the world was bursting into fire
and flame?

Of course, while at college, the young Randolph had
that necessary part of a Southern gentleman's education

in those days, a duel, but there is no reason to suppose that he was given to brawls, and in early life his temper was rather affectionate than harsh. His friendships were strong, and seem to have been permanent. He was intelligent and proud, and may have treated with contempt whatever he thought mean or contemptible. He certainly did quarrel with a Virginian fellow-student, and then shot him, but no one can now say what excuse or justification he may have had. His opponent's temper in after life was quite as violent as his own, and the quarrel itself rose from a dispute over the mere pronunciation of a word.

In the year 1788 he was at college in New York with his elder brother Richard, and we get a glimpse of him in a letter to his stepfather, dated on Christmas Day, 1788:—

"Be well assured, my dear sir, our expenses since our arrival here have been enormous, and by far greater than our estate, especially loaded as it is with debt, can bear; however, I flatter myself, my dear papa, that upon looking over the accounts you will find that my share is by comparison trifling, and hope that by the wise admonitions of so affectionate a parent, and one who has our welfare and interest at heart, we may be able to shun the rock of prodigality upon which so many people continually split, and by which the unhappy victim is reduced not only to poverty, but also to despair and all the horrors attending it."

This was unusual language for a Virginian boy of fifteen! It would have been safe to prophesy that the rock of prodigality was not one of his dangers. Down to the last day of his life he talked in the same strain, always complaining of this old English indebtedness, living with careful economy, but never willing to pay his debt, and never able to resist the temptation of buying land and slaves. The letter goes on:—

"Brother Richard writes you that I am lazy. I assure you, dear papa, he has been egregiously mistaken. I attend every lecture that the class does. Not one of the professors has ever found me dull with my business, or even said that I was irregular. . . . If brother Richard had written you that I did nothing all the vacation, he would have been much in

the dark; neither was it possible for me. We lived in this
large building without a soul in it but ourselves, and it was
so desolate and dreary that I could not bear to be in it. I
was always afraid that some robber, of which we have a
plenty, was coming to kill me, after they made a draught on
the house."

Nervous, excitable, loving warmly, hating more warmly still, easily affected by fears, whether of murderers or
of poverty, lazy according to his brother Richard, neither
dull nor irregular, but timid, according to his own account, this letter represents him as he showed himself
to his parents, in rather an amiable light. It closes with
a suggestion of politics: "Be so good, my dear sir, when
it is convenient, to send me the debate of the convention in our State." He was too true a Virginian not to
oppose the new Constitution of the United States which
Patrick Henry and George Mason had so vehemently
resisted, but that Constitution was now adopted, and
was about to be set in motion. From this moment a new
school was provided for the boy, far more interesting to
him than the lecture-rooms of Columbia College,—a
school which he attended with extraordinary amusement
and even fascination.

"I was at Federal Hall," said he once in a speech to
his constituents; "I saw Washington, but could not hear
him take the oath to support the federal Constitution.
The Constitution was in its chrysalis state. I saw what
Washington did not see, but two other men in Virginia
saw it,—George Mason and Patrick Henry,—the secret
sting which lurked beneath the gaudy pinions of the
butterfly." Wiser men than he, not only in Virginia
but elsewhere, saw and dreaded the centralizing, overwhelming powers of the new government, and are not to
be blamed for their fears. Without boldly assuming that
America was a country to which old rules did not
apply, that she stood by herself, above law, it was impossible to look without alarm at the tendency of the
Constitution; for history, from beginning to end, was
one long warning against the abuse of just such powers.
Were Randolph alive to-day, he would probably feel that
his worse fears were realized. From his point of view
as a Virginian, a slave-owner, a Randolph, it was true
that, although the Constitution was not a butterfly and

did not carry poison under its wings,—for only at Roanoke could a butterfly be found with a secret sting in such a part of its person,—it did carry a fearful power for good or evil in the tremendous sweep of its pinions and the terrible grip of its claws.

Another little incident sharpened Randolph's perception of the poison which lay in the new system. "I was in New York," said he nearly forty years afterwards, "when John Adams took his seat as Vice-President. I recollect—for I was a schoolboy at the time—attending the lobby of Congress when I ought to have been at school. I remember the manner in which my brother was spurned by the coachman of the then Vice-President for coming too near the arms emblazoned on the scutcheon of the vice-regal carriage. Perhaps I may have some of this old animosity rankling in my heart, . . . coming from a race who are known never to forsake a friend or forgive a foe." The world would be an uncomfortable residence for elderly people if they were to be objects of lifelong personal hatred to every boy over whose head their coachman, without their knowledge, had once snapped a whip, and especially so if, as in this case, the feud were carried down to the next generation. Of course the sting did not lie in the coachman's whip. Had the carriage been that of a Governor of Virginia or a Lord Chancellor of England or had the coachman of his own old-fashioned four-horse Virginian chariot been to blame, John Randolph would never have given the matter another thought; but that his brother, a Virginian gentleman of ancient family and large estates, should be struck by the servant of a Yankee schoolmaster, who had neither family, wealth, nor land, but was a mere shoot of a psalm-singing democracy, and that this man should lord it over Virginia and Virginians, was maddening; and the sight of that Massachusetts whip was portentous, terrible, inexpressible to the boy, like the mysterious solitude of his great schoolhouse, which drove him out into the street in fear of robbery and murder.

The Attorney-General of the new government was a Randolph,—Edmund, son of John, and grandson of Sir John, who was brother to Richard of Curles,—and when, in 1790, the seat of administration was transferred to Philadelphia, John Randolph left Columbia

College and went to Philadelphia to study law in the Attorney-General's train. Here, excepting for occasional visits to Virginia, and for interruption by yellow fever, he remained until 1794, occupying himself very much as he liked, so far as is now to be learned. He was not pleased with Mr. Edmund Randolph's theories in the matter of teaching law. He studied systematically no profession, neither law nor medicine, although he associated with students of both, and even attended lectures. He seems to have enjoyed the life, as was natural, for Philadelphia was an agreeable city. "I know," said he many years afterwards, "by fatal experience, the fascinations of a town life,—how they estrange the mind from its old habits and attachments." This "fatal experience" was probably a mere figure of speech; so far as can be seen, his residence in New York and Philadelphia was the most useful part of his youth, and went far to broaden his mind. A few of his letters at this period are extant, but they tell little except that he was living with the utmost economy and was deeply interested in politics, taking, of course, a strongly anti-federalist side.

In April, 1794, he returned to Virginia, to assume control of his property. In after years he complained bitterly of having "been plundered and oppressed during my nonage, and left to enter upon life overwhelmed with a load of debt which the profits of a nineteen years' minority ought to have more than paid; and, ignorant as I was, and even yet am, of business, to grope my way without a clue through the labyrinth of my father's affairs, and, brought up among Quakers, an ardent *ami des noirs,* to scuffle with Negroes and overseers for something like a pittance of rent and profit upon my land and stock." He lived with his elder brother Richard, who was now married, at Bizarre, near Farmville, a place better known to this generation as the town from which General Grant dated his famous letter calling upon General Lee for a surrender of the Confederate Army of Northern Virginia. From here he could direct the management of his own property at Roanoke, some miles to the southward, while he enjoyed the society at Bizarre and economized his expenses.

Nothing further is recorded of his life until in the

spring of 1796 he visited his friend Bryan in Georgia, and during a stay in Charleston came under the notice of a bookseller, who has recorded the impression he made: "A tall, gawky-looking, flaxen-haired stripling, apparently of the age from sixteen to eighteen, with a complexion of a good parchment color, beardless chin, and as much assumed self-confidence as any two-footed animal I ever saw," in company with a gray-headed, florid-complexioned old gentleman, whom he slapped on the back and called Jack,—a certain Sir John Nesbit, a Scotch baronet, with whom he had become intimate, and whom he beat in a horse-race, each riding his own horse. The bookseller at once set him down as the most impudent youth he had ever seen, but was struck by the sudden animation which at moments lighted up his usually dull and heavy face.

After his stay at Charleston, he went on to his friend Bryan's in Georgia, where he proved his convivial powers, as in South Carolina he had proved his superiority in horse-racing. "My eldest brother," wrote Bryan afterwards, "Still bears a friendly remembrance of the *rum ducking* you gave him." This visit to Georgia was destined to have great influence on his later career. He found the State convulsed with excitement over what was long famous as the Yazoo fraud. The legislature of Georgia, in the preceding year, had authorized the sale of four immense tracts of land, supposed to embrace twenty millions of acres, for five hundred thousand dollars, to four land companies. It was proved that, with one exception, every member of the legislature who voted for this bill was interested in the purchase. A more flagrant case of wholesale legislative corruption had never been known, and when the facts were exposed the whole State rose in indignation against it, elected a new legislature, annulled the sale, expunged the act from the record, and finally, by calling a convention, made the expunging act itself a part of the state constitution. With his natural vehemence of temper, Randolph caught all the excitement of his friends, and became a vehement anti-Yazoo man, as it was called, for the rest of his life.

The visit to Georgia accomplished, he turned homewards again, and was suddenly met by the crushing news that his brother Richard was dead. In every way this blow was a terrible one. His brother had been his oldest and closest companion. The widow and two children, one of whom was deaf and dumb from birth, and ultimately became insane, besides the whole burden of the joint establishment, now came under John Randolph's charge. "Then," to use his own words, "I had to unravel the tangled skein of my poor brother's difficulties and debts. His sudden and untimely death threw upon my care, helpless as I was, his family, whom I tenderly and passionately loved.'" Richard's last years had been embittered by a strange and terrible scandal, resulting in a family feud, which John, with his usual vehemence, made his own. These complications would have been trying to any man, but to one of his peculiar temper they were a source of infinite depression and despair.

-◄[II]►-

Virginian Politics

POLITICS MEANWHILE were becoming more and more
violent. The negotiation of Jay's treaty with England,
which took place in 1794, followed by its publication in
June, 1795, and the extraordinary behavior of France,
threw the country into a state of alarming excitement.
Randolph shared in the indignation of those who
thought the treaty a disgraceful one, and there is a
story, told on the authority of his friends, that at a dinner,
pending the ratification, he gave as a toast, "George
Washington,—may he be damned!" and when the company declined to drink it, he added, "if he signs Jay's
treaty." No one can fairly blame the opposition to that
treaty, which indeed challenged opposition; and that
Randolph should have opposed it hotly, if he opposed
it at all, was only a part of his nature; but none the
less was it true that between his Anglican tastes and his
Gallican policy he was in a false position, as he was
also between his aristocratic prejudices and his democratic theories, his deistical doctrines and his conservative
temperament, his interests as a slave-owner and his theories as an *ami des noirs,* and finally in the entire delusion
which possessed his mind that a Virginian aristocracy
could maintain itself in alliance with a democratic polity.

Perhaps these flagrant inconsistencies might have
worked out ten years sooner to their natrual result, had not
John Adams and New England now stood at the head
of the government. If Randolph could wish no better fate for his own countryman, Washington, than that
he might be damned, one may easily imagine what
were his feeling towards Washington's successor, whose
coachman had cracked his whip over Richard Randolph.
For thirty years he never missed a chance to have his

33

fling at both the Adamses, father and son; "the cub,"
he said, "is a greater bear than the old one;" and although he spared no prominent Virginian, neither Washington, Jefferson, Madison, Monroe, nor Clay, yet the
only persons against whom his strain of invective was
at all seasons copious, continuous, and vehement were
the two New England Presidents. To do him justice,
there was every reason, in his category of innate prejudices, for the antipathy he felt; and especially in regard to the administration of the elder Adams there was
ample ground for honest divergence of opinion. For one
moment in the career of that administration the country
was in real danger, and opposition became almost a
duty. When hostilities with France broke out, and under
their cover the Alien and Sedition laws were passed,
backed by a large army, with the scarcely concealed object of overawing threatened resistance from Virginia, it
was time that opposition should be put in power, even
though the opposition had itself undertaken to nullify
acts of Congress and to prepare in secret an armed
rebellion against the national government.

Feeling ran high in Virginia during the year 1798.
Mr. Madison had left Congress, but both he and Mr.
Jefferson, the Vice-President, were busy in organizing
their party for what was too much like a dissolution of
the Union. They induced the legislatures of Virginia
and Kentucky to assert the right of resistance to national laws, and were privy to the preparations making in
Virginia for armed resistance; or if they were not, it
was because they chose to be ignorant. Monroe was
certainly privy to these warlike preparations; for, in
the year 1814, Randolph attacked in debate the conscription project recommended by Monroe, then Secretary of War, and said, "Ask him what he would have
done, whilst Governor of Virginia, and preparing to resist federal usurpation, had such an attempt been made
by Mr. Adams and his ministers, especially in 1800! He
can give the answer." At a still later day, in January,
1817, Randolph explained the meaning of his innuendo.
"There is no longer," said he, "any cause for concealing
the fact that the grand armory at Richmond was built
to enable the State of Virginia to resist by force the
encroachments of the then administration upon her in-
disputable rights." Naturally Randolph himself was in

thorough sympathy with such schemes, and it would be surprising if he and the hot-headed young men of his stamp did not drag their older chiefs into measures which these would have gladly avoided.

Seizing this moment to enter political life, with characteristic audacity he struck at once for the highest office within his reach; at the age of twenty-six, he announced himself a candidate for Congress. Both parties were keenly excited over the contest in Virginia, and the federalists, with Washington at their head, were greatly distressed and alarmed, for they knew what was going on, and after opposing to the utmost Mr. Madison's nullification resolutions, straining every nerve to allay the excitement, as a last resource they implored their old opponent, Patrick Henry, to come to their rescue. Unwillingly enough, for his strength was rapidly failing, Henry consented. Nothing in his life was nobler. The greatest orator and truest patriot in Virginia, a sound and consistent democrat, sprung from the people and adored by them, this persistent and energetic opponent of the Constitution, who had denounced its overswollen powers and its "awful squint towards monarchy," now came forward, not for office, nor to qualify or withdraw anything he had ever said, but with his last breath to warn the people of Virginia not to raise their hand against the national government. Washington himself, he said, would lead an army to put them down. "Where is the citizen of America who will dare lift his hand against the father of his country? No! you dare not do it! In such a parricidal attempt, the steel would drop from your nerveless arm!"

In the light of subsequent history there is a solemn and pathetic grandeur in this dying appeal of the old revolutionary orator, by the tavern porch of Charlotte, at the March court, in 1799,—a grandeur partly due to its simplicity, but more to its association with the great revolutionary struggle which had gone before, and with the awful judgment which fell upon this doomed region sixty-five years afterwards. There was, too, an element of contrast in the composition; for when the old man fell back, exhausted, and the great audience stood silent with the conviction that they had heard an immortal orator, who would never speak again, make an appeal such as defied reply, then it was that John Randolph's

tall, lean, youthful figure climbed upon the platform and
stood up before the crowd.

What he said is not recorded, and would in no case
be very material. He himself, in 1817, avowed in
Congress the main burden of his address: "I was asked
if I justified the establishment of the armory for the
purpose of opposing Mr. Adams' administration. I said
I did; that I could not conceive any case in which the
people could not be intrusted with arms; and that the
use of them to oppose oppressive measures was in principle the same, whether those of the administration of
Lord North or that of Mr. Adams." At this period Randolph did not talk in the crisp, nervous, pointed language of his after life, but used the heroic style which
is still to be seen in the writings of his friend, "the
greatest man I ever knew, John Thompson, the immortal author of the letters of Curtius." The speech could
have been only a solemn defense of states' rights; an
appeal to state pride and fear; an *ad hominem* attack
on Patrick Henry's consistency, and more or less effective denunciation of federalists in general. What he
could not answer, and what must become the more
impressive through his own success, was the splendor of a
sentiment; history, past and coming; the awe that sur-
rounds a dying prophet threatening a new doom deserved.

Vague tradition reports that Randolph spoke for three
hours and held his audience; he rarely failed with a Virginian assembly, and in this case his whole career depended on success. Tradition further says that Patrick
Henry remarked to a by-stander, "I haven't seen the
little dog before, since he was at school; he was a great
atheist then;" and after the speech, shaking hands with
his opponent, he added, "Young man, you call me father; then, my son, I have something to say unto thee:
Keep justice, keep truth,—and you will live to think
differently."

Randolph never did live to think differently, but ended
as he began, trying to set bounds against the power of the
national government, and to protect those bounds, if need
be, by force. Whether his opinions were wrong or right,
criminal or virtuous, is another matter, which has an interest far deeper than his personality, and more lasting
than his fame; but at least those opinions were at that

time expressed with the utmost clearness and emphasis, not
by him but by the legislatures of more than one State; and
as he was not their author, so he is not to be judged harsh-
ly for accepting or adhering to them. Doubtless, as
time passed and circumstances changed, Randolph fig-
ured as a political Quixote in his championship of
states' rights, which became at the end his hobby, his
mania; he played tricks with it until his best friends
were weary and disgusted; but, so far as his wayward
life had a meaning or a moral purpose, it lay in his
strenuous effort to bar the path of that spirit of despotism which in every other age and land had perverted
government into a curse and a scourge. The doctrine
of states' rights was but a fragment of republican dogma in 1800, and circumstances alone caused it to be
remembered when men forgot the system of opinions of
which it made a part: isolated, degraded, defiled by an
unnatural union with the slave power, the doctrine became at last a mere phrase, which had still a meaning
only to those who knew what Mr. Jefferson and the
republicans of America had once believed; but to Randolph it was always an inspired truth which purified
and elevated his whole existence; the faith of his youth,
it seemed to him to sanctify his age; the helmet of this
Virginian Quixote,—a helmet of Mambrino, if one pleas-
es,—it was in Quixote's eyes a helmet all the same.
What warranted such enthusiasm in this threadbare
formula of words? Why should thousands on thousands
of simple-minded, honest, plain men have been willing
to die for a phrase?

The republican party, which assumed control of the
government in 1801, had taken great pains to express
its ideas so clearly that no man could misconceive them.
At the bottom of its theories lay, as a foundation, the
historical fact that political power had, in all experience,
tended to grow at the expense of human liberty. Every
government tended towards despotism; contained some-
where a supreme, irresponsible, self-defined power
called sovereignty, which held human rights, if human
rights there were, at its mercy. Americans believed that
the liberties of this continent depended on fixing a barrier against this supreme central power called national
sovereignty, which, if left to grow unresisted, would
repeat here all the miserable experiences of Europe,

and, falling into the grasp of some group of men, would be the centre of a military tyranny; that, to resist the growth of this power, it was necessary to withhold authority from the government, and to administer it with the utmost economy, because extravagance generates corruption, and corruption generates despotism; that the Executive must be held in check; the popular branch of the legislature strengthened, the Judiciary curbed, and the general powers of government strictly construed; but, above all, the States must be supported in exercising all their reserved rights, because, in the last resort, the States alone could make head against a central sovereign at Washington. These principles implied a policy of peace abroad and of loose ties at home, leaned rather towards a confederation than towards a consolidated union, and placed the good of the human race before the glory of a mere nationality.

In the famous Virginia and Kentucky resolutions of 1798, Mr. Madison and Mr. Jefferson set forth these ideas with a care and an authority which gave the two papers a character hardly less decisive than that of the Constitution itself. The hand which drafted the Declaration of Independence drafted the Kentucky Resolutions; the hand which had most share in framing the Constitution of the United States framed that gloss upon it which is known as the Virginia Resolutions of 1798. Kentucky declared her determination "tamely to submit to *undelegated, and consequently unlimited,* powers in no man or body of men on earth," and it warned the government at Washington that acts of undelegated power, "unless arrested on the threshold, may tend to drive these States into revolution and blood;" that submission to such acts "would be to surrender the form of government we have chosen, and to live under one *deriving its powers from its own will,* and not from our authority; and that the co-States, recurring to their natural right in cases not made federal, will concur in declaring these acts void and of no force." While Kentucky used this energetic language, dictated by Mr. Jefferson, Virginia echoed her words with the emphasis of a mathematical demonstration, and laid down as a general principle of the constitutional compact that, "in case of a deliberate, palpable, and dangerous exercise of other powers not granted by the said compact, the States, who are the parties thereto, have the right, and are in duty bound, to *interpose* for arresting the progress of the evil, and for maintaining, within their respective limits, the authorities, rights, and liberties appertaining to them.

Whether this was good constitutional law need not be discussed at present; at all events, it was the doctrine of the republican party in 1800, the essence of republican principles, and for many years the undisputed faith of a vast majority of the American people. The principle that the central government was a machine, established by the people of the States for certain purposes and no others, was itself equivalent to a declaration that this machine could lawfully do nothing but what it was expressly empowered to do by the people of the States; and who except the people of the States could properly decide when the machine overstepped its bounds? To make the Judiciary a final arbiter was to make the machine master, for the Judiciary was not only a part of the machine, but its most irresponsible and dangerous part. The class of lawyers, trained, as they were, in the common law of England, could conceive of no political system without a core of self-defined sovereignty in the government, and the Judiciary merely reflected the training of the bar. Judiciary, Congress, and Executive, all parts of one mechanism, could be restrained only by the constant control of the people of the States. There can be little doubt that this was the opinion of Patrick Henry in 1800, as it was of Randolph, Madison, and Jefferson; on no other theory, as they believed, could there be a guaranty for their liberties, and certain it is that the opposite doctrine, which made the central machine the measure of its own powers, offered no guaranty to the citizen against any stretch of authority by Congress, President, or Judiciary, but in principle was merely the old despotic sovereignty of Europe, more or less disguised.

Not, therefore, in principle did Randolph differ from Patrick Henry; it was in applying the principle that their ideas clashed so rudely; and this application always embarrassed the subject of states' rights. That the central government was a mere creature of the people of the States, and that the people of those States could unmake as they had made it, was a fact unquestionable and unquestioned; but it was one thing to claim that the people of Virginia had a constitutional right to interpose a protest against usurpations of power at Washington, and it was another thing to claim that they should support their protest by force. Patrick Henry and Mr. Madison shrank from this last appeal to arms, which John Randolph boldly accepted; and, in his defense, it is but fair to say that a right which has nowhere any ultimate sanction of force is, in law, no right at all.

With the correctness of the constitutional theories which have perturbed the philosophy of American politics it is needless to deal, for it is not their correctness which is now in question so much as the motives and acts of those who believed in them. There is no reason to doubt that Randolph honestly believed in all the theories of his party; was deeply persuaded of the corruption and wickedness inherent in every government which defines its own powers; and wished to make himself an embodiment of purity in politics, apart from every influence of power or person. For a generation like our own, in whose ears the term of states' rights has become hateful, owing to its perversion in the interests of negro slavery, and in whose eyes the comfortable doctrines of unlimited national sovereignty shine with the glory of a moral principle sanctified by the blood of innumerable martyrs, these narrow and jealous prejudices of Randolph and his friends sound like systematized treason; but they were the honest convictions of that generation which framed and adopted the Constitution, and the debates of the state conventions in 1788, of Massachusetts as well as of New York and Virginia, show that a great majority of the American people shared the same fears of despotic government. Time will show whether those fears were well founded, but whether they prove real or visionary, they were the essence of republican politics; and Randolph, whatever his faults may have been, and however absurdly in practice his system might work, has a right to such credit as honest convictions and love of liberty may deserve.

On these ideas, advocated in their most extreme form, he contested the field with Patrick Henry, and carried with him the popular sympathies. A few weeks later, Patrick Henry was dead, and young "Jack Randle," as he was called in Virginia, had secured a seat in Congress.

It would be folly to question the abilities of a man who, at twenty-six, could hold his own against such a champion, and win spurs so gilded. The proof of his genius lies in his audacity, in the boldness with which he commanded success and controlled it. More than any other southern man he felt the intense self-confidence of the Virginian, as contrasted with his northern rivals, a moral superiority which became disastrous in the end from its very strength; for the resistless force of northern democracy lay not in its leaders or its political organization, but in its social and industrial momentum, and this was force against which mere individuality strove in vain. Randolph knew Virginia, and knew how far he could domineer over her by exaggerating her own virtues and vices; but he did not so well understand that the world could not be captured off-hand, like a seat in Congress. His intelligence told him the fact, but his ungovernable temper seldom let him practice on it.

Meanwhile the crisis, which for a time had threatened a catastrophe, was passing away; thanks, not to the forbearance of Randolph or his friends, but to the personal interference of that old bear whom Randolph so cordially hated, the President of the United States. Fate, however, seemed bent upon making mischief between these two men. In December, 1799, Randolph took his seat, cordially welcomed by his party in the House, and within a very short time showed his intention to challenge a certain leadership in debate. He was in the minority, but a minority led by Albert Gallatin was not to be despised, when it contained men like John Nicholas of Virignia, Samuel Smith of Maryland, Edward Livingston of New York, Nathaniel Macon of North Carolina, and Joseph Nicholson of Maryland. Randolph was admitted, as of right, into this little circle of leaders, and plunged instantly into debate. He had already addressed the House twice,—the first time on the census bill; the second on a petition from free negroes in favor of emancipation, an act of license which led him to hope "that the conduct of the House would be so decided as to deter the petitioners, *or any persons acting for them*, from ever presenting one of a similar nature hereafter;" and on January 9, 1800, he rose again, and spoke at some length on a motion to reduce the army. The speech, to say the least of it, was not happy: its denunciation of standing armies was not clever enough to enliven the staleness of the idea, and its praise of the

militia system lay open to the same objection; but its
temper was fatal, had the speech been equal to Pitt's
best. Speaking invariably of the army as "mercenaries"
and "hirelings," "loungers who live upon the public,"
"who consume the fruits of their honest industry under
the pretext of protecting them from a foreign yoke," he
at last added, "The people put no confidence in the protection of a handful of ragamuffins." This troubled even
his friends, and the next day he rose again to "exchange," as he expressed it, the term *ragamuffin*. The
same evening he was at the theatre with his friends Macon, Nicholson, Christie of Maryland, and others, when
two young marine officers came into the box behind
them, and made remarks, not *to* Randolph but *at* him:
"Those ragamuffins on the stage are black Virginia ragamuffins;" "They march well for ragamuffins;" "Our mercenaries would do better;" until at length one of them
crowded into the seat by Randolph, and finally, at the
end of the performance, as he was leaving, his collar
was violently jerked from behind, and there was some
jostling on the stairs. The next morning Randolph wrote
a letter to the President, beginning,—

"Sir,—Known to you only as holding, in common with
yourself, the honorable station of servant to the same sovereign people, and disclaiming all pretensions to make to
you any application which in the general estimation of men
requires the preface of apology, I shall, without the circum-
locution of compliment, proceed to state the cause which
induces this address."

Then, after saying in the same astonishing diction that
he had been insulted by two young marine officers, one
of whom was named McKnight, he concluded,—

"It is enough for me to state that the independence of the
Legislature has been attacked, the majesty of the people, of
which you are the principal representative, insulted, and your
authority contemned. In their name I demand that a provision commensurate with the evil be made, and which will be
calculated to deter others from any future attempt to introduce the reign of terror into our country."

To this wonderful piece of bombast the President

made no reply, but inclosed it in a very brief message to the House of Representatives as relating to a matter of privilege "which, in my opinion, ought to be inquired into in the House itself, if anywhere." "I have thought proper to submit the whole letter and its tendencies to your consideration, without any other comments on its matter or style." The message concluded by announcing that an investigation had been ordered.

This reference to the House was very distasteful to Randolph, and when a committee of investigation was appointed he hesitated to appear before it. He was still more annoyed when the committee made its report, which contained a sharp censure on himself for "deviating from the forms of decorum customary in official communications to the chief magistrate," and for demanding redress from the Executive in a matter which respected the privileges of the House, thereby derogating from the rights of that body. In vain Randolph protested that he had not written "Legislature," but "Legislator;" in vain he disavowed the idea that a breach of privilege had taken place, and declared that he had addressed the President only in his military capacity; the majority had him in a position where the temptation to punish was irresistible, and he was forced to endure the stripes.

Even Mr. Gallatin's skillful defense of him was a little equivocal. "As I do not feel myself possessed of sufficient courage," said he, "to support the character of a reformer of received customs, I shall not, when they are only absurd but harmless, pretend to deviate from them, and I do not mean to change my manner in order to assume that used by the gentleman; but he certainly has a right to do it if he thinks proper." One can hardly doubt that the experience of being insulted in public, and censured for it by Congress, though somewhat sharp, did Randolph good. He was more cautious for a long time afterwards; talked less about ragamuffins and hirelings; went less out of his way to challenge attention; and was more amenable to good advice. Indeed, it might be supposed from the index to the reported debates that he did not again open his mouth before the adjournment; but, on the other hand, he has himself said that the best speech he ever made was on the subject of the Connecticut Reserve at this session, and the record shows that on April 4, 1800, he did speak on this subject, although his remarks were not reported. In fact, he took an active share in the public business.

His spirits seem to have been much depressed. "I too am wretched," he wrote to his friend Bryan, in the course of the winter. He says that he meditated resigning his seat and going to Europe. He seems to have been suffering under a complication of trials, the mystery of which his biographers had best not attempt to penetrate; for his wails of despair, sometimes genuine, but oftener the effect of an uncontrolled temperament, tell nothing more than that he was morbid and nervous. "My character, like many other sublunary things, hath lately undergone an almost total revolution." No such change is apparent, but possibly he was really suffering under some mental distress. There is talk even of a love affair, but it is very certain that no affair of the heart had at any time a serious influence over his life.

Nothing, however, is more remarkable than the solemnity with which he regarded himself. It is curious that a man so quick in seeing the weakness of others, and in later life so admirably terse in diction and ideas, should have been able to see nothing preposterous in his own magniloquence, or could have gravely written a letter such as that to the President; but he was writing in a similar vein to his only very intimate friend, Bryan, telling him that "the eagle eye of friendship finds no difficulty in piercing the veil which shrouds you;" that "you seek in vain to fly from misery; it will accompany you; it will rankle in that heart in whose cruel wounds it rejoices to dwell." This was not the tone of his friend, for Bryan had used language which, if profane, was at least natural, and had only said that he "was in a hell of a taking for two or three days," on account of a love affair, and was going to Europe in consequence. Bombast, however, was a fault of the young Virginian school. John Thompson, one of Randolph's intimates, the author of Gracchus, Cassius, Curtius, and Heaven knows how many more classical effusions, wrote in the same stilted and pseudo-Ciceronian sentences. This young man died in 1799, only twenty-three years old; his brother William was another of Randolph's friends, and not a very safe one, for his habits were bad even at twenty, and grew worse as he went on. All these young men seem to have lived on mock heroics. John Thompson, writing to his brother in 1799, mentions that Randolph is running for Congress: "He is a brilliant and noble young man. He will be an object of admiration and terror to the enemies of liberty." William Thompson was, if possible, still more in the clouds than his brother John; his nonsense was something never imagined out of a stage drama of Kotzebue. "Often do I exclaim, Would that you and I were cast on some desert island, there to live out the remainder of our days unpolluted by the communication with man!" In politics, in love, in friendship, all was equally classic; every boyish scrape was a Greek tragedy, and every stump speech a terror to the enemies of liberty. To treat such effusions in boys of twenty as serious is out of the question, even though their ringleader was a member of Congress; but they are interesting, because they show how solemnly these young reformers of 1800 believed in themselves and in their reforms. The world's great age had for them begun anew, and the golden years returned. They were real Gracchi, Curtii, Cassii.

His little collision with the President, therefore, was calculated to do Randolph good. He had come to Washington a devoted admirer of the first Pitt, hoping, perhaps, to imitate that terrible cornet of horse, and, unless likenesses are very deceptive, he studied, too, the tone and temper of the younger Pitt, the great orator of the day, who had been prime minister at twenty-five, and was still ruling the House of Commons, as Randolph aspired to rule the House of Representatives. The sharp check received at the outset was a corrective to these ideas; it made him no less ambitious to command, but it taught him to curb his temper, to bide his time, and not expose himself to ridicule.

-⊰[III]⊱-

In Harness

IN THE autumn of 1800 the presidential election took place, which overthrew the federalist sway, and brought the republican party into power. As every reader knows, Jefferson and Burr received an equal number of electoral votes, a result which, under the Constitution as it then stood, threw the choice into the House of Represensatives, where the vote must be taken by States. This business absorbed attention and left little opening for members to put themselves forward in debate. Randolph, like the rest, could only watch eagerly and write letters, two of which, addressed to Joseph H. Nicholson, then for a few days absent from his seat, are curious as showing his state of mind towards Mr. Jefferson, the idol of his party. The first letter is dated December 17, 1800:—

"There is not a shadow of doubt that the vote will be equal between them [Jefferson and Burr], and if we suffer ourselves to be bullied by the aristocrats they will defeat the election. The only mode for us to adopt is to offer them choice of the men, and see on which horn of the dilemma they will choose to hang themselves. . . . I need not say how much *I* would prefer Jefferson to Burr; but I am not like some of our party, who are as much devoted to him as the feds were to General Washington. I am not a *mon*-archist in any sense."

These ideas seem to have startled Nicholson, who replied with a remonstrance, while in the mean time public opinion in Washington quickly decided that Jefferson alone could be accepted as the republican candidate. On January 1, 1801, a fortnight later, Randolph wrote with a considerable change of tone:—

46

"I have very obscurely expressed, or you have misconceived, my meaning, if you infer from either of my letters that the election, whether of J. or B., to the presidency is in my estimation a matter of indifference."

Then, after explaining that the will of the people would in any case decide his conduct and preferences, he continued:—

" 'T is true that I have observed, with a disgust which I have been at no pains to conceal, a spirit of personal attachment evinced by some of the supporters of Mr. J., whose republicanism has not been the most unequivocal. There are men who do right from wrong motives, if indeed it can be morally right to act with evil views. There are those men who support republicans from monarchical principles; and if the head of that very great and truly good man can be turned by adulatory nonsense, they will endeavor to persuade him that our salvation depends on an individual. This is the essence of monarchy, and with this doctrine I have been, am, and ever will be, at issue."

This was sound doctrine for a man of the people, who held no office and had no object in politics beyond the public good; but in a man himself aspiring to rival the demi-god, and who instinctively disliked what other men adored, it was open to misinterpretation. Mr. Jefferson was quick—no man was quicker—to feel a breath of coldness in his supporters. What would he have thought had Nicholson shown him these letters?

For the present Randolph's independence roused no ill-feeling or suspicion. Mr. Jefferson got his election by the withdrawal of federalist votes. The session passed without bringing to Randolph any special opportunity for distinguishing himself; and on March 4, 1801, the new administration was organized. In every way it was favorable to Randolph's ambition. The President was a Virginian and a blood relation, although perhaps not on that account dearer to Randolph's affections; the Secretary of State was a Virginian; and, still better, the appointment of Gallatin as Secretary of the Treasury removed from the House its oldest and ablest leader.

The summer of 1801 was passed quietly at Bizarre, while Mr. Jefferson was getting his new administration

into order, and preparing a series of measures intended
to purify the Constitution and restore the States to their
proper functions. On July 18, 1801, Randolph writes
thus to his friend Nicholson:—

"If you are not surfeited with politics, I am. I shall therefore say but a word on that subject, to tell you that in this
quarter we think that the great work is only begun, and that
without a *substantial reform* we shall have little reason to
congratulate ourselves on the mere change of *men*. Independent of its precariousness, we disdain to hold our privileges
by so base a tenure. We challenge them as of right, and
will not have them depend on the complexion of an individual. The objects of this reform will at once suggest themselves to you."

In other words, if Mr. Jefferson did not prove reformer enough, Randolph would do his own reforming,
and wished for Nicholson's help. Here already is the
germ of his future development and the clue to his erratic career. The writer goes on:—

"It is no exaggeration when I tell you that there is more
of politics in the preceding page than I have thought, spok-
en, or written since I saw you. During this period I have
been closely engaged in my own affairs, which afford very
little of satisfaction or amusement."

He had passed the last session in the same house
with the Nicholsons, and wished to do so again:—

"Do exert yourself and procure lodgings for us both in
time. I shall want stabling for two horses, and a carriage house . . . By Christmas I expect the leeches of Washington, having disgorged much of their last winter's prey,
will be pretty sharp set. On making up my accounts I find
that, independent of the unlucky adventure of my pocket-
book, I have had the honor of expending in the service of
the United States nearly $1,000, exclusive of their compen-
sation. Such another blood-letting, in addition to the expen-
sive tour which I undertake tomorrow [to the warm springs]
and the fall of produce, will be too much for my feeble
frame to endure. I therefore wish to lay aside the character
of John Bull for a time at least; and, although I will not

live in a sty, wish you to have some eye to economy in the arrangement above mentioned. 'T is the order of the day, you know."

And finally comes a significant little postscript: "What think you of the New Jersey supervisor?" The New Jersey supervisor was James Linn, a member of the last Congress, whose doubtful vote decided the State of New Jersey for Jefferson, and who now received his reward in the profitable office of supervisor. Randolph seems to have questioned the perfect disinterestedness of the transaction on either side.

This glimpse of his private life shows the spirit in which he took up his new responsibilities. He prided himself on independence. These old republicans of the South, Giles, Macon, Nicholson, Randolph, and their friends, always asserted their right to judge party measures by their private standard, and to vote as they pleased; nor was this right a mere theory, for they exercised it freely, and sometimes fatally, to their party interests. Whether they were wise or foolish statesmen, the difference between them and others was simply in this pride, or, as some may call it, self-respect, which made them despise with caustic contempt politicians who obeyed party orders and surrendered their consciences to a caucus. Even in 1801 Randolph would probably have horsewhipped any man who dared tell him he must obey his party, but the whip itself would not have expressed half the bitter contempt his heart felt for so mean a wretch. To be jealous of executive influence and patronage was the duty of a true republican, and to wear the livery of a superior was his abhorrence. Randolph, from the first, was jealous of Mr. Jefferson. Whether he was right or wrong is the riddle of his life.

When Congress met, December 7, 1801, the House chose Nathaniel Macon for its Speaker. Honest, simple-minded, ignorant as a North Carolinian planter in those days was expected to be, and pure as any Cincinnatus ever bred by Rome, Macon was dazzled and bewitched by the charm of Randolph's manner, mind, and ambition. Few southern men could ever resist Randolph's caresses when he chose to caress, and the men who followed him most faithfully and believed in him to the last were the most high-minded and unselfish of south-

erners. Macon was already on his knees to him as before an Apollo, and in spite of innumerable rude shocks
the honest North Carolinian never quite freed himself
from the strange fascination of this young Virginian
Brutus, with eyes that pierced and voice that rang
like the vibration of glass, and with the pride of twenty
kings to back his more than Roman virtue. This con-
ception of Randolph's character may have shown want
of experience, but perhaps Macon had, among his simple theories, no stronger conviction than that Randolph
was, what he himself was not, a true man of the world.
At all events, the Speaker instantly made his youthful
idol chairman of the Ways and Means Committee and
leader of the House. Thus, from the start, Randolph
was put in the direct line of promotion to the Cabinet
and the presidency. During the whole of Mr. Jefferson's
first administration, from 1801 to 1805, he was on trial,
like a colt in training. Long afterwards Mr. Gallatin, in
one of his private letters, ran over the list of candidates
for honors, favored by the triumvirate of Jefferson, Madison, and himself: "During the twelve years I was at
the Treasury I was anxiously looking for some man that
could fill my place there and in the general direction
of the national concerns; for one, indeed, that could
replace Mr. Jefferson, Mr. Madison, and myself. Breckenridge of Kentucky only appeared and died; the eccentricities and temper of J. Randolph soon destroyed
his influence" so that Mr. William H. Crawford of
Georgia became at last the residuum of six great reputations.

Randolph began, like Breckenridge, with marked superiority of will, as well as of talents, and ruled over
the House with a hand so heavy that William Pitt might
have envied him. Even Mr. Jefferson in the White
House, wielding an influence little short of despotic, did
not venture to put on, like Randolph, the manners of a
despot. Outside the House, however, his authority did
not extend. In the Cabinet and in the Senate other men
overshadowed him, and some dramatic climax could hardly
fail to spring from this conflict of forces. The story of Randolph's career as a party leader marks an epoch; round
it cluster more serious difficulties, doubts, problems, par-
adoxes, more disputes as to fact and theory, more contradictions in the estimate to be put on men called

great, than are to be found in any other part of our history. Elsewhere it is not hard for the student to find a clue to right and wrong; to take sides, and mete out some measure of justice with some degree of confidence; but in regard to John Randolph's extraordinary career from 1800 to 1806 it is more than likely that no two historians will ever agree.

From the moment of his first appearance in Congress, Randolph claimed and received recognition as a representative of the extreme school of Virginian republicans, whose political creed was expressed by the Resolutions of 1798. Dread of the Executive, of corruption and patronage, of usurpations by the central government; dread of the Judiciary as an invariable servant to despotism; dread of national sovereignty altogether, were the dogmas of this creed. All these men foresaw what the people of America would be obliged to meet; they were firmly convinced that the central government, intended to be the people's creature and servant, would one day make itself the people's master, and, interpreting its own powers without asking permission, would become extravagant, corrupt, despotic. Accordingly they set themselves to the task of correcting past mistakes, and of establishing a new line of precedents to fix the character of future politics. Every branch of the government except the Judiciary was in their hands. Mr. Jefferson, Mr. Madison, and Mr. Gallantin were their greatest leaders; Macon, the Speaker, was heart and soul with them; Joseph H. Nicholson and Randolph were Macon's closest friends, and by these three men the House of Representatives was ruled. If any government could be saved, this was it.

No one can deny the ability with which Mr. Jefferson's first administration began its career, or the brilliant success which it won. During twelve years of opposition the party had hammered out a scheme of government, forging it, so to speak, on the anvil of federalism, so as to be federalism precisely reversed. The constitution of the republican party was the federalists' constitution read backwards, like a mediæval invocation of the devil; and this was in many respects and for ordinary times the best and safest way of reading it, although followed for only a few years by its inventors, and then going out

of fashion, never again to be heard of except as mere
party shibboleth, not seriously intended, even by its
loudest champions, but strong for them to conjure with
among honest and earnest citizens. In 1801, however,
the party was itself in earnest. Mr. Jefferson and his
Virginian followers thoroughly believed themselves to
have founded a new system of polity. Never did any
party or any administration in our country begin a career of power with such entire confidence that a new
era of civilization and liberty had dawned on earth. If
Mr. Jefferson did not rank among his followers as
one of the greatest lawgivers recorded in history, a re-
splendent figure seated by the side of Moses and Solon,
of Justinian and Charlemagne, the tone of the time
much belies them. In his mind, what had gone before
was monarchism; what came after was alone true republicanism. However absurdly this doctrine may have
sounded to northern ears, and to men who knew the
relative character of New England and Virginia, the
still greater absurdities of leading federalists lent some
color of truth to it; and there can be no doubt that Mr.
Jefferson, by his very freedom from theological prejudices and from Calvinistic doctrines, was a sounder
democrat than any orthodox New Englander could ever
hope to be. Thus it was that he took into his hand the
federalists' constitution, and set himself to the task of
stripping away its monarchical excrescences, and restoring its true republican outlines; but its one serious
excrescence, the only one which was essentially and dan-
gerously monarchical, he could not, or would not, touch;
it was his own office,—the executive power.

When Randolph spoke of a "substantial reform," he
meant that he wanted something radical, something more
than a mere change of office-holders. The federalists
had built up the nation at the expense of the States;
their work must be undone. When he returned to Washington he found what it was that the President and the
party proposed to do by way of restoring purity to the
system. In the executive department, forms were to be
renounced; patronage cut down; influence diminished;
the army and navy reduced to a police force; internal
taxes abandoned; the debt paid, and its centralizing influence removed from the body politic; nay, even the
mint abolished as a useless expense, and foreign coins

to be used in preference to those of the nation, since even a copper cent, the only national coin then in common use, was a daily and irritating assertion of national over state sovereignty. In the legislative department there could be little change except in sentiment, and in their earnest wish to heal the wounds that the Constitution had suffered; but in the Judiciary!—there was the rub!

The test of the party policy lay here. All these Jeffersonian reforms, payment of debt, reduction of patronage, abandonment of etiquette, preference of Spanish dollars, touched only the surface of things. The executive power was still there, though it might not be so visible; the legislative power was also there, dangerous as ever even by its very acts of reform; while, to exorcise these demons effectually, it was necessary to alter the Constitution itself, which neither Mr. Jefferson nor his party dared to do. There was something not merely ridiculous, but contemptible, in abolishing the President's receptions and stopping the coinage of cents, while that terrible clause was left in the Constitution which enabled Congress to make all laws it might choose to think "necessary and proper" to carry out its own powers and provide for the general welfare; or while the Judiciary stood ready at any moment to interpret that clause as it pleased.

Certainly Randolph's own wishes would have favored a thorough revision of the Constitution and the laws; he knew where the radical danger lay, and would have supported with his usual energy any radical measures of reform, but it was not upon him that responsibility rested. The President and the Cabinet shrank from strong measures, and the northern democrats were not to be relied upon for their support. Moreover, the Senate was still narrowly divided, and the federalists were not only strong in numbers, but in ability. Perhaps, however, the real reason for following a moderate course lay deeper than any mere question of majorities. The republican party in 1801 would not touch the true sources of political danger, the executive and legislative powers, because they themselves now controlled these powers, and they honestly thought that, so long as this was the case, states' rights and private liberties were safe. The Judiciary, however, was not within their control, but was wholly federalist, and likely for many years to remain so,— a fortress of centralization, a standing threat to states' rights. The late administration had in its last moments, after the election of Mr. Jefferson, taken a series of measures meant not only to rivet its own hold over the Judiciary, but to widen and strengthen the influence of national at the expense of state courts by reconstructing the judiciary system, reducing to five the number of judges on the supreme bench, and increasing the district courts to twenty-three, thus creating as many new judges. This done, the late President filled up these offices with federalists; the Senate confirmed his appointments; and, to crown all, the President appointed and the Senate confirmed the ablest of the Virginian federalists, the Secretary of State, John Marshall, as Chief Justice of the Supreme Court.

The new President was furious at this manœuvre, and to the last day of his life never spoke of what he called the "midnight appointments" without an unusual display of temper, although it is not clear that a midnight appointment is worse than a midday appointment, or that the federalists were bound to please a President who came into office solely to undo their work. The real cause of Mr. Jefferson's anger, and its excuse, lay beneath the matter of patronage, in the fact that the Judiciary thus established was a serious if not fatal obstacle to his own success; for until the fountain of justice should be purified the stream of constitutional law could not run pure, the necessary legal precedents could not be established, the States could not be safe from encroachments, or the President himself from constant insult.

Thus it was that the most serious question for the new President and his party regarded the Judiciary, and this question of the Judiciary was that which Congress undertook to settle. Randolph, and men of his reckless nature, seeing clearly that Chief Justice Marshall and the Supreme Court, backed by the array of circuit and district judges, could always overturn republican principles and strict construction faster than Congress and the President could set them up, saw with the same clearness that an entire reform of the Judiciary and its adhesion to the popular will were necessary, since otherwise the gross absurdity would follow that four fifths of the people and of the States, both Houses of Congress, the Executive, and the state Judiciaries might go on forever declaring and maintaining that the central government had not the right to interpret its own powers, while John Marshall and three or four old federalists on the supreme bench proved the contrary by interpreting those powers as they liked, and by making their interpretation law. Randolph and his friends, therefore, wished to reconstruct the Judiciary throughout, and to secure an ascendency over the courts of law, but the northern democrats dreaded nothing more than the charge of revolutionary and violent attacks on the Constitution; the President and Cabinet gave no encouragement to hasty and intemperate measures; all the wise heads of the party advised that Chief Justice Marshall and the Supreme Court should be left to the influence of time; and that Congress should be content with abolishing the new circuit system of the federalists, and with getting rid of the new judges.

On January 4, 1802, Randolph moved for an inquiry into the condition of the judiciary establishment, and the motion was referred to a committee of which his friend Nicholson was chairman. Pending their report, a bill came down from the Senate by which the Judiciary Act of 1800 was repealed. The debate which now ensued in the House was long and discursive. The federalists naturally declared that this repealing act put an end forever to the independence of the Judiciary, and that it was intended to do so; they declaimed against its constitutionality; ransacked history and law to prove their positions, and ended by declaring, as they had declared with the utmost simplicity of faith on every possible occasion for ten years past: "We are standing on the brink of that revolutionary torrent which deluged in blood one of the fairest countries in Europe." Yet the Repealing Act was in fact not revolution, but concession; overthrowing a mere outer line of defense, it left the citadel intact, and gave a tacit pledge that the federalist supreme bench should not be disturbed, at least for the present. When it is considered that Chief Justice Marshall, in the course of his long judicial career, rooted out Mr. Jefferson's system of polity more effectually than all the Presidents and all the Congresses that ever existed, and that the Supreme Court not only made war on states' rights, but supported with surprising unani-

mity every political and constitutional innovation on
the part of Congress and the Executive, it can only be
a matter of wonder that Mr. Jefferson's party, knowing
well the danger, and aware that their lives and fortunes
depended, or might probably depend, on their action
at this point, should have let Chief Justice Marshall slip
through their fingers. To remodel the whole bench might
have been revolution, but not to remodel it was to insure the failure of their aim.

The republicans were over-confident in their own
strength and in the permanence of their principles; they
had in fact hoodwinked themselves, and Mr. Jefferson
and John Randolph were responsible for their trouble.
The party had really fought against the danger of an
overgrown governmental machine, but Mr. Jefferson and
John Randolph had told them they were fighting against
monarchy. Setting up, to excite themselves, a scarecrow with a crown upon its head, they called it King
John I., and then, with shouts of delight, told it to go
back to Braintree. The scarecrow vanished at their word,
and they thought their battle won. Randolph saw from
time to time that, so far as there had been any monarchy in question, the only difference was that Thomas
Jefferson instead of John Adams wore the shadow of a
crown, but even Randolph had not the perspicacity or
the courage to face the whole truth, and to strike at the
very tangible power which stood behind this imaginary
throne. He, like all the rest, was willing to be silent
now that his people were masters; he turned away from
the self-defined, sovereign authority which was to grind
his "country," as he called Virginia, into the dust; he
had, it may be, fixed his eyes somewhat too keenly on
that phantom crown, and in imagination was wearing it
himself,—King John II.

The debate on the Judiciary in the session of 1801-2
lacks paramount interest because the states'-rights republicans, being now in power, were afraid of laying
weight on their own principle, although there was then
no taint of slavery or rebellion about it, and although
it was a principle of which any man, who honestly believed in it, must be proud. On the day when Randolph
moved his inquiry, Mr. Bayard of Delaware, in debating
the new apportionment bill, had proposed to make
30,000 instead of 33,000 the ratio of representation,

and had given as his reason the belief that an addition of ten members to the House would do more than an army of 10,000 men to increase its energy, and to give power by giving popularity to the government. Randolph sprang to his feet as Bayard sat down, and burst into a strong states'-rights speech; yet even then, speaking on the spur of his feelings, he was afraid to say what was in his mind,—that the powers of government were already too strong, and needed to be diminished. "Without entering into the question whether the power devolved on the general government by the Constitution exceeds that measure which in its formation I would have been willing to bestow, I have no hesitation in declaring that it does not fall short of it; that I dread its extension, by whatever means, and shall always oppose measures whose object or tendency is to effect it." Throughout the speech he stood on the defensive; he evaded the challenge that Bayard threw down.

The same caution was repeated in the judiciary debate, where there was still less excuse for timidity. The bill could be defended only on the ground that the new Judiciary had been intended to strengthen the national at the expense of the state courts; and that the principle of limited powers could only be maintained by fostering the energies of the States, and especially of the state Judiciaries, and by protecting them from the interference of the general government. Randolph showed himself afraid of this reasoning; his party dreaded it; the President discouraged it; and the federalists would have been delighted to call it out. When, on February 20, 1802, Bayard concluded his long judiciary speech, Randolph again rose to answer him, and again took the defensive. In an ingenious and vigorous argument, as nearly statesmanlike as any he ever made, he defended the repeal as constitutional, and certainly with success. He conceded a great deal to the opposition. "I am free to declare that, if the intent of this bill is to get rid of the judges, it is a perversion of your power to a base purpose; it is an unconstitutional act. The *quo animo* determines the nature of this act, as it determines the innocence or guilt of other acts." What, then, was the *quo animo,* the intent, which constrained him to this repeal? Surely this was the moment for lay-

ing down those broad and permanent principles which
the national legislature ought in future to observe in
dealing with extensions of the central power; now, if
ever, Randolph should have risen to the height of that
really great argument which alone justifies his existence
or perpetuates his memory as a statesman. What was
his "substantial reform"? What were its principles? What
its limits? "If you are precluded from passing this law
lest depraved men make it a precedent to destroy the
independence of your Judiciary, do you not concede
that a desperate faction, finding themselves about to be
dismissed from the confidence of their country, may pervert the power of erecting courts, to provide to an extent for their adherents and themselves?" "We assert
that we are not clothed with the tremendous power of
erecting, in defiance of the whole spirit and express
letter of the Constitution, a vast judicial aristocracy over
the heads of our fellow-citizens, on whose labor it is to
prey." "It is not on account of the paltry expense of
the new establishment that I wish to put it down. No,
sir! It is to give the death-blow to the pretension of rendering the Judiciary an hospital for decayed politicians;
to prevent the state courts from being engulfed by those
of the Union; to destroy the monstrous ambition of ar-
rogating to this House the right of evading all the pro-
hibitions of the Constitution, and holding the nation at
bay."

That is all! Just enough to betray his purpose without justifying it; to show temper without proving courage or forethought! This was not the way in which
Gallatin and Madison had led their side of the House.
Take it as one will, all this talk about "judicial aristocracy" preying on labor, these sneers at "decayed politicians," was poor stuff. Worse than this: without a
thorough justification in principle, the repeal itself was
a blow at the very doctrine of strict construction, since
it strained the powers of Congress by a dangerous precedent, without touching the power of the Judiciary; it
was the first of many instances in which Mr. Jefferson's
administration unintentionally enlarged and exaggerated
the powers of the general government in one or another
of its branches.

By way of conclusion to a speech which, as Randolph
must have felt, was neither candid nor convincing, he

made a remark which showed that he was still jealous of executive influence, and that he wished to act honestly, even where his own party was concerned, in proving his good faith. Mr. Bayard twitted him with being a mere tool of Mr. Jefferson, and the sneer rankled. "If the gentleman is now anxious to protect the independence of this and the other House of Congress against executive influence, regardless of his motives, I pledge myself to support any measure which he may bring forward for that purpose, and I believe I may venture to pledge every one of my friends." Whether Mr. Jefferson would be flattered by this hint that his finger was too active in legislation seems to have been a matter about which Randolph was indifferent.

The Judiciary Bill, however, was not Randolph's work, but was rather imposed upon him by the party. His speech showed that he was in harness, under strict discipline, and rather anxious to disguise the full strength of his opinions than to lay down any party doctrine. The bill passed the house by a large majority and became law, while the practical work of the Ways and Means Committee fell to Randolph's special care, and proved serious enough to prevent his eccentric mind from worrying about possible evils in a distant future. He was obliged to master Gallatin's financial scheme; to explain and defend his economies, the abolition of taxes, and operations in exchange,—details of financial legislation which were as foreign to Randolph's taste and habits of mind as they were natural to Gallatin. This was the true limit of his responsibility, and there is nothing to prove that he was otherwise consulted by the President or the Cabinet.

The federalists, who were better men of business and more formidable debaters than the republican majority, offered the usual opposition and asked the ordinary troublesome questions. At this early day the rules of the House had not been altered; to stop debate by silencing the minority was impossible, and therefore Randolph and his friends undertook to stop debate by silencing themselves, answering no questions, listening to no criticisms, and voting solidly as the administration directed. Such a policy has long since proved itself to be not only dangerous and dictatorial, but blundering, for it gives an irresistible advantage of sarcasm, irony, and argument to the minority,—an advantage which the federalists were quick to use. After a short trial the experiment was given up. The republicans resumed their tongues, a little mortified at the ridicule they had invited, and in future they preferred the more effective policy of gagging their opponents rather than themselves; but there remained the remarkable fact that this attempt to check waste of time was made under the leadershp of John Randolph, who in later years wasted without the least compunction more public time than any public man of his day in discursive and unprofitable talk. The explanation is easy. In 1802 Randolph and his party wished to prove their competence and to make a reputation as practical men of business; they frowned upon waste of time, and wanted the public to understand that they were not to blame for it. Randolph set the example by speaking as little as possible, always to the point, and by indulging his rebellious temper only so far as might safely be allowed; that is to say, in outbursts against the federalists alone.

He gained ground at this session, and was a more important man in May, 1802, when he rode home to Bizarre, than in the previous autumn when he left it. Congress had done good work under his direction. The internal taxes were abolished and half the government patronage cut off; the army and navy suffered what Mr. Jefferson called a "chaste reformation;" the new federalist judiciary was swept away. It is true that, with all these reforms in detail, not one dangerous power had been expressly limited, nor had one word of the Constitution been altered or defined; no federalist precedents, not even the Alien and Sedition laws, were branded as unconstitutional by either House of Congress or by the. Executive. The government was reformed, as an army may be cut down, by dismissing half the rank and file and reducing the expenses, while leaving all its latent strength ready at any moment for recalling the men and renewing the extravagance. There is nothing to show that Randolph now saw or cared for this fact, although he afterwards thought proper to throw upon others the responsibility for inaction.

-◄[IV]►-

A Centralizing Statesman

AFTER THE session closed, early in May, 1802, Randolph retired to Bizarre and remained there, undisturbed by politics, until called back to Washington by the meeting of Congress in December. In the interval events happened which threatened to upset all the theories of the new administration. Napoleon, having made peace with England, turned his attention to America, sending a huge armament to St. Domingo to rescue that island from Toussaint and the blacks, while at the same instant it was made known that he had recovered Louisiana from Spain, and was about to secure his new possession. Finally, at the close of the year, it was suddenly announced that the Spanish Intendant at New Orleans had put an end to the right of deposit in that city, recognized by the Spanish treaty of 1795. The world naturally jumped to the conclusion that all these measures were parts of one great scheme, and that a war with France was inevitable.

Randolph's position was that of a mere mouth-piece of the President, and Mr. Jefferson adopted a policy not without inconvenience to subordinates. To foreign nations Mr. Jefferson spoke in a very warlike tone; at home he ardently wished to soothe irritation, and to prevent himself from being driven into a war distasteful to him. For Mr. Jefferson to act this double part was not difficult; his nature was versatile, supple, gentle, and not contentious; for Randolph to imitate him was not so easy, yet on Randolph the burden fell. He was commissioned by the government to manage the most delicate part of the whole business, the action of the House. It was Randolph who, on December 17, 1802, moved for the Spanish papers; forced the House into secret

61

committee, which he emphatically called "his offspring;" kept separate the public and the secret communications from the President; and held the party together on a peace policy which the western republicans did not like, in opposition to the federalists' war policy which many republicans preferred. Unfortunately, the debates were mostly secret, and very little ever leaked out; this only is certain: the President sent to the House a public and cautious message, with documents; Randolph carried the House into secret session to debate them; there some administration member, either Randolph or Nicholson, produced a resolution, drawn up by Mr. Madison or by the President himself, appropriating two million dollars "to defray any expenses which may be incurred in relation to the intercourse between the United States and foreign nations;" this resolution was referred to a committee, with Nicholson for chairman, who made a report explaining that the object of the appropriation was to purchase East and West Florida and New Orleans, in preference to making war for them; and, on the strength of this secret report, the House voted the money.

The public debate had been running on at intervals while these secret proceedings were in hand, but the reports are singularly meagre and dull. It seems to have been Randolph's policy to hold his party together by keeping open the gap between them and the federalists, and these tactics were not only sound in party policy, but were suited to his temper and talents. The federalists wanted war, not so much with Spain as with Napoleon. Kentucky and Tennessee wanted it, not because they cared for the federalists' objects, but because they were more sure to get the mouth of the Mississippi by fighting than by temporizing. To prevent Kentucky and Tennessee from joining the opposition, it was necessary to repel the federalists, and yet promise war to the western republicans in case the proposed purchase should fail. No task could be more congenial to Randolph's mind than that of repelling insidious advances from federalists. He trounced them vigorously; showed that they had offered to sacrifice the navigation of the Mississippi some years before there had been a federalist party at all, or even a House of Representatives, and after proving their innate wickedness and the virtues of the party now in power, he concluded,—

"When an administration have formed the design of subverting the public liberties, of enriching themselves or their
adherents out of the public purse, or of crushing all opposition beneath the strong hand of power, war has ever been
the favorite ministerial specific. Hence have we seen men in
power too generally inclined to hostile measures, and hence
the opposition have been as uniformly, the champions of
peace, not choosing to nerve with new vigor, the natural
consequence of war, hands on whose hearts or heads they
were unwilling to bestow their confidence. But how shall
we account for the exception which is now exhibited to this
hitherto received maxim? On the one part the solution is
easy. An administration, under which our country flourishes
beyond all former example, with no sinister views, seeking
to pay off the public incumbrances, to lessen the public bur-
dens, and to leave to each man the enjoyment of the fruits
of his own labor, are therefore desirous of peace so long as
it can be preserved consistently with the interests and honor
of the country. On the other hand, what do you see? Shall
I say an opposition sickening at the sight of the public
prosperity; seeking through war, confusion, and a consequent
derangement of our finances, that aggrandizement which
the public felicity must forever forbid? No, sir! My respect
for this House and for those gentlemen forbids this declaration, whilst, at the same time, I am unable to account on any
other principle for their conduct."

In all this matter, so far as general policy was concerned, the administration behaved discreetly and well.
No fault is to be found with Randolph, unless, perhaps,
the usual one of temper. In every point of view, peace
was the true policy; forbearance towards Spain proved
to be the proper course; distrust of the federalists was
fully justified. There was no exaggeration in the picture
of public content which he drew, or in the rage with
which the federalists looked at it. The still unknown
character of Napoleon Bonaparte was the only cloud in
the political horizon; and until this developed itself
there was no occasion for the President to hazard the
success of his pacific policy.

So far as Louisiana was concerned, Randolph's activity
seems to have stopped here. He did his part efficiently,
and supported the administration even more steadily
than usual. In the other work of the session, he was

the most active member of the House; all financial business came under his charge, while much that was not financial depended on his approval; in short, he with his friend Nicholson and the Speaker controlled legislation.

It is not, however, always easy, or even possible, to see how far this influence went. One biographer has said that at this session he spoke and voted for a bill to prevent the importation of slaves; but this was not the case. Some of the States, alarmed at the danger of being inundated with rebel negroes from St. Domingo and Guadaloupe, had passed laws to protect themselves, and, in order to make this legislation effective, a monstrous bill was reported by a committee of Congress, according to which no captain of a vessel could bring into the ports of any State which had passed these laws a negro, mulatto, or person of color, under penalty of one thousand dollars for each. No negro or mulatto, slave or free, fresh from bloody St. Domingo or from the Guinea coast, whether born and educated in Paris, a citizen of France, or a free citizen of the United States, a soldier of the Revolution, could, under this bill, sail into any of these ports without subjecting the master of his vessel to a fine of one thousand dollars. Even the collectors of customs were directed to be governed by the laws of the States. Such a measure excited opposition. Leading republicans from the North pointed out the unconstitutional and impossible nature of its provisions, and moved its recommitment. So far as Randolph is concerned, the report mentions him only as one of those who opposed recommitment, and insisted on the passage of the bill as it stood. The opposition carried its point; the bill was amended and passed on February 17, 1803. Randolph did not vote on its passage, although his name appears at the next division the same day.

He seems to have been beaten again on the subject of the Mint, which he moved to abolish. Indeed, after making one strong effort to overcome opposition to this measure, he was so decidedly defeated that he never touched the subject again, and ceased to sneer at the "insignia of sovereignty." On the other hand, he carried, without serious opposition, the important bill for establishing a fund for schools and roads out of the proceeds of land sales in the Northwestern territory, and he shared with his friend, Nicholson, the burden of impeaching Judge Pickering, whose mental condition rendered him incapable of sitting on the bench.

With this impeachment, on March 4, 1803, the session closed. By the federalists, the attack on Judge Pickering was taken as the first of a series of impeachments, intended to revolutionize the political character of the courts, but there is nothing to prove that this was then the intent of the majority. The most obnoxious justice on the supreme bench was Samuel Chase of Maryland, whose violence as a political partisan had certainly exposed him to the danger of impeachment; but two years had now passed without producing any sign of an intention to disturb him, and it might be supposed that the administration thus condoned his offenses. Unluckily, Judge Chase had not the good taste or the judgment to be quiet. He irritated his enemies by new indiscretions, and on May 13, 1803, nearly three months after Pickering's impeachment, Mr. Jefferson, in a letter to Joseph H. Nicholson, suggested that it would be well to take him in hand:—

"You must have heard of the extraordinary charge of Chase to the grand jury at Baltimore. Ought this seditious and official attack on the principles of our Constitution and on the proceedings of a State to go unpunished? And to whom so pointedly as yourself will the public look for the necessary measures? I ask these questions for your consideration. As for myself, it is better that I should not interfere."

Accordingly, Nicholson took up the matter, and consulted his friends, among others Macon, the Speaker, who, in a letter dated August 6, 1803, expressed grave doubts whether the judge ought to be impeached for a charge to the grand jury, and his firm conviction that, if any attempt at impeachment should be made, Nicholson, at all events, ought not to be the leader. On this hint that no candidate for the judge's office should take the lead, Nicholson seems to have passed on to Randolph the charge he had received from the President.

As usual, Randolph passed his summer at Bizarre. Some of his letters at this period are preserved, but have no special interest, except for a single sentence in one addressed to Gallatin on June 4, which seems to prove that Randolph was not very serious in his parade of devotion to peace. Monroe had been sent to France to negotiate for the purchase of New Orleans, while at home not only the press, but the President, in order to support his negotiation, openly threatened war should he fail. Randolph said,—

"I think you wise men at the seat of government have much to answer for in respect to the temper prevailing around you. By their fruit shall ye know them. Is there something more of system yet introduced among you? Or are you still in chaos, without form and void? Should you have leisure, give me a hint of the first news from Mr. Monroe. After all the vaporing, I have no expectations of a serious war. *Tant pis pour nous!*"

"So much the worse for us!" This sounds little like his comments on the war policy of the federalists.

The criticism, too, on the want of system in the Cabinet reflected on Mr. Jefferson's want of method and grasp. The President, it seems, enforced no order in his surroundings, but allowed each cabinet officer to go his own gait, without consulting the rest. Apparently Gallatin shared this opinion, annoyed at his failure to get Mr. Jefferson's support in efforts to control waste in the navy.

All this grumbling was idle talk. For this time, again, Mr. Jefferson's happy star shone so brightly that cavil and criticism were unnoticed. Little as Randolph was disposed to bow before that star, he could not help himself where such uninterrupted splendor dazzled all his friends. Within a month after this letter was written, the news arrived that Monroe had bought New Orleans; had bought the whole west bank of the Mississippi; had bought, Heaven only knew what! the whole continent! —excepting only West Florida, which had been the chief object of his mission.

The effect of such extraordinary success was instantaneous. Opposition vanished. The federalists kept up a sharp fusillade of slander and abuse, but lost ground every day, and Mr. Jefferson stood at the flood-mark of his immense popularity and power, while Randolph shared in the prestige the administration had gained. His influence in the House became irresistible, and his temper more domineering than ever. In his district he had no rival; in the House he overrode resistance. The next session, of 1903—4, was a long series of personal and party triumphs.

In order to give the new treaty immediate effect, Congress was called for October 17, 1803. Macon was again chosen Speaker; Randolph and Nicholson, at the head of the Ways and Means, were reinforced by Cæsar A. Rodney, who had defeated Bayard in Delaware. The House plunged at once into the Louisiana business. Although the federalists were very imperfectly informed, they divined the two weak points of the treaty: for France had sold Louisiana without consulting Spain, although she was pledged not to alienate it at all, and could convey no good title without Spain's assent; she had sold it, too, without defining its boundaries, and on this account Spain became again a party to the bargain. Spain had protested against the sale as invalid; it was to be expected that, even if she withdrew her protest against the sale, she would insist on defining the boundaries to suit herself. The federalists naturally wanted to know what Spain had to say on the subject, and they moved for the papers. The republicans were determined not to gratify them, and Randolph refused the papers.

This was treading very closely in federalist footsteps, for few acts of the federalists had excited more criticism than their refusal of papers in the dispute over Jay's treaty. Randolph rejected the federalist doctrine that the House had nothing to do but to carry the treaty into effect, yet he followed it so closely in practice that his majority almost rebelled, and even Nicholson could not be induced to go with him. This, however, was not all. Only some four months before, he had written to Gallatin himself, the only consistent advocate of peace in the whole government, that it would be the worse for us if we had not a serious war. Like many if not most southern men, he wanted a war with Spain, and was pacified only by the assurance that Florida would certainly be ours without it. Mr. Jefferson and Mr. Madison, Mr. Monroe and Mr. Livingston, had all written or said, more or less privately, that under the treaty a fair claim could be set up to West Florida as having at one time been included in Louisiana. There was hardly a shadow of substance in this assumption, in itself an insult to Spain, put forward without the sanction of France, and calculated to embarrass relations with both powers; yet Randolph, as though in order to force the hands of government, boldly stated this shadowy claim as an express title: "We have not only obtained the command of the mouth of the Mississippi, but of the Mobile, with its widely extended branches, and there is not now a single stream of note, rising within the United States and falling into the Gulf of Mexico, which is not entirely our own, the Apalachicola excepted." On the strength of this assertion, which he afterwards confessed to be unfounded, he reported a bill which authorized the President, whenever he should deem it expedient, "to erect the shores, waters, and inlets of the bay and river of Mobile, and of the other rivers, creeks, inlets, and bays emptying into the Gulf of Mexico east of the said river Mobile," into a collection district of the United States, with ports of entry and with the necessary officers of revenue. This bill passed through Congress and was signed by the President, although it actually annexed by statute the whole coast of Florida on the Gulf. As for Spain, Randolph ignored her existence; he considered her right of reclamation as not worth notice. Nothing could have tended more directly to bring on the war, which the act indirectly authorized the President to begin.

Nevertheless, there was one point in this Louisiana business which Randolph, of all living men, was most certain to mark and expose. Mr. Jefferson had instantly seen it, and had lost no time in explaining it to his confidants. What effect would the acquisition and the mode of acquisition have upon states' rights and on the Constitution? No one could doubt the answer, for it was plain that the Louisiana purchase, in every possible point of view, was fatal to states' rights. From the ground which Mr. Jefferson and his friends had consistently taken, the Constitution was a carefully considered compact between certain States, with a view to union for certain defined objects; any measure likely to alter the fixed relations and the established balances of the Constitution without an amendment required the consent of all the parties; it might even be argued, as Timothy

Pickering actually did assert, that in an extreme case a State had the right to treat the Constitution as abrogated if the status were altered against her single will. The Louisiana purchase was such an extreme case. No one doubted, and Randolph least of all, that it completely changed the conditions of the constitutional compact; rendering the nation, independent of the States, master of an empire immensely greater than the States themselves; pledging the nation in effect to the admission of indefinite new States; insuring an ultimate transfer of power from the old original parties in the compact to the new States, thus forced on their society; and foreboding the destruction of states' rights by securing a majority of States, without traditions, history, or character, the mere creatures of the general government, thousands of miles from the old Union, inhabited in 1803, so far as the territory was populated at all, only by Frenchmen, Spaniards, or Indians, and fitted by climate and conditions for a people different from that of the Atlantic seaboard. There was, indeed, no end to the list of instances in which this purchase affected the original Union. No federalist measure had ever approached it in constitutional importance. The whole list of questionable federalist precedents was insignificant beside this one act.

By what authority was the Union to put on this new character and to accept this destiny, of which no man had an idea on July 3, 1803, and which was an accomplished fact on the next day? Who did it? It was the perfectly independent act of President Jefferson and twenty-six senators. This constitutional cataclysm was effected by the treaty-making power; Congress had not been otherwise consulted; the States had not been called upon in any other way to assent; the central government, not the States, was party to the new contract.

Mr. Jefferson, in this far-reaching action, scandalized even himself. "The Executive," said he, "has done an act beyond the Constitution. The legislature must ratify it, and throw themselves on the country for an act of indemnity." He drew the necessary amendment to the Constitution, consulting his Cabinet, and getting official opinions; writing to his friends, and soon receiving letters in reply. Shocked to find that his party, perverted by the possession of power, would not hear of amending the Constitution or seeking indemnity, he supplicated them to listen to him: "Our peculiar security is in the possession of a written Constitution. Let us not make it a blank paper by construction." He said that this new rule of construction abolished the Constitution. His supporters persisted in their own contrary opinion, and in the end he acquiesced.

Randolph was probably the most thorough-going states'-rights man in the republican party, for he had assailed Patrick Henry, and was one day to stand by Calhoun on this favorite creed. So extreme were his views that at a later period he boasted of having never voted for the admission of any new State into the Union, not even for that of Ohio in the session of 1802. Now that the federalists were out of office, they too had become alive to the importance of this principle, for, at bottom, Massachusetts was as jealous as Virginia of any stretch of power likely to weaken her influence. The federalist leaders in Congress, accordingly, now attacked the administration for exceeding its powers, and Mr. Griswold of New York, in a temperate and reasonable speech, took precisely the ground which Mr. Jefferson had taken in his private letters, that the annexation of Louisiana and its inhabitants by treaty was a plain violation of the Constitution. Randolph replied, and the reply was a curious commentary on his past and future political life. Not a word fell from his lips which could be construed into a states'-rights sentiment. He who had raged with the violence of a wild animal against the constitutional theories of Washington and John Adams did not whisper a remonstrance against this new assumption of power, which, according to Mr. Jefferson, made blank paper of the Constitution. He advanced an astonishing argument to show that a right to acquire territory must exist, because the national boundaries in certain directions, under the treaty of 1783, were disputed or doubtful, and because the government had obtained territory at Natchez and elsewhere without raising the question. The federalists, he said, had wanted to seize New Orleans by force, and were therefore estopped from reasoning that it could not be annexed by treaty. The conditions of acquisition, moreover, being a part of the price, were involved in the right to acquire; for if the Constitution covered the right to purchase terri-

tory, it covered also the price to be paid for that territory, whether this included the naturalization of the inhabitants or special privileges to foreign nations. Acting
doubtless under the advice and instructions of Mr. Madison, he denied that there was any unconstitutional stipu-
lation in the treaty; he even denied that the pledge
given in it, that "the inhabitants of the ceded territory
shall be incorporated in the Union," meant that they
should be incorporated into the Union of States, or that
the further pledge, that they should be "admitted as
soon as possible, according to the principles of the federal Constitution, to the enjoyment of *all* the rights,
advantages, and immunities of citizens of the United
States," meant that they were to enjoy any political
rights.

If this reasoning satisfied Randolph, it should certainly
have pleased those who had labored for fifteen years,
against the bitterest opposition from Randolph and his
friends, to strengthen the national government; but how
Mr. Randolph, after making such an argument, could
ever again claim credit as a champion of states' rights
is a question which he alone could answer. Under such
rules of construction, according to Mr. Jefferson's view,
the President and two thirds of the senators might abolish
the States themselves and make serfs of every Randolph in Virginia, as indeed, some sixty years afterwards, was done. This is no captious criticism. Mr.
Jefferson's language is emphatic. He declared that this
construction "would make our powers boundless," and
it did so. Randolph himself acknowledged his mistake.
"We were forewarned!" he cried in 1822. "I for one,
although forewarned, was not forearmed. If I had been,
I have no hesitation in declaring that I would have said
to the imperial Dejanira of modern times, 'Take back
your fatal present!' " From this moment it became folly
to deny that the general government was the measure
of its own powers, for Randolph's own act had changed
theory into fact, and he could no more undo what he
had done than he could stop the earth in its revolution.

Having swallowed without even a grimace this enormous camel, Randolph next strained at a gnat. A bill
came down from the Senate authorizing the President to
take possession of the new territory and to exercise
all the powers of government until Congress should make

provision on the subject. Of course the authority thus conveyed was despotic, but so was the purchase itself; circumstances allowed no delay, and the President was properly responsible for his trust, which would last only so long as Congress permitted. Randolph, however, was vigilant in his watchfulness against the danger of executive encroachments. "If we give this power out of our hands, it may be irrevocable until Congress shall have made legislative provision; that is, a single branch of the government, the executive branch, with a small minority of either House, may prevent its resumption." Had he refused to confer this dictatorial power at all, he would at least have had a principle to support him, but he was ready to approve despotic principles for four months, till the session ended, though not a moment longer. In the end he allowed the President to govern Louisiana with the powers of a King of Spain until a rebellion became imminent.

Of other measures, only two were of enough interest to deserve notice. While the regular business of the session went on, exacting that attention which the chairman of Ways and Means must always expect to give, two subjects came before the House, which were to decide Randolph's future career,—the impeachment of Judge Chase and the Yazoo claims. Thus far all had gone well with him; his influence had steadily increased with every year of his service; his control over the House was great, for among the republicans who obeyed his lead, there was not a single member competent to dispute it. Already the federalists dreaded this aristocratic democrat, who, almost alone in his party, had the ability and the courage to act upon his theories; and they looked on with a genuine feeling of terror, as though they saw in his strange and restless face a threat of social disaster and civil anarchy, when, with the whole power of the administration behind him and a majority of two to one in the House, he rose in his place to move the impeachment of Judge Chase.

⊸❪ V ❫⊷

Vaulting Ambition

THERE IS nothing to show that Randolph was the real author of Judge Chase's impeachment; on the contrary, it appears from the letters already quoted that Mr. Jefferson himself was the man who set this engine in motion, and that it was Nicholson through whom the President acted. Nicholson impeached Judge Pickering, and was the only prominent manager in that cause, of which he was now in charge. Nicholson, too, had made all the preparations for this second, more serious exercise of the impeaching power. However readily the scheme may have fallen in with Randolph's wishes and prejudices, it was certainly Nicholson who urged him to action, and provided him with such law as he could not do without. Properly, therefore, the credit or discredit of the measure should have fallen upon Nicholson and Mr. Jefferson, but Randolph willingly relieved them of the load.

Judge Chase's recent charge to the Baltimore grand jury in May, 1803, offensive as it certainly was, seemed hardly such a high crime or misdemeanor as to render his conviction certain, and the impeachers thought it safer to strengthen their cause by alleging other offenses of earlier date. Yet Chase had sat on the bench and administered justice for three years since Mr. Jefferson's election without a sign of impeachment, and without complaint from the suitors in his court. To go back four years, and search old court records for offenses forgotten and condoned, was awkward. Could the impeachers excuse themselves and their House for permitting this notorious criminal to wear his robes and expound the Constitution and the laws for so many years, without an attempt on their part to relieve a groaning

73

people from the tyranny of a worse than Jeffries or
Scroggs? Could the House venture to set out on this crusade against a coördinate and independent branch of the
government, without at least an invitation from the Executive? Mr. Jefferson, however, would not burn his
fingers in such a flame. "As for myself, it is better that I
should not interfere." Nicholson and Randolph were hot-
headed men! They had the courage of their convictions,
and they accepted the difficult task.

Mr. Jefferson was a little too apt to evade open responsibility; the number of instances in which he encouraged others to do what he would not do himself is
so large as to strike even careless attention. He would
have shuddered at the idea of betraying friends, but it
is not to be denied that a sanguine temperament and
perfect faith in his own honest purposes sometimes
caused him to lead those friends into difficulties from
which, in case of failure, he could not extricate them.
Had Randolph been a wise or cautious man, he would
have insisted that nothing should induce him to touch
the impeachment until the President had sent to the
House some official message, as in the case of Judge
Pickering, upon which an inquiry might be founded.
Being neither wise nor cautious, but on the contrary
deeply jealous of Mr. Jefferson and his interference,
Randolph undertook to act alone. Perhaps, like many
another man, his mind was overmastered by the splendor
of the Hastings trial, then so recent, which has dazzled
the good sense of many politicians; perhaps he was deluded
by the ambition to rival his great teacher, Edmund Burke;
but more probably he was guided only by the political
faith of his youth, by the influence of Nicholson, and his
own impatient temper.

On January 5, 1804, Randolph rose to move for an
inquiry into the conduct of Judge Chase. No official
document existed on which to found such a motion,
and he condescended to act a little comedy, not so
respectful to the House or the country as might have
been expected from a Randolph, whose sense of truth
and honor was keen. In the course of the last session,
a bill had been introduced to change the circuits, by
which Judge Chase was assigned to that of Pennsylvania, and one of the Pennyslvanian members, John
Smilie, made a speech on February 16, 1803, in con-

nection with this bill. In order to explain why Mr. Chase should be put on some other circuit, where he would not be obnoxious to the bar and the people, he recalled the well-known stories of Chase's arbitrary conduct at the trial of Fries in April, 1800. These remarks were of so little importance in Mr. Smilie's mind that he put no weight upon them except for the passing object they were meant to serve. The idea of impeachment did not enter his head.

There was, therefore, a certain grimace of fun in the solemnity with which Randolph now rose and said that Mr. Smilie's remarks on that occasion and the facts stated by him were of such a nature as the House was bound to notice. "But the lateness of the session (for we had, if I mistake not, scarce a fortnight remaining) precluding all possibility of bringing the subject to any efficient result, I did not then think proper to take any steps in the business. Finding my attention, however, thus drawn to a consideration of the character of the officer in question, I made it my business, considering it my duty as well to myself as to those whom I represent, to investigate the charges then made, and the official character of the judge in general."

Mr. Smilie was a very respectable but not very weighty member of the House, and this sudden elevation to the rank of public accuser, which Mr. Jefferson, if any one, could alone fill with sufficient authority, was a stroke of Randolph's wit, characteristic of the man. As for the whole statement with which Randolph introduced his motion, it is curious chiefly because it is, to say the least, inconsistent with the facts. Mr. Smilie's speech had no more than the oration of Cicero against Clodius to do with Randolph's sudden zeal. Smilie's speech was made on February 16, 1803; Chase's address to the grand jury at Baltimore was made nearly three months afterwards, on May 2, 1803; and it was only then that the idea of impeachment was suggested. Yet this invocation of Smilie in place of Mr. Jefferson was less amusing than the coolness with which the speaker required the House to believe that his only knowledge of Judge Chase's conduct at the trial of Fries was derived from a few remarks made in Congress three years after the offense. The trial of Fries had taken place in Philadelphia, in April, 1800, within twenty rods of the building where

Randolph was then sitting as a member of Congress, and excited great attention, especially among the members, many of whom were present at it; Mr. Dallas, the most prominent republican lawyer in the State, closely connected with all the leaders of his party, acted as counsel for Fries, and threw up his brief on account of the judge's conduct; William Lewis, one of the best lawyers Pennsylvania ever had, and a federalist by previous tastes, was also in the case and guided the course of Dallas: yet, in spite of this notoriety, and the dissensions afterwards caused by President Adams's pardon of Fries, Randolph still asserted that the subject was new to him when Mr. Smilie, in February, 1803, made his passing allusion to it. "It is true that the deliberations of Congress were then held in Philadelphia, the scene of this alleged iniquity, but, with other members, I was employed in discharging my duties to my constituents, not in witnessing in any court the triumph of my principles. I could not have been so employed." Even if this were true, did his ignorance excuse the inaction of his whole party? Or would his effrontery go so far as to assert that he and his friends had never heard of Callender's trial at Richmond, which was to constitute other counts in the indictment?

Mr. Smilie, thus put forward as official accuser, told his story over again. Without other evidence, after a long debate, the inquiry was ordered, and Randolph, with his friend Nicholson, was put at the head of the committee. On March 26, 1804, they reported seven articles of impeachment: the first and second covering the case of Fries; the third, fourth, and fifth that of Callender; the sixth that of Judge Chase's refusal to discharge the grand jury at Newcastle in June, 1800, until they should have indicted a Delaware printer; and the seventh embracing that charge to the grand jury at Baltimore in May, 1803, which had stirred up President Jefferson to set the whole movement afoot. With this the session ended, and the trial went over to the next year.

The Yazoo claims came before the House in the regular course of business. The story of these claims is long and complicated, but it is so closely entwined with the thread of Randolph's life that to omit or slur it would be to sever the connection of events, and to miss one of the decisive moments of his career.

The rescinding act, already mentioned as passed by the State of Georgia in the year 1796 at the time when Randolph was visiting his friend Bryan, did not end the matter of the Yazoo grants, and the very pains taken to fortify that act by incorporating it in the state Constitution showed doubt as to its legality. The companies had, in fact, paid their money, obtained their grants, and sold considerable portions of the land to private individuals throughout the Union; and these persons, in their turn, wherever there was money to be made by it, had transferred the property to others. A wild speculation followed, involving some two million dollars in Massachusetts alone. Were the companies and these third parties innocent purchasers? Were they, or any of them, ignorant that the title of Georgia to the lands in question was doubtful, that the grants had been obtained by corruption, and that the State of Georgia would certainly revoke them? The only evidence that the purchasers knew their risk was that the companies in all cases declined to give a warranty as against any defect in their title from the State of Georgia.

When Georgia rescinded and expunged the act of 1795, a certain number of the purchasers surrendered their titles and received back their money. The United States government next intervened as protector of the Indians, who actually owned and occupied the land; and at length, in 1802, Mr. Jefferson succeeded in obtaining from Georgia the cession of such rights as she had over all that vast territory which now makes the States of Alabama and Mississippi. The purchasers under the Yazoo grants who still clung to their titles gave due notice of their claims, and the law which authorized the treaty of cession provided for a compromise with these claimants. The Secretary of State, Mr. Madison, the Secretary of the Treasury, Mr. Gallatin, and the Attorney-General, Mr. Levi Lincoln, commissioners for arranging the terms of settlement, reported, on February 14, 1803, that although in their opinion the title of the claimants could not be supported, yet they believed that "the interest of the United States, the tranquillity of those who may hereafter inhabit that country, and various equitable considerations which may be urged in favor of most of the present claimants" rendered it expedient to enter into a compromise on reasonable terms.

They proposed, therefore, that five million acres be set aside, within which, under certain restrictions, the claimants might locate the quantity of land allotted to them, or from the sale of which they were to receive certificates for their proportion of the proceeds, something like one sixth or one eighth of their claim.

Thus the matter now stood, and it should be mentioned, by way of parenthesis, that when, in 1810, the subject came before the Supreme Court, in the case of Fletcher against Peck, Chief Justice Marshall delivered the opinion of the court that the legislature of Georgia had, by its act of 1795 and its grants of land, executed a contract with the claimants; that the rescinding act of 1796 impaired the obligation of that contract, and was therefore repugnant to the Constitution of the United States; that it could not devest the rights acquired under the contract; and that the court would not enter into an inquiry respecting the corruption of a sovereign State.

It is plain, therefore, that any one who intended to resist the Yazoo claims had a difficult task on his hands. The President, Mr. Madison, Mr. Gallatin, and Mr. Lincoln were against him; several acts of Congress stood in his way; the Supreme Court was behind him, ready to trip him up; a very large number of most respectable citizens were petitioners for the settlement. The compromise suggested would cost nothing to Georgia, for she had given the lands to the United States, and would cost nothing to the United States, for they held the lands as a gift from Georgia. A refusal to compromise would throw the whole matter into the courts, with the result of retarding settlement, multiplying expenses, and probably getting in the end an adverse decision. It would create serious political ill-feeling in the party, and, on the other hand, what possible object could be gained by it?

Randolph was equal to the occasion. On February 20, 1804, he opened his attack on the commissioners' report by moving a string of resolutions: first, that the Georgia legislature had not the power of alienating territory "but in a rightful manner and for the public good;" second, that it is "the inalienable right of a people" to abrogate an act passed with bad motives, to the public detriment; the third and fourth recited the cir-

cumstances of the case; the next affirmed the right of
a legislature to repeal the act of a preceding legislature,
"provided such repeal be not forbidden by the Constitution of such State, or of the United States;" the sixth
affirmed that the rescinding act of Georgia "was forbidden neither by the Constitution of that State, nor by
that of the United States," the seventh declared that the
claims had not been recognized either in the cession by
Georgia, or in any act of the federal government; and
the last forbade any part of the reserved five million
acres to be used in satisfying the claims.

These resolutions covered the whole ground; they
swept statements of fact, principles of law, theories of
the Constitution, considerations of equity, like a flock of
sheep into one fold to be sheared. Randolph, too, was
in deadly earnest, and in his most domineering temper.
When he saw that the Committee of the Whole showed
signs of evading a vote on his resolutions, he stood
over them like an Egyptian taskmaster, and cracked
his whip as though they were his own negroes. "No
course that can be pursued shall prevent me from bringing out the sense of the House. Whether the question
on these resolutions shall be attempted to be got rid of
by the previous question, or by a postponement, I will
have the sense of the House expressed to the public;
for this is one of the cases which, once being engaged in, I can never desert or relinquish till I shall
have exercised every energy of mind and faculty of
body I possess in refuting so nefarious a project." He
was warmly supported, and as warmly opposed. "Persons of every political description," said he, "are mar-
shaled in support of these claims. We have had to
contend against the bear of the arctic and the lion of
the torrid zone." Matthew Lyon, once a martyr to the
sedition law, the man most famous as having spit in
Roger Griswold's face and rolled with him on the floor
of the House, was in fact a supporter of the compromise; and, being a man of strong sense and courage, did
not shrink from Randolph's whip. He made a sensible
speech in reply to this challenge, keeping his temper
on this occasion at least. At length, after two days' debate, a vote was reached, not on the question of adopting, but of postponing, the resolutions. On the first
Randolph defeated his opponents by the narrowest pos-

sible majority, 52 to 51. On all the others he was
beaten by majorities varying from 2 to 7, and after
this postponement of his other resolutions he himself
ecquiesced in abandoning the first. The object he had
in view was gained; he had forced the House to delay
legislation for another year.

If, now, the Yazoo affair be considered without prejudice or feeling, it must be acknowledged to involve a
serious doubt. That Randolph was right need not be
argued; that he was wholly in the wrong is not to be
lightly admitted. The people of Georgia believed themselves betrayed by their agents, who had, in their name,
entered into a contract against public interest, induced
thereto by corrupt motives. Were the people to be forever bound by the corrupt and dangerous bargain of
their representatives?

They had instantly, publicly, violently disavowed those
agents and repudiated their act, calling upon all the
parties who had meanwhile paid value for lands, under
the obnoxious grants, to receive back their money and
surrender their titles. What more could they have done?
What more should they be required to do?

In 1796, and even in 1804, the law was not yet
decided. The case of Fletcher against Peck, that of Ter-
rett against Taylor, and the still more famous Dartmouth College case, lay in the breast of Chief Justice
Marshall, waiting till Mr. Jefferson's day should be
over. Yet, even now, with all the weight of those decisions and many more, it is hard for laymen to surrender their judgment on this subject. Were a state
legislature to-day bribed by a great railroad company
to confer a grant of exclusive privileges, fatal to the
public interests, for a nominal consideration, it would be
dangerous to the public safety to affirm that the people
could never free themselves from this servitude. To
overcome the difficulty by resorting to some theory
like that of eminent domain is merely John Randolph's
proposition under another form; it is state sovereignty,
to which we must come at last. Was it not simpler to
assume at once an implied right, in every grant, to
alter or amend it, if contrary to public interest? Was it
politically safe, even though legally correct, to make
this hazardous experiment of tying the limbs of sovereignty with the thin threads of judge-made law?

Randolph's resolutions turned on state sovereignty, but when he came to debate he used a weapon more effective for the moment, because states' rights sound less persuasively in the ears of the party in power than in those of the opposition. He denounced the Yazoo settlement as a corrupt job, to be forced through Congress by an interested lobby, and declared, doubtless with perfect honesty, that the purity of government was gone forever if this gross outrage on decency were to succeed. In taking this position, Randolph was consistent; he stood on solid party ground, opposing a combination of northern democrats, federalists, and executive influence, which he thought corrupt. To do this required no little courage, and if there were selfish or personal motives behind his action they are not to be seen. If he struck also at Mr. Jefferson and Mr. Madison, he struck also at Mr. Gallatin, his strongest friend; and if he made enemies of the northern democrats, it was because he knew the weakness of their party principles. Mean ambition does not work in such paths; only a classical, over-towering love of rule thus ventures to defy the opinion of others. Had Randolph wanted office he would, like Mr. Jefferson and Mr. Madison, have conciliated the northern democrats and smoothed the processes of corruption; he would have shut his eyes to what was going on in the lobby, well aware that his blind war against his party must do more harm than good. Office he did not want, and he willingly flung his chances away, but only to grasp at the higher, moral authority of a popular tribune. He believed that the administration, backed by northern democrats, was forgetting the principles on which it had claimed and won confidence and power; he foresaw an over-powerful Executive purchasing influence by jobs and patronage, the experience of all past ages, and falling at last into the hands of a Cæsar or a Bonaparte. In his eyes, all the easy roads of doubtful virtue led to this. Debt, taxes, armies, navies, and offices of every sort; executive intermeddling, legislative jobs, and all expenditure of any kind that fed an interest; all assumptions of power, all concessions to influential fraud,—were mere steps to Roman degradation. Madman he may have been, but his madness had a strong element of reason and truth. He told his party that they were going wrong; the time was near at hand when he was to tell them that he could no longer share their offices and honors.

Thus far, although touching the extreme limit of propriety in the manner of his opposition, he had not passed beyond bounds, and, what told most in his favor, he won his single-handed battle; the path of compromise was blocked, and he himself was now a great political power, for never before had any man, living or dead, fought such a fight in Congress and won it. Feared by the federalists for having by an arbitrary act, avowedly his own, impeached Judge Chase for offenses long ago tacitly condoned, he was still more formidable to Mr. Jefferson and the Cabinet. With such dictatorial power over the House of Representatives, what might he not do should he oppose a vital measure of the administration, as he had resisted the Yazoo compromise? Even at this early moment, shrewd observers might calculate the orbit of this political comet, and no extraordinary knowledge of mathematics was needed to show them where to look for a coming collision.

The session, however, was now at an end, and Randolph buried himself again at Bizarre. As a curiosity, the following extracts from a letter written by him to Joseph H. Nicholson, on August 27, 1804, are worth reading. The famous duel between Aaron Burr and Alexander Hamilton had just taken place, and Burr's political ruin, caused chiefly by the enmity of De Witt Clinton and by the bitter persecution of De Witt Clinton's newspaper, the "American Citizen," edited by an Englishman named Cheetham, was the excitement of the day.

RANDOLPH TO NICHOLSON

"I have not seen, although I have heard, of the attack which you mention, upon Gallatin, in the 'Aurora.' That paper is so long in reaching me, and, moreover, is so stuffed with city, or rather suburb, politics, that I seldom look at it. Indeed, I have taken a disgust at newspapers ever since the deception and disappointment which I felt in the case of Langdon's election. If the 'Boston Chronicle,' published almost upon the spot, should so grossly misrepresent a plain matter of fact, so easily ascertained, what reliance can be placed

upon a newspaper statement? My incredulity refused to
credit Hamilton's death, which I thought it very likely would
be contradicted by the next mail; and, until I saw Morris's
wretched attempt at oratory, regarded it merely as a matter
of speculation. You ask my opinion on that subject; it differs
but little, I believe, from your own. I feel for Hamilton's
immediate connections real concern; for himself, nothing;
for his party and those *soi-disant* republicans who have been
shedding crocodile tears over him, contempt. The first are
justly punished for descending to use Burr as a tool to divide their opponents; the last are hypocrites, who deify
Hamilton merely that they may offer up their enemy on his
altars. If Burr had not fallen, like Lucifer, never to rise
again, the unprincipled persecution of Cheetham might do
him service. (By the way, I wonder if Dennie adverted to
Cheetham's patronage of General Hamilton's memory when
he said that, 'except the imported scoundrel,' etc., etc., all
bewailed is loss.) As it is, those publications are calculated
to engage for him the pity even of those who must deny
their esteem. The people, who ultimately never fail to make
a proper decision, abhor persecution, and, while they justly
refuse their confidence to Mr. Burr, they will detest his op-
pressors. They cannot, they will not, grope in the vile mire
of seaport politics, not less vitiated than their atmosphere.
Burr's is indeed an irreparable defeat. He is cut off from all
hope of a retreat among the federalists, not so much because
he has overthrown their idol as because he cannot answer
their purpose. If his influence were sufficient to divide us,
Otis and Morris would to-morrow, ere those shoes were old
in which they followed Hamilton to the grave, go to the
hustings and vote for Burr; and if his character had no
other stain upon it than the blood of Hamilton, he should
have mine, for any secondary office. I admire his letters,
particularly that signed by Van Ness, and think his whole
conduct in that affair does him honor. How much it is to be
regretted that so nice a perception of right and wrong, so
delicate a sense of propriety, as he there exhibits should have
had such little influence on his general conduct! In his correspondence with Hamilton, how visible is his ascendency
over him, and how sensible does the latter appear of it!
There is an apparent consciousness of *some* inferiority to his
enemy displayed by Hamilton throughout that transaction,
and from a previous sight of their letters I could have inferred the issue of the contest. On one side there is labored

obscurity, much equivocation, and many attempts at eva-
sion, not unmixed with a little blustering; on the other, an
unshaken adherence to his object and an undeviating pursuit of it, not to be eluded or baffled. It reminded me of a
sinking fox pressed by a vigorous old hound, where no
shift is permitted to avail him. But perhaps you think me
inclined to do Burr more than justice. I assure you, however, that when I first saw the correspondence, and before
my feelings were at all excited for the man, as they have
been in some degree by the savage yell which has been
raised against him, I applauded the spirit and admired the
style of his compositions. They are the first proof which I
ever saw of his ability."

One more letter is worth a little attention. The Louisiana business was rapidly taking a new phase. The Spanish minister at Washington, the Marquis of Casa Yrujo,
irritated by the cavalier manner in which his country
had been treated, made himself very disagreeable to
Mr. Madison, and in return was charged by William
Jackson, editor of the "Political Register," of Philadelphia, with an attempt to corrupt the press by Spanish
gold. Mr. Charles Pinckney of South Carolina, our minister at Madrid, had, without the authority of government, undertaken to break off his relations with the
government of Spain. W. C. C. Claiborne, the new
Governor of Louisiana, had managed to irritate New
Orleans. The British frigates Cambrian and Leander
were searching every vessel that entered or left the har-
bor of New York, and seizing men and ships without
mercy. It is well to know what Randolph, in his private
talk, had to say about matters so loudly discussed by
him at a later time.

On October 14, 1804, he wrote from Bizarre to the
Secretary of the Treasury, Albert Gallatin:—

RANDOLPH TO GALLATIN.

"On my return from Fredericksburg, after a racing campaign, I was very agreeably accosted by your truly welcome
letter, to thank you for which, and not because I have anything, stable news excepted, to communicate, I now take
up the pen. It is some satisfaction to me, who have been
pestered with inquiries that I could not answer on the sub-

ject of public affairs, to find that the Chancellor of the
Exchequer and First Lord of the Treasury is in as comfortable a state of ignorance as myself. Pope says of governments, that is best which is best administered. What idea,
then, could he have of a government which was not administered at all? The longer I live, the more do I incline to
somebody's opinion that there is in the affairs of this world
a mechanism of which the very agents themselves are ignorant, and which, of course, they can neither calculate
nor control. As much free will as you please in everything
else, but in politics I must ever be a necessitarian. And this
comfortable doctrine saves me a deal of trouble and
many a twinge of conscience for my heedless ignorance. I
therefore leave Major Jackson and his Ex. of Casa Yrujo to
give each other the lie in Anglo-American or Castilian fashions, just as it suits them; and when people resort to me for
intelligence, instead of playing the owl and putting on a
face of solemn nonsense, I very fairly tell them, with perfect
nonchalance, that I know nothing of the matter,—from
which, if they have any discernment, they may infer that I
care as little about it,—and then change the subject as
quickly as I can to horses, dogs, the plough, or some other
upon which I feel myself competent to converse. In short, I
like originality too well to be a second-hand politician when
I can help it. It is enough to live upon the broken victuals
and be tricked out in the cast-off finery of you first-rate
statesmen all the winter. When I cross the Potomac I leave
behind me all the scraps, shreds, and patches of politics
which I collect during the session, and put on the plain
homespun, or, as we say, the 'Virginia cloth,' of a planter,
which is clean, whole, and comfortable, even if it be homely.
Nevertheless, I have patriotism enough left to congratulate
you on the fullness of the public purse, and cannot help
wishing that its situation could be concealed from our San-
grados in politics, with whom depletion is the order of the
day. On the subject of a navy, you know my opinion con-
curs with yours. I really feel ashamed for my country that,
whilst she is hectoring before the petty corsairs of the coast
of Barbary, she should truckle to the great pirate of the
German Ocean; and I would freely vote a naval force that
should blow the Cambrian and Leander out of water. Indeed, I wish Barron's squadron had been employed on that
service. I am perfectly aware of the importance of peace to
us, particularly with Great Britain, but I know it to be equal-

ly necessary to her; and in short, if we have any honor as a nation to lose, which is problematical, I am unwilling to surrender it.

"On the subject of Louisiana you are also apprised that my sentiments coincide with your own, and it is principally because of that coincidence that I rely upon their correctness. But as we have the misfortune to differ from that great political luminary, Mr. Matthew Lyon, on this as well as on most other points, I doubt whether we shall not be overpowered. If Spain be 'fallen from her old Castilian *faith, candor,* and *dignity,'* it must be allowed that we have been judicious in our choice of a minister to negotiate with her; and Louisiana, it being presumable, partaking something of the character which distinguished her late sovereign when she acquired that territory, the selection of a *pompous nothing* for a Governor will be admitted to have been happy. At least if the appointment be not defensible on that principle, I am at a loss to discover any other tenable point. In answer to your question I would advise the printing of—thousand copies of Tom Paine's answer to their remonstrance, and transmitting them by as many thousand troops, who can speak a language perfectly intelligible to the people of Louisiana, whatever that of their Governor may be. It is, to be sure, a little awkward, except in addresses and answers, where each party is previously well apprised of what the other has to say, that, whilst the eyes and ears of the admiring Louisianians are filled with the majestic person and sonorous periods of their chief magistrate, their understandings should be utterly vacant. If, however, they were aware that, even if they understood English, it might be no better, they would perhaps be more reconciled to their situation. You really must send something better than this mere ape of greatness to these Hispano-Gaulo. He would make a portly figure delivering to 'my lords and gentlemen' a speech which Pitt had previously taught him; we want an *automaton,* and a puppet will not supply his place."

This letter, which otherwise contains nothing remarkable except perhaps its egotism, might equally well have been written by a federalist in opposition to government. The writer shows irritation at his want of influence in public affairs; he will vote a navy to blow British ships out of water; he is ready to face a war rather than surrender the national honor; he wishes to send some thousands of troops to overawe his fellow-citizens at New Orleans; and he has none but words of contempt for all the President's appointments. What else could a federalist have said, and how could he have shown less respect for the sentiments of 1800? Randolph, however, was a fault-finder by profession; what he wrote in this jocular way is perhaps not to be taken as serious. Eccentric, as his friends acknowledged, it was not always easy to tie him down to one opinion; nor was it even quite certain that he himself remembered his own opinions from one month to another. Yet in regard to the most notable idea expressed in this letter, he was so far consistent as to repeat it in a still more emphatic form during the next session of Congress; for when, on December 6, 1804, the bill for "the more effectual preservation of peace in the ports and harbors of the United States" came before the House, he delivered a violent harangue on the subject:—

"I would be glad to see a remedy more complete than the one mentioned in this bill.... I would like to see the armed vessels employed in disturbing our peaceable commerce blown out of the water. I wish to see our American officers and seamen lying yard-arm and yard-arm in the attack, and the question of peace or war staked on the issue, if the conduct of such marauders were justified by the government of the nation to which they belong. This language may appear different from what I have constantly used, but our situation is also different. Heretofore I was not disposed to engage in hostilities for the protection of our navigation, but we then had no maritime force. We have since created one. If we had no navy, we could not meet them on the ocean; but having one, I would apply it to the best purpose, that of efficaciously defending our ports and harbors, and would struggle till the whole of our marine was annihilated, if in the contest Britain should not leave us a single ship. Though we lost all, we should not lose our national honor; though we should not beat her on the ocean, we should save our reputation; but to suffer insult to be added to injury is indeed a degradation of national honor, and ought never to be borne with, let it come from any nation whatever."

There was no exaggeration in the mild remark that

this language might appear different from that which he had constantly used; but why and how was the situation different? In the name of common truth and consistency, who made the American navy? Who laid it up? Who persisted, during the utmost perils of our government, in vehement assertions that a navy was a mere invitation of insult? Who for years vomited fire and blood against the federalist party for trying to be prepared against war? In the course of American history the reader may meet with many mad inconsistencies, but he will never find one more bewildering than this. In Randolph's later life there would have been no loss for an explanation, but in this case he had nursed his new patriotism for two entire months; it was no flash of sudden excitement; it was mere temper. He was angry, and had forgotten his principles.

-⟨ VI ⟩-

Yazoo and Judge Chase

CONGRESS MET on November 5, 1804, a month earlier than usual, and Randoph came to Washington in the temper which his letter to Gallatin indicates. He was irritable, nervous, extravagant, and had doubtless many excuses for being so. More jealous than ever of executive influence, he seemed at last alive to the mistakes he had made in straining party principles; he began to lecture his followers with the pragmatic air of a pedagogue, and sought out occasions to worry them with small discipline. As chairman of the Committee on Ways and Means he reported against the remission of duties on books intended for the use of colleges and seminaries of learning, and his report dogmatized thus:—

"The Constitution of the United States was a grant of limited powers for general objects which Congress had no right to exceed. . . . Its leading feature was an abhorrence of exclusive privileges. . . . On the privilege asked for. . . . we refer to the eighth section of the first article, where it is declared that Congress shall have power to levy and collect taxes, duties, imposts, and excises; but all duties, imposts, and excises shall be uniform throughout the United States. The impost shall be uniform, . . . that is to say . . . there shall not be two measures to mete with. If Congress undertake to exempt one class of people from the payment of the impost, they may exempt others also. . . . Indeed, it cannot be seen where they are to stop. . . . Perhaps it may be said that . . . philosophical apparatus is exempted from duty when imported for the benefit of seminaries of learning, . . . but I believe that law to be an unconstitutional law, as well as some others passed by former Congresses."

This was strict construction run riot; on such princi-

89

ples it would not have been difficult to prove that Congress could lay no imposts at all, because, in the sense contended, no possible impost could be uniform; one or another class of people might always be exempt from its burden, unless light, air, and water could be made dutiable; but granting that Randolph was correct, he might at least have consoled the petitioners by telling them that a means of evading the difficulty existed; that to obtain their object they need only to go to the President and invoke the treaty-making power which brought Louisiana, all its inhabitants and all their property, real and personal, through the custom house, made them all citizens, and gave them special privileges of foreign trade, without offense to the Constitution, or authority from an act of Congress.

Two days after thus teaching the House its business, Randolph, Nicholson, Macon, and the whole body of strict constructionists undertook to tell it that Congress could not embank or bridge the Potomac, because Virginia and Maryland had a right of navigation there, although navigation might even be improved by the change. These petty attempts to restrict a power which had just been declared sufficient to subvert, by a mere treaty, the existing status of the Union, were vexatious and irritating. They drove the northern democrats into silent rebellion. The House allowed Randolph to say what he liked, but paid no attention to his lectures, and he harmed only his own cause. "Mere metaphysical subtleties," said Mr. Jefferson openly before a large company at his own table; and he added: "they ought to have no weight."

With Randolph in this state of incessant irritation, it is easy to understand the excitable temper with which he approached the Yazoo claim when, on January 29, 1805, it made its appearance before the House. At his coolest moments the word Yazoo was to him what the sight of a bodkin was to Sir Piercie Shafton; but in his present condition of mind the effect was beyond all measure violent. He took the floor, and after speaking for a few minutes with apparent self-control broke out into a tirade such as the House had never yet heard from him, or from any other man:—

"Past experience has shown that this is one of those

subjects which pollution has sanctified; that the hallowed
mysteries of corruption are not to be profaned by the eye
of public curiosity. No, sir, the orgies of Yazoo speculation
are not to be laid open to the public gaze. None but the
initiated are permitted to behold the monstrous sacrifice of
the best interests of the nation on the altars of corruption.
When this abomination is to be practiced, we go into conclave. Do we apply to the press, that potent engine, the dread
of tyrants and of villains, but the shield of freedom and of
worth? No, sir, the press is gagged! On this subject we have
a virtual sedition law, not with a specious title, but irresistible in its operation, which, in the language of a gentleman
from Connecticut, goes directly to the object. The demon of
speculation at one sweep has wrested from the nation their
best, their only defense, and closed every avenue of information. But the day of retribution may yet come. If their
rights are to be bartered away and their property squandered,
the people must not, they shall not, be kept in ignorance by
whom or for whom it is done."

After much more of this wild denunciation,
which should have been stopped by the Speaker at
once; after imputing to the House corrupt motives and
"public plunder" and "out-of-door intrigues" under "exact discipline,"—he tried to re-state his case and to
argue upon it; but his arguments were as wild as his
invective, and he always returned to the easier task of
denunciation. Gideon Granger, the Postmaster-General,
had very improperly undertaken to act as agent of the
claimants, and Randolph fell foul of him with tremendous virulence:—

"His gigantic grasp embraces with one hand the shores
of Lake Erie, and stretches with the other to the bay of Mobile. Millions of acres are easily digested by such stomachs!
The retail trade of fraud and imposture yields too slow
and small a profit to gratify their cupidity. They buy and
sell corruption in the gross, and a few millions, more or
less, is hardly felt to the account. . . . Is it come to this? Are
heads of executive departments of the government to be
brought into this House, with all the influence and patronage
attached to them, to extort from us now what was refused
at the last session of Congress?"

He felt it an outrage that he should be obliged to
fight such a battle. He raged like a maniac because his
party had gone off after false leaders, and left him to
prophesy destruction and woe to the echoes of the
chamber. A party that had come to power only four
years ago, saying and believing that they had created
for the first time in man's history a system of pure and
democratic government, under which corruption was impossible, now forced their leader to devote his most passionate energies to the task of convincing them that
the Postmaster-General, the master of executive patronage, should not be a lobbyist for private claimants on
the floor of Congress. These methods of influencing legislatures Randolph had always charged on the federalists
as their own dishonest European practices, the fruit of
their monarchical theories; he was genuinely tortured
to find himself wrong, and to see that his own followers had turned federalist. He had the courage to tell
them so:—

"What is the spirit against which we now struggle and
which we have vainly endeavored to stifle? A monster gen-
erated by fraud, nursed in corruption, that in grim silence
awaits its prey! It is the spirit of federalism,—that spirit
which considers the many as made only for the few, which
sees in government nothing but a job, which is never so
true to itself as when false to the nation! When I behold a
certain party supporting and clinging to such a measure,
almost to a man, I see only men faithful to their own principles; pursuing with steady step and untired zeal the uniform
tenor of their political life. But when I see, associated with
them, in firm compact, others who once rallied under the
standard of opposite principles, I am filled with apprehension and concern. Of what consequence is it that a man
smiles in your face, holds out his hand, and declares himself the advocate of those political principles to which you
are also attached, when you see him acting with your adversaries upon other principles, which the voice of the nation has put down, never to rise again in this section of
the globe?"

What Randolph thus said was to a great extent true.
The republican party, when in opposition, set up an
impossible standard of political virtue, and now that

they were in power found that government could not
be carried on as they had pledged themselves to conduct it. Randolph himself shared their inconsistencies.
He had talked and voted as his interests or passions
dictated, supporting the constitutionality of the Louisiana
purchase, intriguing for war with Spain, inciting to war
with England, governing by military power the people
of New Orleans, without a thought of the precedents he
helped to establish, but he had the merit of seeing
others' mistakes if not his own. He had the courage to
proclaim the offenses of his party. This it was which
gave him the confidence and support of friends and
constituents. They believed in his honesty of purpose,
and pardoned all else.

The debate went on for several days with increasing
violence. Language unprecedented was used. Randolph
attacked Granger with savage ferocity. He found the
whole weight of the administration, and especially the
influence of Mr. Madison, thrown into the scale against
him, and he struggled desperately against it. Beaten by
five votes on the division, he still carried his point in
preventing actual legislation by this Congress, and stood
in the gap with a courage fairly to be called heroic, had
it not been to so great an extent the irrational outcome
of an undisciplined and tyrannical temper. A true statesman, with some concession and good management, might
perhaps have carried all his points, thus overawing his
party, reëstablishing his favorite states' rights, and breaking in advance the force of Marshall's law. Nay, it was
not impossible that by dexterity and steady persistence
he might shut up the Dartmouth College case forever
in gremio magistratus, or drive the Chief Justice from
the bench. Randolph clutched with both hands at Marshall's throat, but to be victor in such a contest he
needed Marshall's mind.

The Yazoo debate closed on Saturday, February 2,
and on February 9 Randolph appeared with his brother managers before the Senate to open the impeachment
of Judge Chase. It was the weightiest moment of his
public life; for an instant he challenged a place in history beside the masters of oratory and power. Where all
others, including Mr. Jefferson himself, shrunk back, he
stood forward, while the object of his ambition, if

gained, assured him high rank among the great men of his century.

The impeachment of Justice Chase is a landmark in American history, because it was here that the Jeffersonian republicans fought their last aggressive battle, and, wavering under the shock of defeat, broke into factions which slowly abandoned the field and forgot their discipline. That such a battle must one day be fought for the control of the Judiciary was from the beginning believed by most republicans who understood their own principles. Without controlling the Judiciary, the people could never govern themselves in their own way; and although they might, over and over again, in every form of law and resolution, both state and national, enact and proclaim that theirs was not a despotic but a restricted government, which had no right to exercise powers not delegated to it, and over which they, as States, had absolute control, it was none the less certain that Chief Justice Marshall and his associates would disregard their will, and would impose upon them his own. The people were at the mercy of their creatures. The Constitutions of England, of Massachusetts, of Pennsylvania, authorized the removal of an obnoxious judge on a mere address of the legislature, but the Constitution of the United States had so fenced and fortified the Supreme Court that the legislature, the Executive, the people themselves, could exercise no control over it. A judge might make any decision, violate any duty, trample on any right, and if he took care to commit no indictable offense he was safe in office for life. On this license the Constitution imposed only one check: it said that all civil officers should be removed from office "on impeachment for, and conviction of, treason, bribery, or other high crimes and misdemeanors." This right of impeachment was as yet undefined, and if stretched a little beyond strict construction it might easily be converted into something for which it had not been intended; might even be made to serve for the British removal of judges by address. That, in order to do this, the strict constructionists must strain the language of the Constitution out of its true sense was evident, but they had, without flinching, faced the same difficulty in the Louisiana purchase. The actual disregard of the Constitution would hardly be so flagrant in regard to impeachment as it had been in regard to the treaty-making power.

This suggestion was actually carried out by the impeachment of Judge Pickering in 1803—4. In this case twenty senators had voted Judge Pickering's removal from office on a simple hearing of the case, without defense or even the appearance of the accused by counsel. The final vote had not declared Pickering guilty either of high crimes or misdemeanors, but simply "guilty as charged." The proceeding was a mere inquest of office under a judicial form. In the eyes of Randolph, Nicholson, Macon, Giles, and the Virginian school in general, an impeachment and a removal from office by this process need imply no criminality; it was a declaration by Congress that a judge held dangerous opinions, which made it necessary for the public safety that another man should be substituted in his place. In their eyes the Senate was not to be considered a court of justice, but simply a part of the constitutional machine for making appointments and removals.

In theory this view was very simple and reasonable; in practice it met with difficulties. The conviction of Pickering in March, 1804, was carried by nineteen votes in a Senate of thirty-four members, and, even after conviction, only twenty senators voted for his removal. Five administration senators absented themselves; several others voted unwillingly, and the immediate impeachment of Chase on the very day of Pickering's conviction startled these hesitating republicans, whose consciences were already so heavy laden. Other difficulties were still more certain. A summary vote of expulsion from office, which was feasible enough in the case of a friendless, absent, unknown, and imbecile New Hampshire district judge, was out of the question when a venerable justice of the Supreme Court appeared at the bar of the Senate, backed by a body-guard of the ablest lawyers in America, who were considerably less afraid of Congressmen than Congressmen of them. There could be no summary process here. There must be a regular, formal trial, according to the rules and principles of law. The Senate must be a court.

Cogent reasons, therefore, forced Randolph at the outset to abandon his own theory of impeachment, and, what was much more fatal, to establish a precedent tending to break this theory down. He began by accepting the whole paraphernalia of the law, and by demanding the conviction of Chase as a criminal. By thus admitting that criminality of a deep nature alone warranted the removal of a supreme judge, Randolph's victory would have made impeachment as useless as his defeat made it, for there never sat on the Supreme Bench another judge rash enough to imitate Chase by laying himself open to such a charge. To restore its usefulness he must have fought another battle under great disadvantages.

Judge Chase's offenses were serious. The immediate cause of impeachment, his address to the grand jury at Baltimore on the 2d May, 1803, proved that he was not a proper person to be trusted with the interpretation of the laws. In this address he said that those laws were rapidly destroying all protection to property and all security to personal liberty. "The late alteration of the federal Judiciary," said he, "by the abolition of the office of the sixteen circuit judges, and the recent change in our state Constitution by the establishing of universal suffrage, and the further alteration that is contemplated in our state Judiciary, if adopted, will, in my judgment, take away all security for property and personal liberty. The independence of the national Judiciary is already shaken to its foundations, and the virtue of the people alone can restore it." That by this reference to the virtue of the people he meant to draw a contrast with the want of virtue in their government was made clear by a pointed insult to Mr. Jefferson: "The modern doctrines by our late reformers, that all men in a state of society are entitled to enjoy equal liberty and equal rights, have brought this mighty mischief upon us, and I fear that it will rapidly progress until peace and order, freedom and property, shall be destroyed." These opinions were formidable, because they were held by every member of the Supreme Court; for they were the opinions of the federalist party, whose leaders were at this moment, on the same system of reasoning, preparing for a dissolution of the Union.

There was gross absurdity in the idea that the people who, by an immense majority, had decided to carry on their government in one way should be forced by one of their own servants to turn about and go in the op-

posite direction; and the indecorum was greater than the
absurdity, for if Judge Chase or any other official held
such doctrines, even though he were right, he was
bound not to insult officially the people who employed
him. On these grounds Mr. Jefferson privately advised
the impeachment, and perhaps Randolph might have
acted more wisely had he followed Mr. Jefferson's hint
to rely on this article alone, which in the end came
nearer than any other to securing conviction. In so cum-
bersome a procedure as that of impeachment, it was
peculiarly necessary to narrow the field of dispute, to
exclude doubtful points of law, and avoid cumulative
charges.

Randolph thought otherwise. Conscious that he would
meet with strong opposition in the Senate, he determined
to make his attack overwhelming by proving criminality,
even though in doing it he gave up for the time his
theory that impeachment need imply no criminal offense;
and therefore, placing the real cause of impeachment
last in the order of his articles, he threw into the fore-
ground a long series of charges, which concerned only
questions of law. Going back to the year 1800 and the
famous trials of Fries and Callender, he made out of
these materials no less than six complicated articles, embracing numerous charges. Still another article was
framed to cover a complaint founded on the judge's
treatment of the grand jury at Newcastle in the same
year. Thus these seven heads of impeachment, intended
as they were to support each other with irresistible cumulative power, withdrew the trial from the region of
politics, and involved it beyond extrication in the meshes
of legal methods and maxims. Bristling with difficult
points of pure law; turning on doubtful questions of
practice; involving a flat assumption of numerous abstract propositions, they required a categorical, off-hand
decision on the rules of evidence, the reciprocal rights
and duties of judge, counsel, and jury, the customs in
different courts and in different places, the legality of
bad manners, and the humanity of strict law, only to
prove that Justice Chase had been actuated by corrupt
and criminal motives,—for it seemed at first to be conceded that no mere error of judgment would warrant
his conviction.

The articles of impeachment which Randolph presented to the House on March 26, 1804, and which were, he claimed, drawn up with his own hand, rested wholly on the theory of Chase's criminality; they contained no suggestion that impeachment was a mere inquest of office. But when Congress met again, and, on December 3, the subject came before the House, it was noticed that two new articles, the fifth and sixth, had been quietly interpolated, which roused suspicion of a change in Randolph's plan. No one could say that the original charges involved any other victim than the one named in them; they could not be tortured into an attack on the court as a whole; but the two new articles wore a threatening look. The fifth charged that Judge Chase had issued a capias against the body of Callender, whereas the law of Virginia required a summons to appear at the next court; it alleged no evil intent, as all the other articles had done, and by thus making a mere error impeachable it put the whole court at the mercy of Congress. The sixth went farther. Assuming that the statute required the federal courts to follow in each State of the Union the modes of process usual in that State, this article impeached Judge Chase for having held Callender to trial at the same term at which he was indicted. Although the sixth, unlike the fifth article, alleged that this act was done "with intent to oppress" it was peculiarly alarming, because one of the earliest decisions of the Supreme Court had been directly contrary to the doctrine that the United States courts were bound to follow the modes of process usual in the state courts, and there was not a judge on the supreme bench whose practice in this respect had not rendered him liable to impeachment on the same charge. No one could doubt that Randolph and his friends, seeing how little their ultimate object would be advanced by a conviction on the old charges, inserted these new articles in order to correct their mistake and to make a foundation for the freer use of impeachment as a political weapon.

The behavior of Giles and his friends in the Senate strengthened this suspicion. He made no concealment of his theories, and labored earnestly to prevent the Senate from calling itself a court, or from exercising any functions that belonged to a court of law. To some extent he succeeded, but when at last he declared that the

Secretary had no right to administer an oath, and that a magistrate must be called in for the purpose; when he was led still further to acknowledge that on his doctrine the Senate itself had no right to issue writs, summonses, and subpœnas, so that all the proceedings against Judge Pickering had been unconstitutional and his removal illegal,—the Senate lost patience and rebelled. From that moment the fate of Randolph was sealed.

In all these transactions Giles and Randolph acted in the closest alliance. Their idea of impeachment was honestly held and openly avowed; they did their utmost tɔ force it on their party, and it is clear that, except on such a theory, Randolph was absurdly out of place in trying to conduct a trial of such importance. For an inquest of office, whatever such a proceeding might be, he was perhaps as competent as another but that a Virginian planter, who occasionally sat on a grand jury, should be vain enough to suppose himself capable of arguing the most perplexed questions of legal practice was incredible; and when, in addition, he was obliged to fling his glove in the faces of the best lawyers in America, his rashness became laughable. Even though he had all the resources of his party in the House to draw upon, including Joseph H. Nicholson and Cæsar A. Rodney, both fair lawyers, yet at the bar before him he saw not only Justice Chase, keen, vigorous, with long experience and ample learning, but also, at Chase's side, counsel such as neither Senate nor House could command, at whose head, most formidable of American advocates, was the rollicking, witty, audacious Attorney-General of Maryland; boon companion of Chase and the whole bar; drunken, generous, slovenly, grand; bulldog of federalism, as Mr. Jefferson called him; shouting with a schoolboy's fun at the idea of tearing Randolph's indictment to pieces and teaching the Virginian democrats some law,—the notorious reprobate genuis, Luther Martin.

If the sight of these professional enemies were not enough to disturb Randolph's self-confidence as he rose to open the case under their contemptuous eyes, the sight of the senate chamber might have done so without their aid. In spite of all his party influence, Randolph saw few men before him upon whose friendly sympathy he could count. Hated by the northern democrats, he saw the head and front of northern democracy, Aaron Burr, presiding over the court. The supreme bench, led by Chief Justice Marshall, a man whom Randolph deeply respected, was looking on with sympathies which were certainly not with him. Among southern senators, his closest associate was Giles of Virginia, whom no man ever trusted without regret. The thirty-four senators consisted of eleven northern democrats, fourteen democrats from the South, and nine federalists. If from his own party Randolph could expect little genuine regard, it is easy to conceive the intensity of ill-will with which the federalist senators listened to his argument. Moderate men, like Bayard of Delaware, and Dayton of New Jersey, had little patience with him or his opinions, while the New England senators regarded him with extreme antipathy and contempt as hearty as that which he had so freely showered on them and their friends. To face the humor of Tracy, the senator from Connecticut, was more trying than to defy the bitter tongue of Timothy Pickering, which spared not even his own personal and party friends, or to ignore the presence of Pickering's colleague, the "cub," who was "a greater bear than the old one," and whose capacity for expressing contempt was exceeded only by his right to feel it,—Mr. J. Q. Adams of Massachusetts.

Before this unsympathetic band of critics, on the 9th February, 1805, Randolph and his associates appeared, and in a speech of about one hour and a half, which by its unusual caution proved that, if now cowed, he was at least for once subdued by the occasion and the audience, he unfolded to the Senate his articles of impeachment. On no other occasion in Randolph's life was he compelled to follow a long and consecutive train of thought within the narrow bounds of logical method, and his arguments at this trial are therefore the only exact test of his reasoning powers. His failure was decided. From the point of view which lawyers must take, his arguments, if arguments they can be called, are not even third-rate; they are the feeblest that were made in the course of this long trail. He undertook to speak as an authority upon the law, when he knew no more law than his own overseer; naturally given to making assertion stand for proof, he asserted legal principles calculated to make Luther Martin's eyes sparkle with delight. From first to last he never rose above the atmosphere of a court room. Avoiding all discussion of impeachment as a theory, and leaving unnoticed the political meaning of his eighth article, he deliberately tangled his limbs in the meshes of law, and offered himself a willing victim to the beak and claws of the eagles who were marking him for their sport.

To analyze such an address is useless. Not even the warmest of his friends has ever thought it a good example of his merits, and no one will care to waste time in proving self-evident defects. Nevertheless, the peroration has been often quoted as a specimen of his more carefully studied eloquence, and since this peroration illustrates the best as well as the worst of the speech it shall stand as a fair test of its value.

"The respondent hath closed his defense by an appeal to the great Searcher of hearts for the purity of his motives. For his sake I rejoice that by the timely exercise of that mercy, which for wise purposes has been reposed in the Executive, this appeal is not drowned by the blood of an innocent man crying aloud for vengeance; that the mute agony of widowed despair and the wailing voice of the orphan do not plead to Heaven for justice on the oppressor's head. But for that intervention, self-accusation before that dread tribunal would have been needless. On that awful day the blood of a poor, ignorant, friendless, unlettered German, murdered under the semblance and color of law, would have risen in judgment at the throne of grace against the unhappy man arraigned at your bar. But the President of the United States, by a well-timed act at once of justice and mercy (and mercy, like charity, covereth a multitude of sins), wrested the victim from his grasp, and saved him from the countless horrors of remorse by not suffering the pure ermine of justice to be dyed in the innocent blood of John Fries."

These words closed the speech, and were doubtless carefully considered, probably committed to memory in advance, and intended to produce a deep effect on the Senate; but they will not bear analysis. In drawing the articles of impeachment, Randolph had carefully avoided the allegation that John Fries was "an innocent man." The managers had no idea of taking evidence in support of such a theory; they preferred to avoid it, because they knew that Fries was guilty, under aggravated circumstances, of what the law called treason; that in any case he must have been convicted; that his counsel had thrown up their brief, against Judge Chase's prayers, solely because they saw no other ground on which to found an appeal for executive pardon; and, finally, that Judge Chase had made no mistake in his rulings. All this was well known to Randolph, who would certainly, in his articles of impeachment, have alleged that Fries was innocent, had there been the smallest possibility of proving it. With what decent apology, then, could Randolph venture upon so gross and evident a misstatement of fact? What treatment could he expect from Luther Martin?

"The President of the United States, by a well-timed act at once of justice and of mercy, wrested the victim from his grasp." What made the Executive pardon an act of justice? What proved it? What evidence did the managers propose to offer on that head? None whatever. President Adams pardoned Fries as an act of mercy, rather than hang, for the first time in the national history, a political criminal, who had thrown himself, undefended, on the court. Judge Chase, then, was to be held guilty because President Adams had not hung Fries. Curran is said to have claimed a verdict from an Irish jury on the ground that his only witness had been spirited away by the attorney for the defense. Randolph claimed a conviction on the ground that, had the President not spirited away all excuse for complaint, there might have been a grievance, although none was alleged in the indictment. The whole array of Chase's counsel must have joined in broad laughter over this novel idea, as they drank that night to the confusion of democratic lawyers, and promised themselves a pleasure to come.

Their pleasure came in due time. If any student of American history, curious to test the relative value of reputations, will read Randolph's opening address, and then pass on to the argument of Luther Martin, he will feel the distance between show and strength, between intellectual brightness and intellectual power. Nothing can be finer in its way than Martin's famous speech. Its rugged and sustained force; its strong humor, audacity, and dexterity; its even flow and simple choice of language, free from rhetoric and affectations; its close and compulsive grip of the law; its good-natured contempt for the obstacles put in its way,—all these signs of elemental vigor were like the forces of nature, simple, direct, fresh as winds and ocean, but they were opposite qualities to those which Randolph displayed. The contrast with Randolph's closing address is much more striking; for whether it were that the long excitement had broken his strength, or that the arguments of Martin, Harper, Hopkinson, and Key had shattered his indictment and humiliated his pride, or whether, in this painful effort to imitate legal minds and logical methods, he at last flung himself like a child on the ground, crushed by the consciousness that his mind could not follow out a fixed train of thought, could not support the weight of this intellectual armor which it had rashly put on, certain it is that Randolph appeared in his closing speech more like a criminal fearing sentence than like a tribune of the people dragging a tyrant to his doom.

On February 27, 1805, he appeared before the Senate to make this closing address. He was ill and unprepared, although he had surely been engaged on the subject long enough to need little more preparation than a single night of hard work. He no longer had the lash of Luther Martin to fear, for his own word was to be the last; while it was clear that, as the case stood, conviction was more than doubtful, and Randolph's own reputation and authority could now be saved only by some serious effort. In spite of all these motives for exertion, he astonished the Senate by the desultory and erratic style of his address. Soon he broke down. He was forced to apologize: he had lost, he said, his voluminous notes; but it was only too evident that these could not have helped him; it would have been quite in character had he, in his disgust, flung his notes into the fire, conscious that he was helpless to deal with their mass of unmanageable matter. With or without notes, no man of a clear mind could possibly have run wild, as he now did. This closing argument or harangue, great as the occasion was, hardly rises to the level of Randolph's ordinary stump-speeches; equally weak in arrangement and reasoning, equally inexact in statement and violent in denunciation, it has fewer gleams of wit, fewer clever illustrations, and none of those occasional flashes of inspired prophecy which sometimes startled hostile hearers into admiration. When Randolph sat down he had betrayed his own weakness; he was no longer dangerous, except to his friends.

To reproduce or analyze an harangue like this, of which Randolph himself was keenly ashamed, would be unfair. He was honest in acknowledging his failure, and it is useless to prove what he was first to confess and proclaim. The task, he said, was one for which he felt himself "physically as well as morally incompetent." "My weakness and want of ability prevent me from urging my cause as I could wish, but it is the last day of my sufferings and of yours." Again and again he apologized to the Senate for his incompetency in a manner almost abject, as though he were crushed under it. He did more: he pleaded the fact in deprecation of criticism. The newspapers of the time show how complete was the impression of his failure; but among the eye-witnesses of the scene was one who recorded on the spot the effect made upon him by Randolph and his speech. "On the reopening of the court," wrote Mr. J. Q. Adams, "he began a speech of about two hours and a half, with as little relation to the subject-matter as possible,—without color, connection, or argument; consisting altogether of the most hackneyed commonplaces of popular declamation, mingled up with panegyrics and invectives upon persons, with few well-expressed ideas, a few striking figures, much distortion of face and contortion of body, tears, groans, and sobs with occasional pauses for recollection, and continual complaints of having lost his notes. He finished about half past two. Mr. Harper then made a very few observations on one of the authorities he had produced, to which he replied with some petulance."

Mr. Adams was certainly a warm partisan of Judge Chase, but he made no such comments on the speeches of other managers, and indeed paid a small compliment to Rodney, who had spoken the day before. His description of the contents of Randolph's speech is accurate enough to create confidence in his account of its delivery, and it is only to be regretted that he said nothing about that voice which Virginian hearers were apt to think the most melodious in the world.

On March 1 Randolph's defeat was at last seen in all
its overwhelming completeness. When the senators came
to a vote, only the third, fourth, and eighth articles received even a majority of their voices. The highest point
reached by the impeachers was in the vote of 19 to 15
on the eighth article, Mr. Jefferson's peculiar property.
Five democratic senators from northern States and Gaillard of South Carolina refused to follow Randolph's lead.
Worse than this, so thoroughly had Luther Martin and
his brother counsel broken into atoms the suspicious fifth
and sixth articles of Randolph's indictment that not a
single senator sustained the one, and only four supported the other, although Randolph's honor was at
stake, for Martin had openly charged him with having
misquoted the law of Virginia; "How this hath happened is not for me to say," and no defense was offered
to the charge. Wrathful beyond measure, Randolph and
Nicholson hurried back to the House of Representatives, and on the spot moved that two new articles be
added to the Constitution. Randolph's amendment declared that all judges should be removed by the President on a joint address of both Houses; while Nicholson
proposed that senators should be removable at any time
by the legislatures of their own States. These resolutions
were made the order of the day for the first Monday in
December, when Congress was to meet. The same evening Mr. J. Q. Adams made another curious entry in
his diary. Informed in society of what had taken place
in the House, he added: "I had some conversation on
the subject with Mr. Madison, who appeared much di-
verted at the petulance of the managers on their
disappointment." Considering the source from which the
impeachment sprang, Mr. Madison's diversion would perhaps have seemed to be in better taste had it been less
openly displayed.

This was the end of Judge Chase's impeachment, a
political mistake from its inception by Mr. Jefferson
down to its last agonies in Randolph's closing address.
As though every act of Randolph's life, no matter what
its motive or its management, were fated to injure all
that he most regarded, and to advance every interest
he hated, so this impeachment made the Supreme Court
impregnable; for the first time the Chief Justice could
breathe freely. Not only had Randolph proved impeach-

ment to be a clumsy and useless instrument as applied
to judicial officers, but he seemed reckless in regard to
the fate of his proposed constitutional amendment, and
was clearly more angry with the Senate than with the
court. As though not satisfied with allowing Nicholson
to throw a gross insult in the very faces of senators by
an amendment to the Constitution which branded them
as false to their constituents, Randolph would not allow
the House to appropriate money for any expenses of
Judge Chase's trial except such as should be certified by
himself, and in no case for the expenses of witnesses
for the defense. Whether he was right or wrong in principle was a matter of little consequence, for, in the
temper of the two Houses, the bill thus passed was a
positive insult to the Senate. Even Giles took up the
challenge, and declared that as he had drawn the form
of summons by which all the witnesses had been commanded to attend, without indicating on whose behalf
they were called, he could not admit that any distinction should be made in paying them. The Senate unanimously insisted on amending the bill, and Randolph
insisted with equal obstinacy that the bill should not be
amended. The two Houses were thus driven into a quarrel
and the bill was lost. Randolph then, in flat contradiction of every financial doctrine he had ever professed, wished the House to pay his witnesses out of the
contingent fund, and was defeated only by the withdrawal of the federalist members, which left the House
without a quorum whenever the resolution was brought
up. In the midst of this mischievous confusion, the session ended at half past nine o'clock on the evening of
March 3, 1805, three days after Chase's acquittal.

-◄[VII]►-

The Quarrel

THE RESULT of Chase's trial was disastrous to the influence of Randolph and his whole sect. It widened the breach between him and the northern democrats, and deepened his distrust of Mr. Jefferson and Mr. Madison, who had taken such good care not to allow their own credit to be involved with his. The Yazoo quarrel added intensity to the feeling of bitterness with which the session closed. When, after March 4, 1805, he went home to Bizarre, he was oppressed with feelings of disappointment and perhaps of rage. There is no proof that he held the President or Mr. Madison responsible for the defeat of the impeachment; certainly he never brought such a charge; but he thought them to blame for the lax morality of the Yazoo bill, and he was particularly irritated with Mr. Madison, whose brother-in-law, John G. Jackson, a member of Congress from Virginia, had been a prominent supporter of that bill, and had sharply criticised Randolph's course in a speech to the House at a time when Randolph's authority was trembling on the verge of overthrow. A few extracts from letters written during the summer to Joseph Nicholson will show the two correspondents and friends in their own fairest light:—

RANDOLPH TO NICHOLSON.

"BIZARRE, 29 *March*, 1805.... My sins against Monroe, in whose debt I have been for near five months, would have excited something of compunction in me were I any longer susceptible of such sensations; but I will write to him immediately on your subject; and, take my word for it, my good friend, he is precisely that man to whom your spirit

107

would not disdain to be obliged. For, if I know you, there are very few beings in this vile world of ours from whom you would not scorn even the semblance of obligation. In a few weeks I shall sail for London myself. . . . I gather from the public prints that we are severely handled by the feds and their new allies. Not the least equivocal proof, my friend, that the trust reposed in us has not been betrayed. I hope to be back in time to trail a pike with you in the next campaign. . . . I wish very much to have if it were but half an hour's conversation with you. Should you see Gallatin, commend me to him and that admirable woman his wife. What do you augur from the vehement puff of B[urr]? As you well know, I never was among his persecutors, but this is overstepping the modesty of nature. Besides, we were in Washington at the time, and heard nothing of the miraculous effects of his valedictory. Rely upon it, strange things are at hand. Never did the times require more union and decision among the real friends of freedom. But shall we ever see decision or union? I fear not. To those men who are not disposed to make a job of politics, never did public affairs present a more awful aspect. Everything and everybody seems to be jumbled out of place, except a few men who are steeped in supine indifference, whilst meddling fools and designing knaves are governing the country under the sanction of their names."

"30 *April.* Of all the birds of the air, who should light upon me to-day but our dapper sergeant-at-arms. His presence would have been of litle moment had he not informed me that he left you in Washington in your usual good health and spirits. You know Wheaton, and will not be surprised when I tell you that from his impertinences I picked up some intelligence not altogether uninteresting. The ex-Vice [Burr] and Dayton, between whom, you know, there has long subsisted a close political connection, and my precious colleague Jackson, who is deeply concerned with this last in some very masterly speculations, together with J. Smith of Ohio, himself no novice, and whose votes on a late occasion you cannot have forgotten, have given each other the rendezvous in the northwestern corner of our Union. The pious Æneas and faithful Achates are, I understand, about to reconnoitre lower Louisiana. As to the upper district, I have no doubt they can safely trust that province to their well-tried coadjutor, the new Governor [Wilkinson]. Nicholson, my good friend, rely upon it, this conjunction of

malign planets bodes no good. As Mr. J. is again seated in
the saddle for four years, with a prospect of reëlection for
life, the whole force of the adversaries of the man, and,
what is of more moment, of his principles, will be bent to
take advantage of the easy credulity of his temper, and
thus arm themselves with power, to set both at defiance
as soon as their schemes are ripe for execution. I do not
like the aspect of affairs. ... If you have not amused yourself with the Dean of St. Patrick's lately, let me refer you
to his 'Free Thoughts on the Present State of Affairs' for a
description of a race of politicians who have thriven wonderfully since his time. The 'whimsicals' advocated the
leading measures of their party until they were nearly ripe
for execution, when they hung back, condemned the step
after it was taken, and on most occasions affected a glorious
neutrality."

"23 October. ... I saw the great match for three thousand dollars: Mr. Tayloe's Peacemaker, 5 years old, lbs.
118, against Mr. Ball's ch. c. Florizel, 4 years old, lbs.
106, both by Diomed; four mile heats. It was won with
perfect ease by Florizel, beating his adversary in a canter.
. . . Thus, you see while you turbulent folks on the east of
Chesapeake are wrangling about Snyder and McKean, we
old Virginians are keeping it up, *more majorum*. De gustibus
non est disputandum, says the proverb; nevertheless, I
cannot envy the taste of him who finds more amusement in
the dull scurrility of a newspaper than in 'Netherby's Calendar,' and prefers an election ground to a race-field. That
good fellow Rodney has taken the trouble to send me a
Philadelphia print, full of abuse against myself, for which I
had to pay 7/6 postage. If there had been any point in the
piece I should have thought it very hard to be obliged to
pay for having my feelings wounded; and as it is, to see a
nameless somebody expose himself in an attempt to slander
me is not worth the money. I do not understand their act-
ings and doings in our neighbor State. As Dr. Doubly says, I
fear there is something wrong on both sides. On the one
hand indiscretion, intemperance, and rashness; on the other,
versatility and treachery. I speak of the leaders. As to the
mass of society, they always mean well, as it never can
become their interest to do ill. Before the election for Governor was decided in Pennsylvania, I was somewhat dubious
whether we should be able to reinstate Macon in the Speaker's chair. I am now seriously apprehensive for his election;

and more on his account than from public considerations, although there is not a man in the House, himself and one other excepted, who is in any respect qualified for the office. I cannot deny that the insult offered to the man would move me more than the injury done the public by his rejection. Indeed, I am not sure that such a step, although productive of temporary inconvenience, would not be followed by permanent good effects. It would open the eyes of many well-meaning persons, who, in avoiding the Scylla of innovation, have plunged into the Charybdis of federalism. ... Do not fail to be in Washington time enough to counteract the plot against the Speaker, and pray apprise such of his friends as are within your reach of its existence."

When we reflect that these letters were written by one angry politician to another, and that Randolph's relations with Nicholson were absolutely confidential, it must be agreed that on the whole they give an agreeable impression of Randolph. We see him, with Nicholson, Macon, and a few other very honest men, looking on with anxiety while Burr and Dayton were hatching their plot, and working on the "easy credulity" of Mr. Jefferson's temper. Their anxiety was not without ample cause, although Mr. Jefferson did not share it until too late to prevent the danger. We see them watching "meddling fools and designing knaves" who surrounded the administration, and their estimates of character were not very far from right. We see, too, the contempt with which Randolph's group regarded the "whimsicals" of their party, and "my precious colleague Jackson," brother-in-law of the Secretary of State, and John Smith of Ohio, Burr's friend, who had voted for Justice Chase's acquittal. There is no sign of violence or revenge in these letters; in reading them one is forced to believe that in this Virginian character there were two sides, so completely distinct that the one had no connection with the other. The nobler traits, shown only to those he loved, were caught by Gilbert Stuart in a portrait painted in this year, when Randolph was thirty-three. Open, candid, sweet in expression, full of warmth, sympathy, and genius, this portrait expresses all his higher instincts, and interprets the mystery of the affection and faith he inspired in his friends. If there were other expressions in this mobile face which the painter did not care to render, he at least succeeded in showing artists what the world values most—how to respect and dignify their subject.

Randolph's letters to Nicholson were not more temperate or sensible than those he wrote to Gallatin at the same time, which covertly suggest without openly expressing two of the writer's antipathies, the Smiths of Maryland and Mr. Madison. Robert Smith was Secretary of the Navy, and Mr. Madison was a rival with Mr. Monroe for the succession to the presidency.

RANDOLPH TO GALLATIN.

"28 *June*, 1805. . . . I do not understand your manœuvres at headquarters, nor should I be surprised to see the Navy Department abolished, or, in more appropriate phrase, swept by the board, at the next session of Congress. The nation has had the most conclusive proof that a head is no necessary appendange to the establishment."

"25 *October*. . . I look forward to the ensuing session of Congress with no very pleasant feelings. To say nothing of the disadvantages of the place, natural as well as acquired, I anticipate a plentiful harvest of bickering and blunders; of which, however, I hope to be a quiet if not an unconcerned spectator. . . . I regret exceedingly Mr. Jefferson's resolution to retire, and almost as much the premature annunciation of that determination. It almost precludes a revision of his purpose, to say nothing of the intrigues which it will set on foot. If I were sure that Monroe would succeed him, my regret would be very much diminished. Here, you see, the Virginian breaks out; but, like the Prussian cadet, 'I must request you not to make this known to the Secretary of the Treasury.' "

The sudden announcement of Mr. Jefferson's withdrawal now made Madison a candidate for the presidency in 1808, and, in Randolph's opinion, Madison was a Yazoo man, a colorless semi-federalist, an intriguer with northern democrats and southern speculators, one who never set his face firmly against an intrigue or a job. Holding the man at this low estimate, it was out of the question for Randolph to support him, and he turned to Monroe, who alone could contest with Madison the State of Virginia. As luck would have it,

Mr. Madison, unknown to Randolph, was doing much
to justify this hostility. Between him and the President
at Washington, and Mr. Monroe and Mr. Charles
Pinckney at Madrid, the Spanish dispute had been
brought to a pass which only Randolph's tongue could
describe. After claiming West Florida as a part of
the Louisiana purchase, and allowing Randolph to erect
Mobile by law into a collection district for the United
States customs, they had been compelled to receive a
terrible castigation from the Marquis of Casa Yrujo at
Washington, and to hear his bitter severities supported
at Madrid and indorsed at Paris. Their own minister
at Madrid, Charles Pinckney, undertaking to bully the
Spanish government into concessions, actually made a
sort of public declaration of war, which Mr. Madison
hastily disavowed by sending Monroe to Madrid. Monroe suffered ignominious defeat. The Spanish government, which, as must be owned, was wholly in the right,
listened very civilly to all that Monroe had to say, and
after keeping him five months hanging about Madrid
declined to yield a single point, and left him to travel
back to Paris in high dudgeon. At Paris, M. Talleyrand
coldly announced that an attack upon Spain was an
attack upon France, and that Spain was right in every
particular. Monroe returned to his legation at London,
not a little bewildered and mortified, just in time to find
that Mr. Pitt, during his absence, had upset the rules
hitherto recognized as regulating the subject of neutral
commerce, and that Sir William Scott had announced
in his Admiralty Court a new decision, which swept
scores of innocent American ships, without warning, as
good prize into British ports.

Here was a list of misadventures well calculated to
keep Mr. Madison busily at work, with very little prospect of repairing them. For a time during the summer
of 1805, every one at Washington, except the Secretary
of the Treasury, fulminated war against Spain. On re-
flection, however, the President thought better of it. This
pacific turn took place about October 23, when Randolph was writing so mildly to Nicholson and Gallatin;
and it was caused ostensibly by the war news in Europe.
At a cabinet meeting on November 12, Mr. Jefferson
accordingly suggested a new overture to Bonaparte. "I
propose," said he in his manuscript memoranda, "we

should address ourselves to France, informing her it was a last effort at amicable settlement with Spain, *and offer to her or through her a sum of money for the rights of Spain east of Iberville,* say the Floridas." "It was agreed unanimously, and the sum to be offered fixed not to exceed five million dollars." Not only was it distinctly understood and stated in Mr. Jefferson's own hand at the time that this money "was to be the exciting motive for France, to whom Spain is in arrears for subsidies," but in the course of the next week dispatches arrived from Paris containing an informal offer from Talleyrand to effect the object desired on condition of a payment of seven millions, which were of course to go to France; and this proposition from Talleyrand was instantly accepted as the groundwork of the new offer of five millions.

The President wished to send instructions on the spot authorizing General Armstrong, our minister at Paris, to pledge government for the first installment of two millions, but was overruled, and it was decided to wait an appropriation from Congress. Then the question rose, How was the subject to be got before Congress? Secrecy was required, for in this whole transaction everything was to be secret; but to conceal measures which must be confided to two hundred men was not a light task, and Mr. Jefferson, with his easy temper, forgot that John Randolph was not so easy-tempered as himself.

At length the President arranged the plan. He sent to Congress his annual message, containing a very war-like review of the Spanish difficulties, and a few days later he followed up this attack by sending papers showing, among other things, that trespasses had been committed in the Mississippi territory by two parties of Spanish subjects. To these communications Congress was to respond in a series of belligerent resolutions, drawn by the President himself. This done, he was to send a secret message requesting an appropriation of two millions towards buying Florida, and this secret message was to be made the subject of a confidential report from a special committee, to be followed by an immediate appropriation.

In due time the matter was arranged. Congress met on December 2. Macon, after a sharp contest, was reëlected Speaker, the northern democrats at last working

up their courage so far as fairly to rebel against the
tyranny of the Virginian group. Randolph and Nicholson were again put at the head of the Ways and Means
Committee. The annual message, sounding war, was sent
in on December 3; the secret message, inviting Congress to make provision for a settlement, followed on
December 6: both were referred to committees at the
head of which Randolph and Nicholson were placed,
and the President restlessly waited for the echo of his
words.

The echo did not come. On the contrary, a series of
lively scenes followed such as no comic dramatist, neither Sheridan nor Mark Twain himself, could represent
with all the humor of the reality. Either dramatist or
novelist would be taxed with gross exaggeration who
should describe the events of this winter as grotesquely
as they occurred, or should paint the queer figure of
Randolph, booted, riding-whip in hand, flying about
among the astonished statesmen, and flinging, one after
the other, Mr. Jefferson, Mr. Madison, and dozens of
helpless congressmen headlong into the mire. The instant
Randolph grasped the situation, he saw that Mr. Madison had converted the Spanish dispute into a French
job. He put the President's messages in his pocket.
Honestly indignant at what he considered a mean attempt to bribe one nation to join in robbing another, he
thought the whole transaction only worthy of Madison's
groveling character. All his prejudices were strengthened
and his contempt for the Secretary was turned into a
passion. Meanwhile, he had found that Mr. Madison's
partisans were extremely active, and that his candidacy
was to be prevented only by vigorous resistance. "One
of the first causes of surprise," said he, "which presented
itself to me, on coming to the seat of government, was
that, while the people of the United States thought all
eyes were fixed on the shores of the Atlantic, all eyes
were in fact fixed on the half-way house between this
and Georgetown; that the question was not what we
should do with France or Spain or England, but who
should be the next President." " I came here disposed to
coöperate with the government in all its measures. I
told them so." Mr. Madison's avowed candidacy and the
disclosure of the two-million job cut all pacific plans

short; he had no choice but to interpose; he felt himself forced into a dilemma.

For a time he hesitated. Calling his committee together, he affected to see nothing in the secret message that could be construed as a request for money to purchase Florida, and a majority of the committee joined him in this view. He went to see Mr. Madison, and, according to his account, the Secretary told him that France was the great obstacle to the compromise of Spanish difficulties; that she would not permit Spain to settle her disputes with us because France wanted money, and we must give her money or have a Spanish and French war,—all which, whether Mr. Madison said it or not, was true, but put a terrible weapon into Randolph's hands. He called on the President, always affecting total ignorance as to executive plans, and professing a wish to coöperate with the government so far as his principles and judgement would permit; yet when Mr. Jefferson explained that he wanted two millions to buy Florida, Randolph replied without reserve that he would never consent, because the money had not been asked for in the message, and he would not take on his own shoulders or those of the House the proper responsibility of the Executive; but even if the money had been expressly asked, he should have been averse to granting it, because, after the failure of every attempt at negotiation, such a step would disgrace us forever; because France would be encouraged to blackmail us on all occasions, and England would feel contempt for our measures and attitude towards herself. He did not mince his words.

The meeting of the committee and the interviews with Mr. Madison and the President seem all to have taken place on December 7 and 8. Randolph now waited a week, and then on December 14 coolly set out for Baltimore, where he passed another week, while the administration was fuming in Washington, unable to call the committee together. On December 21 he returned, and by this time the excitement had waxed high, so that even his friend Nicholson remonstrated. The committee was instantly called, and Randolph, booted and spurred, as he had ridden from Baltimore, was hurrying to the committee-room, when he was stopped by his friend Gallatin, who put into his hands a paper headed "Pro-

vision for the purchase of Florida." Randolph broke
out upon him with a strong expression of disgust. He
declared that he would not vote a shilling; that the
whole proceeding was highly disingenuous; that the
President said one thing in public, another in private,
took all the honor to himself, and threw all the odium
on Congress; and that true wisdom and cunning were
utterly incompatible in the management of great affairs.
Then, striding off to his committee, he put his opinions
into something more than words. Except for Mr. Bidwell of Massachusetts, the committee was wholly under
his control, and, instead of reporting the two-million appropriation proposed by Mr. Bidwell, the majority directed Randolph to ask the Secretary of War what force
was needed to protect the southwest frontier. When the
Secretary's answer was received, the committee met
again, and a second time Mr. Bidwell moved the resolution to appropriate the two millions. Randolph induced
the committee to reject the motion, and then himself
drafted a warlike report, which closed with a resolution
to raise troops for the defense of the southwest frontiers
"from Spanish inroad and insult."

He seems to have dragged Nicholson with him by
main force, for among Judge Nicholson's papers is a
slip of Randolph's handwriting, carefully preserved and
indorsed in the Judge's hand: "John Randolph's note relative to the vote of two millions for the Floridas. Last
of December, 1805, or first of January, 1806, just before the report was made."

RANDOLPH TO NICHOLSON

"I am still too unwell to turn out. My bowels are torn all
to pieces. If *you* persist in voting the money, the committee will alter its report. Write me on this subject, and tell
me what you are doing. How is Edward to-day? I've heard
from St. George. He got to Norfolk in time for the Intrepid,
on the 24th, Tuesday. She was loaded, and only waiting for
a fair wind. If the southeaster of Friday did not drive her
back into the Chesapeake, she has by this time crossed the
Gulf Stream. The poor fellow was very seasick going down
the bay. Yours truly,   J.R.
"MR. NICHOLSON of Maryland."

Nicholson did not persist, and accordingly the report as Randolph drafted it was adopted by the aid of federalist votes in committee, and was presented to the House on January 3, 1806. This serio-comic drama had now consumed a month, during which time Randolph was gravely undertaking to govern the country in spite of itself, and, by tactics of delay, resistance, and dictation, to defeat the will of the President and the party. He had succeeded in checking the Yazoo compromise by like tactics, and he did not altogether fail in this new struggle, although no sooner had the House recovered possession of the subject than it went into secret session, flung Randolph's report aside, and took up in its place the President's two-million appropriation. Randolph, whose temper never allowed him to play a losing game with coolness or skill, threw himself with a sort of fury into the struggle over his report, and day after day for a week occupied the floor in committee of the whole House. Beaten in committee, and forced to see the appropriation reported, he kept up his opposition at every stage in its passage, while the federalists smiled approval and the northern democrats sulkily voted as they were bidden. On January 11 Randolph's warlike report was rejected by a vote of 72 to 58, and on the 14th the House adopted Bidwell's resolution by a vote of 77 to 54, the federalists and twenty-seven republicans voting with Randolph against the administration.

At length the House reopened its doors, and the world asked curiously what had happened in the long conclave. Randolph was not the man to let himself be overridden in secret. His method of attack was always the same: to spring suddenly, violently, straight at the face of his opponent was his invariable rule; and in this sort of rough-and-tumble he had no equal. In the white heat of passionate rhetoric he could gouge and kick, bite off an ear or a nose, or hit below the waist; and he did it with astonishing quickness and persistence. No public man in America ever rivaled him in these respects; it was his unapproached talent. With a frail figure, wretched health, and despondent temperament, he could stand on the floor of the House two or three hours at a time, day after day, and with violent gesticulation and piercing voice pour out a continuous stream of vituperation in well-chosen language and with sparkling illustration. In the spring of 1806 he was new in the rôle, and still wore some of the shreds and patches of official dignity. The world was scandalized or amused, according to its politics, at seeing the President's cousin and friend, Virginian of Virginians, spoiled child of his party and recognized mouthpiece of the administration, a partisan railer against federalism, whose bitter tongue had for years spit defiance upon everything smacking of federal principles, now suddenly turn about and rail at Mr. Jefferson and Mr. Madison, as he had railed at Washington and John Adams, while he voted steadily with federalists and exercised diabolical ingenuity to thwart and defeat the measures of friends. His melodramatic success was largely one of scandal, but there was in it also an element of respectability. To defy power requires courage, and although Randolph's audacity too closely resembled mere bad temper, yet it was rare, and to the uncritical public admirable. Moreover, there could be no doubt of the infernal ability with which he caught and tortured his victims; and finally, although the question of fact was unfortunately little to the purpose even then, and now only interests mere fumblers of historical detail, it is quite certain that in his assertions he was essentially correct, and that the sting of his criticisms lay in their truth.

On March 5, 1806, he began his long public career of opposition. Mr. Gregg of Pennsylvania had offered a resolution for prohibiting the importation of British goods, in retaliation for Mr. Pitt's attack on our carrying trade. Mr. Crowninshield of Salem supported the measure in a speech strongly warlike in tone, which certainly promised more than was afterwards achieved as a result of our future conquests, besides suggesting confiscation of British debts to the amount of forty million dollars. Mr. Crowninshield was a New England democrat, a thorough supporter of Mr. Jefferson, a "Yazoo man," who had lately allowed himself to be made Secretary of the Navy and declined to serve. On all these accounts he was an object of hatred to Randolph, who rose when he sat down.

First he gave Mr. Crowninshield a stinging blow in the face: "I am not surprised to hear men advocate these wild opinions, to see them, goaded on by a spirit of mercantile avarice, straining their feeble strength to excite the nation to war, when they have reached this stage of infatuation that we are an overmatch for Great Britain on the ocean. It is mere waste of time to reason with such persons. They do not deserve anything like serious refutation. The proper arguments for such statesmen are a strait-waistcoat, a dark room, water gruel, and depletion." Then, after a few words on the dispute with England, adopting the extreme ground that the carrying trade was a mushroom, a fungus, not worth a contest, an unfair trade, to protect which we were to be plunged into war by the spirit of avaricious traffic, he hit one of his striking illustrations: "What! shall this great mammoth of the American forest leave his native element, and plunge into the water in a mad contest with the shark! Let him beware that his proboscis is not bitten off in the engagement. Let him stay on shore, and not be excited by the mussels and periwinkles on the strand." Then he touched on the policy of throwing weight into the scale of France against England, and on the effects of foreign war in subverting the Constitution, gradually coming round to the proposed confiscation of British debts in order to strike another ugly blow at Mr. Crowninshield's face: "God help you, if these are your ways and means for carrying on war; if your finances are in the hands of such a chancellor of the exchequer! Because a man can take an observation and keep a log-book and a reckoning, can navigate a cock-boat to the West Indies or the East, shall he aspire to navigate the great vessel of state,—to stand at the helm of public councils? *Ne sutor ultra crepidam!*"

This, however, was mere by-play; it was not Crowninshield at whom his harangue was aimed, but far more important game, and his audience could see him approach nearer and nearer his real victim, as though he were himself drawn on against his own judgment by the fascination of hatred.

"You may go to war for this excrescence of the carrying trade, and make peace at the expense of the Constitution; your Executive will lord it over you." "I have before protested, and I again protest, against secret, irresponsible, overruling influence. The first question I asked when I saw the gentleman's resolution was, 'Is this a measure of the Cabinet?' Not of an open, declared Cabinet, but of an in-

visible, inscrutable, unconstitutional Cabinet, without responsibility, unknown to the Constitution! I speak of back-stairs
influence,—of men who bring messages to this House,
which, although they do not appear on its journals, govern
its decisions. Sir, the first question I asked on the subject of
British relations was, 'What is the opinion of the Cabinet?'
'What measures will they recommend to Congress?' Well
knowing that, whatever measures we might take, they
must execute them, and therefore that we should have their
opinion on the subject. My answer was, and from a Cabinet
minister, too, *'There is no longer any Cabinet.'* Subsequent
circumstances, sir, have given me a personal knowledge of
the fact."

This attempt to drag Mr. Gallatin into the business of
discrediting the President and Secretary of State was a
serious if not a fatal mistake; but Randolph was already out of his head. After alienating Gallatin, he
insulted the whole House, exasperating poor Sloan of
New Jersey as he had already embittered Crowninshield: "Like true political quacks, you deal only in
hand-bills and nostrums. Sir, I blush to see the record
of our proceedings; they resemble nothing but the adver-
tisements of patent medicines. Here you have 'the worm-
destroying lozenges;' there 'Church's coughdrops;' and,
to crown the whole, 'Sloan's vegetable specific,' an in-
fallible remedy for all nervous disorders and vertigoes of
brain-sick politicians,—each man earnestly adjuring you
to give his medicine only a fair trial." This done, he
suddenly shot another arrow within the sacred circle of
the administration into the secret and mysterious Spanish embroglio: "And where are you going to send your
political panacea, resolutions and hand-bills excepted,
your sole arcanum of government, your king cure-all?
To Madrid? No! You are not such quacks as not to
know where the shoe pinches. To Paris!" "After shrink-
ing from the Spanish jackal, do you presume to bully
the British lion?" Another foul blow, for his lips were
sealed on what had been done in secret session; but it
brought him at last to his end. *"Unde derivatur?*
Whence comes it," this non-importation bantling?
"Some time ago, a book was laid on our tables, which,
like some other bantlings, did not bear the name of its
father." This was Mr. Madison's well-known examination

into the British doctrine of neutral trade. "If, sir, I were the foe, as I trust I am the friend, of this nation, I would exclaim, 'Oh that mine enemy would write a book!' At the very outset, in the very first page, I believe, there is a complete abandonment of the principle in dispute. Has any gentleman got the work?" Then he read a few lines from the book, and flung it aside. Again sweeping away over a long, discursive path of unconnected discussion about Spain, France and England, New Orleans, Holland, and a variety of lesser topics, including remarks made by "the greatest man whom I ever knew, the immortal author of the letters of Curtius," he closed by another challenge to the administration:—

"Until I came into the House this morning I had been stretched on a sick-bed; but when I behold the affairs of this nation, instead of being where I hoped and the people believed they were, in the hands of responsible men, committed to Tom, Dick, and Harry, to the refuse of the retail trade of politics, I do feel, I cannot help feeling, the most deep and serious concern. If the executive government would step forward and say, 'Such is our plan, such is our opinion, and such are our reasons in support of it,' I would meet it fairly, would openly oppose or pledge myself to support it. . . . I know, sir, that we may say and do say that we are independent (would it were true!), as free to give a direction to the Executive as to receive it from him; but do what you will, foreign relations, every measure short of war, and even the course of hostilities, depend upon him. He stands at the helm, and must guide the vessel of state. You give him money to buy Florida, and he purchases Louisiana. You may furnish means; the application of those means rests with him. Let not the master and mate go below when the ship is in distress, and throw the responsibility upon the cook and the cabin-boy!"

The next day he returned to the attack, and assailed Mr. Madison's pamphlet with a sort of fury. "No, sir; whatever others may think, I have no ambition to have written such a book as this. I abjure the very idea." He called it "a miserable card-house of an argument, which the first puff of wind must demolish." "Sir, I have tried, but I could not get through this work. I found it so wiredrawn, the thread so fine, that I could neither see nor feel it; such a tangled cobweb of contradictions that I was obliged to give it up." Flinging it violently upon the floor, as though it were only fit to be trampled on, he maintained that England was justifiable in all her measures, even in impressing our seamen; impressment was a necessity of war. He attacked the navy department for waste. He affirmed that Great Britain was the sole bulwark of the human race.

This was the man who, barely a year before, had been crying out that the navy should be employed to blow the British frigates out of water, and who wished to see our officers and seaman lying yard-arm and yard-arm in the attack. "Though we lost all, we should not lose our national honor." Within the year Great Britain had made more than one additional onslaught upon our national honor, but Randolph would now listen to no thought of war, and derided the use of our navy. After all, there was much to be said on this side of the question, and, as events proved, had Mr. Jefferson followed his first impulse in the summer of 1805, and seized the moment for going to war with Spain and France, he might perhaps have checkmated the aggressive tories in England, prevented the war of 1812, and probably saved himself, his successor, and his party from being driven into a false position in regard to the liberties of Europe and the states' rights of America. Randolph, however, did not advocate this policy now, when he might have done so with effect. Repeatedly and emphatically he declared himself opposed to war with Spain or France or any other nation. "There was no party of men in this House or elsewhere in favor of war." "We were not for war; we were for peace." His only recommendation, repeated over and over again, was one of the most extraordinary, as coming from his mouth, that human wit could have imagined:—

"I can readily tell gentlemen what I will not do. I will not propitiate any foreign nation with money. I will not launch into a naval war with Great Britain. . . I will send her money, sir, on no pretext whatever, much less on pretense of buying Labrador or Botany Bay, when my real object was to secure limits which she formally acknowledged at the peace of 1783. I go farther. I would, if anything, have laid an embargo. This would have got our property home, and our adversary's into our power. If there is any wisdom left among us, the first step towards hostility will always be an embargo. In six months all your mercantile megrims would vanish. As to us, although it would cut deep, we can stand it." "What would have been a firm measure? An embargo. That would have gone to the root of the evil."

With what interest and amusement, with what fury and unconcealed mortification, such speeches were listened to by the House may be easily conceived. That they were desultory, and skipped from subject to subject with little apparent connection, was an additional charm. No one could tell where or when his sudden blows were to fall. He dwelt on nothing long enough to be tedious. He passed hither and thither, uttering sense and nonsense, but always straining every nerve to throw contempt on Mr. Madison and his supporters. In his next speech he avowed himself to be no longer a republican; he belonged to the third party, the *quiddists* or *quids,* being that a *tertium quid,* that "third something," which had no name, but was really an anti-Madison movement, an "anti-Yazoo" combination. When at last, on April 5, 1806, he dragged the Spanish embroglio before the open House under pretext of correcting the secret journal, the personal bias of his opposition became still more strongly marked. He told how Mr. Madison had said to him that France wanted money, and we must give her money. "I considered it a base prostration of the national character to excite one nation by money to bully another nation out of its property, and from that moment and to the last moment of my life my confidence in the principles of the man entertaining those sentiments died, never to live again." No answer to this charge was ever made; no satisfactory answer was possible. Mr. Madison's counter-statement, which may be seen in the third volume of his printed correspondence (p. 104), is equivocal and disingenuous. The "two-million" transaction was one of the least defensible acts of Mr. Jefferson's administration; but this does not affect the fact that Randolph was merely using it, and the private knowledge which Mr. Madison's confidence had given him, in order to carry out an attempt at political assassination. His deepest passions were not

roused by the "two-million job," but by Madison's overpowering influence. From the first this domination had
galled him: in the Yazoo contest it strove to defeat him
on his own ground; it crowed over him on his own
dunghill; and he had fought and beaten it with the desperate courage of his Virginian game-cocks. Even at this
moment he was proclaiming the fact in his speeches.
"The whole executive government has had a bias to
the Yazoo interest ever since I had a seat here. This is
the original sin which has created all the mischiefs which
gentlemen pretend to throw on the impressment of our
seamen and God knows what! This is the cause of
those mischiefs which existed years ago." "The Yazoo
business is the beginning and the end, the Alpha and
Omega of our alphabet." Mr. Madison's influence had
been brought into the House and pitted against his own;
he was now retaliating by an attack on Mr. Madison
before the country. A rumor ran through Washington
that he meant to impeach Madison for attempting to get
the two millions to Europe before receiving authority
from Congress, and he did in fact make a desperate
attempt to drag Gallatin into support of this charge.

Unluckily for Randolph, it was not directly Mr. Madison, but the President, who had invented and carried
out the whole "two-million" scheme down to its smallest
detail. All the Cabinet knew this fact, and the President's conscience was of course active in stimulating
him to protect his Secretary. The party could not let
Mr. Madison perish as a martyr before the altar of
Jeffersonian popularity. To sustain him was no matter
of choice, but a necessity. The northern democrats never
faltered in their discipline, and the southern republicans
were slowly whipped back to their ranks. Randolph's
wild speeches between March 5 and April 21, 1806,
were fatal only to himself. In his struggle against the
administration on the two-million policy, early in January, he carried with him some twenty-seven republicans,
including a majority of the Virginia delegation; but his
withdrawal from the party in April, and his unexpected
devotion to England, left these followers in an awkward
place, where little could be done by resisting Madison
within the party, and still less by following Randolph
into opposition. One by one they fell away from their
eccentric and extravagant chief.

Meanwhile, Randolph showed an astonishing genius for destroying his own influence and strengthening his opponents. He obstructed the business of the House, and then sneered at the majority for the condition their affairs were in. He brought up the navy appropriations with a blank for contingent expenses, and told the House to fill it up as they pleased; their decision would be no check on the expenditure; whether they provided the money or not, the department would spend it. He kept back the appropriation bills till late in the session, and then rose to inform the House, with a contemptuous smile, that All-Fools' Day was at hand, when, if they did not pass the bill for the support of government, they would look like fools indeed. He made the most troublesome attempts to abolish taxes. He had another bout with the Yazoo men, and managed to procure the rejection of their bill. He tore the mask of secrecy from the Spanish negotiation, and succeeded in defeating all chance of its success. He even irritated Napoleon against the government, and helped to confirm both France and Great Britain in their meditated aggressions. His vehemence of manner was equal to the violence of his language and acts. One of the members, Sloan, of the "vegetable specific," described him on the floor of the House inviting the attacks of his enemies, and representing them as crying out, "Away with him! Away with him! Clap on the crown of thorns!" (clapping his hands on the top of his head). "Crucify him!" Crucify him!" (whirling his arm about). On another occasion, it seems, he shook his fist at a member, and not only ordered him to sit down, but to go down the back stairs. Finally he charged Mr. Findley of Pennsylvania, once his "venerable friend" and "political father," not only with "mumbling," but with being an old toothless driveler, in his second dotage.

Yet in his most violent passions he kept his coolness of head, and knew well how to subordinate an enmity to an interest. Even while most bitterly charging Mr. Madison with subservience to France, and proving his charge by betraying private conversations, as no man of true self-respect could have done, he was himself helping the Secretary to put the country on its knees before Napoleon in an attitude more humiliating than the United States had ever yet assumed towards a foreign

power. In the session of 1804—5 Congress, out of deference to France and to the obligations of international
law, passed an act to regulate the trade with revolted St.
Domingo, and to restrain it within proper and peaceful
limits. In the summer of 1805 Napoleon, still unsatis-
fied, issued an order that the United States government should stop the trade altogether. His peremptory
note on the subject to Talleyrand, dated August 10,
1805, is curious, not only as an example of his extraordinary ignorance, but still more as a specimen of
his emphasis. "I want you to send a note to the American minister here, . . . and declare to him that it is time
to stop this." M. Talleyrand obeyed. General Turreau,
also, his minister at Washington, notified Mr. Madison
that "this system must continue no longer (*ne pourrait
pas durer*)." These letters were called for and printed,
while Congress, in December, 1805, and January, 1806,
were considering a bill introduced by Senator Logan of
Pennsylvania to prohibit the trade in question. That Logan's bill was in reality a subordinate but essential part
of the two-million scheme is self-evident; but Randolph,
not Mr. Jefferson or Mr. Madison, is the subject of this
story, and it is interesting to ask whether Randolph denounced the bill and exposed the shame to which the
administration was privy.

To prohibit the trade with St. Domingo was to make
the United States government a party in the attempt to
reëstablish French influence in the American hemisphere;
it was to help Napoleon in his plan of reënslaving the
negroes whom France had declared free; it was to en-
force a French sham blockade by our legislation, to
bolster up a mere pretense of French occupancy, to
throw the whole trade of this rich market into the hands
of England, and to endanger the life of every American
in St. Domingo. Mr. Madison had resisted the measure
as long as he dared. He now yielded, partly to the
mandate of Napoleon, partly to the outcry of the southern slaveholders, who were wild with fear of the revolted Haytian negroes, and who seized with avidity
upon the bill. They forced it through the House with
unreasoning arrogance, at the time when Randolph, an
ami des noirs, a hater of slavery, was angriest at the
attempt of Mr. Madison to bribe the French government with five million dollars. This new proof of the

"base prostration of the national character" inherent in the Florida negotiation might have been a terrible weapon in Randolph's hands had he chosen to use it, but, so far from using it, he imitated Mr. Madison's own conduct: he hid himself from sight. "I voted in favor of it," said he in 1817. He was mistaken. He did not vote at all; he gave the bill his silent support. "I voted in favor of it because I considered St. Domingo as an anomaly among the nations of the earth, and I considered it my duty, . . . as a representative above all of the southern portion of the United States, to leave nothing undone which could possibly give to the white population in that island an ascendency over the blacks." For such a purpose he could consent to use the powers of centralization in defiance of international law, in contempt of the rights of northern merchants, and in forgetfulness of constitutional theories; but if he held the arbitrary prohibition of trade with St. Domingo to be constitutional, how was he afterwards to denounce as unconstitutional either the embargo, or the non-intercourse, or the law abolishing the coastwise slave-trade?

Thus, at length, on April 21, 1806, this extraordinary session closed, one of the most remarkable in the history of our government. Randolph was left a political wreck; the true Virginian school of politics was forever ruined; Macon was soon driven from the speakership; and Nicholson forced on to the bench; Gallatin was paralyzed; Mr. Jefferson, Mr. Madison, and ultimately Mr. Monroe were thrown into the hands of the northern democrats, whose loose political morality henceforward found no check; the spirit of intrigue was stimulated, and the most honest and earnest convictions of the republican party were discredited. That Mr. Jefferson had steadily drifted away from his original theories was true, and that his party, like all other parties, was more or less corrupted by power can hardly be denied; but Randolph's leadership aggravated these evils, deprived him and the better southern republicans of all influence for good, and left corrupt factions to dispute with each other the possession of merely selfish power.

-❦[VIII]❦-

Monroe and the Smiths

OF ALL republican factions the most mischievous was that which gathered round Robert Smith, the Secretary of the Navy, and his brother, Samuel Smith, the senator from Maryland. The latter, during this turbulent session, had contributed not a little to vex and worry Mr. Jefferson and Mr. Madison by an attempt to force himself upon them as a special envoy to London to aid or supplant Monroe in his difficult negotiations on the neutral trade. The first effect of Randolph's violent outburst was to drive General Smith back to discipline; the remote result was to give him more influence than before. As Smith wrote to his brother-in-law, Wilson Cary Nicholas, on April 1, 1806:—

"The question was simply, Buy or Fight! Both Houses by great majorities said, Buy! The manner of buying appears a little disagreeable. Men will differ even on that subject. Politicians will believe it perfectly honest to induce France, 'by money,' to coerce Spain to sell that which she has absolutely declared was her own property, and from which she would not part. Mr. R. expects that this public explosion of our views and plans will render abortive this negotiation, and make the Executive and poor little Madison unpopular. Against this last he vents his spleen. However, he spares nobody, and by this conduct has compelled *all* to rally round the Executive for *their own* preservation. From the Potomac, north and east, the members adhere to the President; south, they fall off daily from their allegiance."

Although Mr. Jefferson irritated the Smiths by passing directly over their heads and taking another Maryland man, the federalist lawyer William Pinkney, as his new

128

minister to England, General Smith could now only submit in silence to this sharp rebuke, the more marked
because the new appointment was not laid before the
Cabinet or discussed in advance. Randolph's revolt had
instantly stiffened the party discipline, and the Smiths
were forced to wait.

The Smiths, however, knew when to wait and when
to intrigue, while Randolph knew neither the one nor
the other. To do him justice, he was a wretched intriguer and no office-seeker. He and his friends were
remarkably free from the meaner ambitions of political
life; they neither begged patronage nor asked for money, nor did they tolerate jobbery in any form. Mr.
Madison always believed otherwise, and his followers
openly charged Randolph with having sought an office,
and with having persecuted Mr. Madison for refusing
it; but this story merely marked a point in the quarrel;
it was a symptom, not a cause. Certain members of
Congress urged Randolph's appointment as minister to
England, to fill the office which Monroe held, which
General Smith wanted, and which William Pinkney got;
but Randolph himself did not know of the suggestion or
hear of the President's refusal until after the whole
transaction was closed. Then he was told of the matter
by the member who had been most active in it and,
according to an account published in the "Richmond
Enquirer," evidently by himself, he replied, "If I did
not know you so well, I should suppose you were sent
to me by the Executive to buy off my opposition, which
they fancy must take place from the course they pursue." For years Randolph had been steadily coming
nearer a quarrel with his party leaders: he was striving,
as he believed, to drag them back to their purer principles of 1800; they were pleasantly drifting with the easy
current of power. The rupture was a mere matter of
time. Randolph's political isolation was in any case inevitable, if Madison were to fill the executive chair, for
Mr. Madison, the President of the United States, was a
very different character from Mr. Madison the author of
the Virginia Resolutions.

He went back to Bizarre in April, 1806, a ruined
statesman, never again to represent authority in Congress or to hope for ideal purity in government. His
illusions of youth were roughly brushed away. He saw,

what so few Virginians were honest enough to see, that the Virginian theory had been silently discarded by its own authors, and that through it pure government could never be expected. Henceforward he must be only a fault-finder, a common scold, whose exaggerated peculiarities of manner would invite ridicule, and whose only means of influence must lie in the violence of his temper and the sharpness of his tongue. Among thousands of honest and enthusiastic young men who in every generation rush into public life, with the generous confidence that at last government shall be made harmless and politics refined, Randolph was neither the greatest nor the best; his successes and failures were not the most alluring, and his fate was not more tragic than that of others: but it is the misfortune of these opal-winged dragon-flies of politics that from the moment their wings become tarnished and torn they themselves become objects of disgust. After conceiving the career of a Pericles or a Cæsar, to fall back among common men with vulgar aims and mean methods is fatal to self-respect. When his theories broke down, and his Virginian leaders decided that their own principles were visionary, Randolph had nothing to do in political life but to accept what other men accepted, or to look on and grumble at evils which he no longer hoped to cure. He had failed as a public man, and had dragged with him in his failure all his friends and his principles. Though he remained forever before the public, he could not revive dead hopes or bring back the noble aspirations of 1800.

To follow him through five-and-twenty years of miserable discontent and growing eccentricities would be time thrown away. He represented no one but himself; he had very few friends, and mere rags and tatters of political principles. His party flung him aside, and Mr. Jefferson, for a time very bitter against him, soon learned that he was as little to be feared as to be loved. Randolph, on his side, dubbing his old leader with the contemptuous epithet of "St. Thomas of Cantingbury," lost no chance of expressing for Mr. Jefferson a sort of patronizing and humiliating regard. In his eyes Mr. Jefferson as President had weakly betrayed all the principles he had preached in opposition. The time was to come when Mr. Jefferson would return to those principles, but meanwhile Randolph was ruined. He knew it, and it drove him mad.

For a while, however, he still hoped to retrieve himself by bringing Mr. Monroe forward as the candidate of Virginia for the next general election in 1808. His letters to Nicholson during the summer of 1806 give glimpses of his situation before it was made wholly desperate by the collapse of Monroe's treaty with England in March, 1807, and the caucus nominations of Mr. Madison in January, 1808.

RANDOLPH TO NICHOLSON.

"BIZARRE, 3 *June*, 1806 ... The public prints teem with misrepresentations, which it would be vain to oppose, even if an independent press could be found to attempt it. The torrent is for the present resistless. I long for the meeting of Congress, an event which hitherto I have always deprecated, that I may face the monster of detraction.... Nothing will be left undone to excite an opposition to me at the next election, but I have no expectation that it will be effected, or of its success in case it should. There are too many gaping idolaters of power among us, but, like you, we have men of sterling worth; and one thing is certain,— that, however we may differ on the subject of the present administration, all parties here (I speak of the republicans) unite in support of Monroe for President. I have heard of but one dissenting voice, Giles, who is entirely misled; all his information is from E[ppes], his representative. They talk of an expression of the opinion of our legislature to this effect at their next meeting. An inefficient opposition is making to Garnett. Thompson, I believe, will have an opponent likewise, but this is not yet determined on. From what I have written above you are not to infer that I mean to yield a bloodless victory to my enemies. You know me well enough, I hope, to believe that a want of perseverance is not among my defects. I will persevere to the last in the cause in which I am embarked."

"24 *June*, 1806.... As to politics, lies are your only sort of wear nowadays. Some artificial excitement has been produced in favor of administration, but it will affect no election, unless perhaps Thompson's, and, on second thoughts, Mercer's. Beau Dawson and his friend Bailey are in a fair way of promotion. I can't tell what provision the President that is to be can make for these two worthy *chevaliers d'industrie*, unless he gives them foreign embassies. As to his respectable brother-in-law, he will succeed, I suppose, to the vacant Secretaryship of State, and will be every way qualified to draw the instructions and receive the dispatches of the two illustrious diplomates.... You ask what are our prospects in Virginia. Depend upon it, a very large majority of us are decidedly opposed to Madison's pretensions; and if the other States leave it to Virginia, he never will be President."

"*7 July* ... From what I can learn, my name is the general theme of invective in the Northern prints, and there are not wanting some of us (one of this district) who are very willing to lend a helping hand to pull me down. Giles, I am told, has been very violent, and has even descended to unworthy means of which I had deemed him incapable. I have no favors to ask. I want nothing. Let justice be done to my motives, which I know to have been upright, and I am content. No member of the administration has reason to think them otherwise, I am sure; and if they suppose they have, they shall not dare to say so with impunity ... About the close of the last session of Congress, Granger inquired of a gentleman from Richmond, then at Washington, whether there was not such a character as Creed Taylor in my district, and if he would not be brought forward to oppose me. Giles (who had always professed to despise Mr. T.) has been busy making the same inquiries. I am told that He (G.) has shown a letter which I wrote him in full confidence during the winter, to my prejudice. "Where dwelleth honor?""

These letters to Nicholson are far less notable than the series of letters which Randolph was now writing to Monroe. Of all the great names in American history, that of Monroe seems to the keen eyes of critics to stand on the smallest intellectual foundation. Individuality, originality, strong grasp of principles, he had to a less degree than any other prominent Virginian of his time; but, while usually swept along by the current of prevailing opinion, he enjoyed general respect as a man whose personal honesty was above dispute, and whose motives were sincerely pure. As Mr. Madison's chief rival in popularity, although absent in England, he now became a disturbing force in Virginian politics, and Mr. Jefferson on one side, Randolph, Nicholson, Taylor,

Tazewell, and their friends on the other, disputed fierce-
ly the possession of this ally. Far away in London, Mr.
Monroe began to receive letters filled with such honeyed
flattery as few men except those who wield power and
dispense patronage are so happy as to hear. No reader
can help noticing that Randolph could flatter, and perhaps, for the moment, he may have believed his flattery
sincere. He had reason, too, in feeling kindly towards
Mr. Monroe, for Monroe was showing much kindness
to Randolph's poor deaf and dumb nephew, St. George,
who had been sent abroad. The following extracts from
Randolph's letters show the man in a new character,—
that of political manager. The first was written in the
full excitement of his winter struggle.

RANDOLPH TO MONROE.

WASHINGTON, *March* 20, 1806 . . . There is no longer a
doubt but that the principles of our administration have
been materially changed. The compass of a letter (indeed, a
volume would be too small) cannot suffice to give you even
an outline. Suffice it to say that everything is made a business of bargain and traffic, the ultimate object of which is
to raise Mr. Madison to the presidency. To this the old
republican party will never consent, nor can New York be
brought into the measure. Between them and the supporters
of Mr. Madison there is an open rupture. Need I tell you
that they (the old republicans) are united in your support?
that they look to you, sir, for the example which this nation
has yet to receive to demonstrate that the government can
be conducted on open, upright principles, without intrigue or
any species of disingenuous artifice? We are extremely rejoiced to hear that you are about to return to the United
States. Much as I am personally interested, through St.
George, in your stay in Europe, I would not have you remain one day longer. Your country requires, nay demands,
your presence. It is time that a character which has proved
invulnerable to every open attack should triumph over insidious enmity."

"ALEXANDRIA, *April* 22, 1806. . . . Last night Congress ad-
journed, under circumstances the most extraordinary that I
ever witnessed. It would be impossible for me, even if it
were advisable, to give you a sketch, much less a history, of
our proceedings. The appointment of Mr. Pinkney to the

Court of London will, no doubt, be announced to you, at least as soon as this letter can reach the place of its destination. A decided division has taken place in the republican party, which has been followed by a proscription of the anti-ministerialists. Among the number of the proscribed are Mr. Nicholson, who has retired in strong disgust; the Speaker, who will soon follow him from a like sentiment; and many others of minor consequence, such as the writer of this letter, *cum multis aliüis.* My object at present is merely to guard you, which your own prudence, perhaps, renders an unnecessary caution, against a compromitment of yourself to men in whom you cannot wholly confide. Be assured that the aspect of affairs here and the avowed characteristics of those who conduct them have undergone a material change since you left America. In a little while I hope you will be on the spot to judge for yourself, to see with your own eyes and to hear with your own ears. All the statements of our public prints are, at present, garbled, owing to the peculiar situation of the place which is the established seat of our government."

"BIZARRE, *July* 3, 1806. . . . There is a system of which you are not informed, but in which, nevertheless, every effort will be made, indeed is making, to induce you to play a part so as to give a stage effect that may suit a present purpose. I wish it were in my power to be more explicit. Be assured, however, that you have friends, whose attachment to you is not to be shaken, and from whose zeal you have at the same time nothing to fear. I need not tell you, I hope, that the fervor of my attachment has never betrayed me into a use of your name on any occasion, except where your public dispatches, laid by government before Congress, called for and justified the measure."

"BIZARRE, *September* 16, 1806. . . . If heretofore I had been at a loss to fix upon the individual the most disinterested and virtuous whom I have known, I could *now* find no difficulty in determining; nor do I hesitate to declare that the very arguments which you adduce to dissuade your friends from supporting you at the next presidential election form with me an invincible motive for persisting in that support, since they exhibit the most irrefragable proof of that superior merit which you alone are unwilling to acknowledge. Yet I must confess there are considerations amongst those presented by you that would have great and perhaps decisive influence upon my mind where the preten-

sions of the candidates were nearly equal. But in this case
there is not only a strong preference for the one party, but
a decided objection to the other. It is not a singular belief
among the republicans that to the great and acknowledged
influence of this last gentleman [Mr. Madison] we are in-
debted for that strange amalgamation of men and principles
which has distinguished some of the late acts of the administration, and proved so injurious to it. Many, the most
consistent and influential, of the old republicans, by whose
exertions the present men were brought into power, have
beheld, with unmeasurable disgust, the principles for which
they had contended, and, as they thought, established, neu-
tralized at the touch of a cold and insidious moderation. I
speak not of the herd of place-hunters, whose sole view in
aiding to produce a change in the administration was the
advancement of themselves and their connections, but of
those disinterested and generous spirits who served from
attachment to the cause alone, and who neither expect nor
desire preferment. Such men, of whom I could give you a
list that would go near to fill my paper, ascribe to the bane-
ful counsels of the Secretary of State that we have been
gradually relaxing from our old principles, and relapsing
into the system of our predecessors; that government stands
aloof from its tried friends, whilst it hugs to its bosom men
of the most equivocal character, and even some who have
been and still are unequivocally hostile to that cause which
our present rulers stand pledged to support; and that you
are at this moment associated with a colleague whom former administrations deemed a fit instrument to execute the
ever-memorable treaty of London! They are, moreover, determined not to have a Yazoo President if they can avoid
it, nor one who has mixed in the intrigues of the last three
or four years at Washington. There is another consideration, which I know not how to touch. You, my dear sir,
cannot be ignorant, although of all mankind you, perhaps,
have the least cause to know it, how deeply the respectability of any character may be impaired by an unfortunate
matrimonial connection. I can pursue this subject no further.
It is at once too delicate and too mortifying. Before the
decision is ultimately made I hope to have the pleasure of
communicating fully with you in person. With you, I believe
the principles of our government to be in danger, and union
and activity on the part of its friends indispensable to its existence. But that union can never be obtained under the

presidency of Mr. Madison... I will never despair of the
republic whilst I have life, but never could I see less cause
for hope than now. I have beheld my species of late in a
new and degrading point of view, but at the same time I
have met with a few Godlike spirits, who redeem the whole
race in my good opinion."

The story of Randolph's famous quarrel with his party
has now been told in a spirit as friendly to him as his
friends can require or expect,—has been told, so far as
possible, in his own words, without prejudice or passion,
and shall be left to be judged on its merits. There
are, however, a few questions which students of American history will do well to ask themselves before taking
sides with or against the partisans of Jefferson, Madison,
Randolph, and Monroe. Did or did not Randolph go
with his party in disregarding its own principles down
to the moment when he became jealous of Madison's
influence? Was that jealousy a cause of his feud? Was
the Yazoo compromise a measure so morally wrong as
to justify the disruption of the party? Had he reason to
think Monroe a safer man than Madison? Had he not
reason to know that Mr. Jefferson himself and Mr.
Gallatin were quite as responsible as Madison for "that
strange amalgamation" which he complained of? Or,
to sum up all these questions in one, was Randolph
capable of remaining true to any principle or any friendship that required him to control his violent temper and
imperious will?
Upon this point Randolph's Virginian admirers will
listen to no argument: they insist that he was their only
consistent statesman; they reject Mr. Jefferson, Mr.
Madison, and Mr. Monroe, and utterly repudiate President Washington, Patrick Henry, and John Marshall,
in order to follow this new prophet of evil. Without
Randolph, the connection of Virginian history would, in
their eyes, be lost. Perhaps they are right. Readers must
solve the riddle as truth and justice shall seem to require.
Meanwhile Randolph fretted at Bizarre, and wrote
long letters, signed "Decius," to the "Richmond Enquirer," until the much-desired month of December
came, and he returned to fight his battles at Washington. Passions, however, had now cooled. Calmer himself,

h₃ found all parties ready to meet him in a formal
truce. Nicholson had gone upon the bench, but Macon
was still Speaker, and Randolph himself, until March 4,
1806, could not be deposed from his chairmanship of
the Ways and Means Committee. Mr. Jefferson's message, very different in tone from that of the year before,
was calculated to soothe party quarrels and to satisfy
Randolph's wishes. In reality the President's belligerency
of December, 1805, had been intended as a ruse and a
false demonstration to cover a retreat from foreign difficulties; and Randolph, knowing this, had made use of
his knowledge to worry the administration and to damage
Mr. Madison by affecting at one time to take these
belligerent threats as serious, and by throwing ridicule
upon them at other times as quackery. In December,
1806, the President, satisfied that the ruse of last year
had failed, sent in a message breathing only peace and
the principles of 1800. Randolph chose to look upon it
as a triumph for himself, and wrote to Nicholson accordingly:—

RANDOLPH TO NICHOLSON

"GEORGETOWN, 10 *December,* 1806.... The message of
the 3d was, as you supposed, wormwood to certain gentry.
They made wry faces, but, in fear of the rod and in hopes
of sugar-plums, swallowed it with less apparent repugnance
than I had predicted. .. Of all the men who have met me
with the greatest apparent cordiality, old Smilie is the last
whom you would suspect. I understand that they (you know
who *they* are) are well disposed towards a truce. The higher
powers are in the same goodly temper, as I am informed.
I have seen nobody belonging to the administration but
the Secretary of the Navy, who called here the day before
yesterday, and whose visit I repaid this morning. You may
remember, some years ago, my having remarked to you the
little attention which we received from the grandees, and
the little disposition which I felt to court it. I have therefore
invariably waited for the first advance from them, because
at home I conceive myself bound to make it to any gentleman who may be in my neighborhood."

Burr's conspiracy now broke out, startling the nation
out of its calm, and proving, or seeming to prove, the

justice of Randolph's suspicions and anxieties. For a time a sort of panic reigned in Washington except among the federalists. Randolph and his friends sneered at the last year's work; Smith and his friends grumbled at the supineness of this year. The expressions of both these factions in their private letters were very characteristic.

On December 26, 1806, Macon wrote to Nicholson, "The doings here will surely convince every candid man in the world that the republicans of the old school were not wrong last winter. Give truth fair play and it will prevail." A fortnight later, January 9, 1807, General Smith wrote to his brother-in-law, W. C. Nicholas:—

"My ambition is at an end. I sicken when I look forward to a state of things that would require exertions. We have established theories that would stare down any possible measures of offense or defense. Should a man take a patriotic stand against those destructive and seductive fine-spun follies, he will be written down very soon. Look at the last message! It in some sort declared more troops to be unnecessary. It is such, however, that the President cannot recommend (although he now sees the necessity) any augmentation of the army. Nay, *I,* even *I,* did not dare to bring forward the measure until I had first obtained his approbation. Never was there a time when executive influence so completely governed the nation."

General Smith's comments on the "destructive and seductive fine-spun follies," which he so detested, forgot to note that, whether destructive or not, they sprang straight from the theories of his party, which had no moral existence except on and in those principles. John Adams had been sent back to Braintree for no other avowed reason than that Smith might establish, as the practice of government, what he now called "fine-spun follies." Randolph felt the shame of such an inconsistency. The meeting of two extremes is always interesting, and the moment of their contact is portentous. While General Smith on one side was repudiating the theories he had "established" in 1800, and was frankly going back to his old federalist policy, Randolph, who still believed in the "fine-spun follies" of his youth, was also confessing that in practice they had failed, and that the night of corruption and violence was again closing upon mankind. On February 15, 1807, a few weeks after General Smith's letter to Nicholas, Randolph wrote to Joseph Nicholson:—

"I do now believe the destiny of the world to be fixed, at least for some centuries to come. After another process of universal dominion, degeneracy, barbarian irruption and conquest, the character of man may, two thousand years hence, perhaps, begin to wear a brighter aspect. Cast your eyes backward to the commencement of the French Revolution; recall to mind our hopes and visions of the amelioration of the condition of mankind, and then look at things as they are! I am wearied and disgusted with this picture, which perpetually obtrudes itself upon me."

The republican party had broken up in factions, and even its best members had lost faith in their own theories. Among these factions Randolph's group of "old republicans" held a sort of monopoly in pure republican principles, while the rest were contented with carrying on the government from day to day, disputing, not about principles, but about offices. Randolph looked down on them all with bitter contempt. His letters to Nicholson became gall.

RANDOLPH TO NICHOLSON

"COMMITTEE ROOM, 17 *February,* 1807.... Bad as you suppose matters to be, they are even worse than you apprehend. What think you of that Prince of Prigs and Puppies, G. W. C[ampbell] for a judge of the Supreme Court of the United States!!! *Risum teneas?* You must know we have made a new circuit, consisting of the three western States, with an additional associate justice. A caucus (excuse the slang of politics) was held, as I am informed, by the delegations of those States for the purpose of recommending some character to the President. Boyle was talked of, but the interest of C. finally prevailed. This is 'Tom, Dick, and Harry' with a vengeance. .. If Mr. 'American,' whom, by the way, I never see, should persevere in the attack which you tell me he is making upon me, I shall issue letters of marque and reprisal against his principals. The doughty general [Samuel Smith] is vulnerable at all points, and his plausible brother [Robert Smith] not much better defended.

The first has condemned in terms of unqualified reprobation the general measures pursued by the administration, and lamented that, such was the public infatuation, no man could take a position against it without destroying himself and injuring the cause which he attempted to serve,—with much more to the same tune. I called some time since at the navy office to ask an explanation of certain items of the estimate for this year. The Secretary called up his chief clerk, who knew very little more of the business than his master. I propounded a question to the head of the department; he turned to the clerk like a boy who cannot say his lesson, and with imploring countenance beseeches aid; the clerk with much assurance gabbled out some commonplace jargon, which I would not take for sterling; an explanation was required, and both were dumb. This pantomine was repeated at every new item, until, disgusted, and ashamed for the degraded situation of the principal, I took leave without pursuing the subject, seeing that my object could not be attained. There was not one single question relating to the department that the Secretary could answer."

Randolph's temper was now ugly beyond what was to be expected from a man whose objects were only to serve the public and to secure honest government. His hatred of the northern democrats broke out in ways which showed a wish to rule or ruin. When the bill for prohibiting the slave-trade was before the House, a bill chiefly supported by the Varnums and Bidwells, Sloans, Smilies, and Findleys, whom he so much disliked, he broke out in a startling denunciation of the clause which forbade the coastwise slave-trade in vessels under forty tons. This provision, he said, touched the right of private property; he feared it might one day be made the pretext for universal emancipation; he had rather lose the bill, he had rather lose all the bills of the session, he had rather lose every bill passed since the establishment of the government, than agree to the clause; it went to blow the Constitution into ruins; if ever the time of disunion should arrive, the line of severance would be between the slave-holding and the non-slave-holding States. Besides attempting thus to stir up trouble between the South and North, he made a desperate effort to put the Senate and House at odds, and showed a spirit of pure venom that went far to sink his character as an honest man.

On March 3, 1807, his means of effecting further mischief were to be greatly curtailed, for on that day the Ninth Congress came to an end, and Randolph lost his hold on the Ways and Means Committee. This was not his only disatser, for, on the same day, Mr. Erskine, the British minister at Washington, received from London a copy of the new treaty which Mr. Monroe and Mr. Pinkney had barely succeeded in negotiating with the British government. Hurrying with it to Mr. Madison, the minister supposed that an extra session of the Senate would be immediately called for March 4; but instead of this, the President declined to send the treaty to the Senate at all, and contented himself with denouncing it in very strong language to all the senators who called upon him. The treaty was indeed a very bad one, but it carried on its shoulders the fortunes of the old republicans, and its humiliating reception was a fatal blow to Randolph's hope of retrieving his own fortunes by attaching them to those of James Monroe. Randolph of course felt no doubt as to the motives which prompted so stern a rebuke before an expectant nation. He wrote to Monroe accordingly:—

RANDOLPH TO MONROE.

"Bizarre, *March* 24, 1807. . . . Mr. T. M. Randolph suddenly declines a reëlection, in favor of Wilson Nicholas, whose talents for intrigue you well know, I presume. Had I known of Mr. Purviance's arrival, I should certainly have remained in Washington for the purpose of seeing him, and procuring better information concerning the treaty than the contradictory accounts of the newspapers furnish. I have considered the decree of Berlin to be the great cause of difficulty; at the same time, I never had a doubt that clamor would be raised against the treaty, be it what it might. My reasons for this opinion I will give when we meet. They are particular as well as general. Prepare yourself to be surprised at some things which you will hear."

The old republicans were now in despair. Recognizing the fact that Monroe was out of the race, they turned their attention to New York. Of all northern democracy, the democrats of New York and Pennsylvania, the Cheethams and Duanes, had been most repulsive to Randolph, but in his hatred for Mr. Madison he was now ready to unite with these dregs of corruption, rather than submit to the Secretary of State; he was ready to make George Clinton President, and to elevate De Witt Clinton, most selfish, unscrupulous, and unsafe of democrats, into a position where the whole government patronage would lie at his mercy. He wrote again to Monroe, evidently to prepare him for being gently set aside:—

RANDOLPH TO MONROE

"RICHMOND, *May* 30, 1807. . . . The friends of Mr. Madison have left nothing undone to impair the very high and just confidence of the nation in yourself. Nothing but the possession of the government could have enabled them to succeed, however partially, in this attempt. In Virginia they have met with the most determined resistance, and although I believe the executive influence will at last carry the point, for which it has been unremittingly exerted, of procuring the nomination of electors favorable to the Secretary of State, yet it is not even in its power to shake the confidence of the people of this State in your principles and abilities, or to efface your public services from their recollection. I should be wanting in my duty to you, my dear sir, were I not to apprise you that exertions to diminish the value of your character and public services have been made by persons, and in a manner that will be scarcely credible to you, although at the same time unquestionably true. Our friend Colonel Mercer, should you land in a northern port, can give you some correct and valuable information on this and other subjects. Meanwhile, the republicans of New York, sore with the coalition effected by Mr. John Nicholas between his party and the federalists (now entirely discomfited), *and knowing the auspices under which he acted,* are irreconcilably opposed to Mr. Madison, and striving to bring forward Mr. Clinton, the Vice-President. Much consequently depends on the part which Pennsylvania will take in this transaction. There is a leaning, evidently, towards the New York candidate. Whether the executive influence will be able to overcome this predisposition yet remains to be seen. In the person of any other man than Mr. M. I have no doubt it would succeed. But the republicans of Pennsylvania, setting all other considerations aside, are indignant at the recollection that in all their struggles with the combined parties of McKean, etc., and the federalists, and so far as it has been exerted they *choose* to ascribe [it] to the exertions of Mr. M. Such is, as nearly as I can collect, the posture of affairs at present. Wilson C. N[icholas] and Duane are both in town at this time. Some important result is no doubt to flow from this conjunction. When you return, you will hardy know the country. A system of espionage and denunciation has been organized which pervades every quarter. Distrust and suspicion generally prevail in the intercourse between man and man. All is constraint, reserve, and mystery. Intrigue has arrived at a pitch which I hardly supposed it would have reached in five centuries. The man of all others who, I suppose, would be the last suspected by you is the nucleus of this system. The maxim of Rochefoucauld is in him completely verified, 'that an affectation of simplicity is the refinement of imposture.' Hypocrisy and treachery have reached their acme amongst us. I hope that I shall see you very soon after your arrival. I can then give you a full explanation of these general expressions, and proof that they have been made upon the surest grounds. Amongst your unshaken friends you may reckon two of our chancellors, Mr. Nicholson of Maryland, Mr. Clay of Philadelphia, Col. Jno. Taylor, and Mr. Macon."

At the same time, Judge Nicholson wrote to Monroe a letter which is worth a moment's notice on account of the support it gave to Randolph's views:—

JOSEPH H. NICHOLSON TO MONROE

"BALTIMORE, *April* 12, 1807. . . . As to the public sentiment, I cannot readily state what it is. Perhaps there is none. The President's popularity is unbounded, and his will is that of the nation. His approbation seems to be the criterion by which the correctness of all public events is tested. Any treaty, therefore, which he sanctions will be approved of by a very large proportion of our people. The federalists will murmur, but as this is the result of system, and not of principle, its impression will be neither deep nor extensive. A literal copy of Jay's treaty, if ratified by the present administration, would meet their opposition, while the same instrument, although heretofore so odious to some of us, would now command the support of a large body who call themselves democrats. Such is our present infatuation. To this general position, however, there are some honest exceptions. There is a portion who yet retain the feelings of 1798, and whom I denominate the old republican party. These men are personally attached to the President, and condemn his measures when they think him wrong. They neither wish or nor expect anything from his extensive patronage. Their public service is intended for the public good, and has no view to private emolument or personal ambition. But it is said they have not his confidence, and I lament it. You must have perceived from the public prints that the most active members in the House of Representatives are new men, and I fear that foreign nations will not estimate American talent very highly if our congressional proceedings are taken as the rule. If you knew the Sloans, the Alstons, and the Bidwells of the day, and there are a great many of them, you would be mortified at seeing the affairs of the nation in such miserable hands. Yet these are styled exclusively the President's friends. . . . These facts will enable you to form an early opinion as to the necessity of remaining in England. You know Mr. Jefferson perfectly well, and can therefore calculate the chances of his approving anything done not in precise conformity to his instructions. He is, however, somewhat different from what he was. He feels at present his own strength with the nation, and therefore is less inclined to yield to the advice of his friends. Your return is anxiously wished for by many who, I presume you know, are desirous of putting you in nomination for the presidency. My own expectations are not very sanguine on this subject. Great efforts are making for and by another. The Virginia and New York elections which take place in the course of the present month will determine much. The point is made throughout Virginia, I believe, and much solicitude is felt and expressed by the candidate for the presidency as to the result of the several elections. It is to be hoped, therefore, that you will return as early as possible."

What course things might have taken had nothing occurred to disturb domestic politics must be left to conjecture. Fate now decreed that a series of unexpected events should create an entirely new situation, and bury in rapid oblivion all memory of old republican principles. The aggressions of Europe forced America out of her chosen path.

-◀[IX]▶-

"A Nuisance and a Curse"

RANDOLPH'S LETTERS to Nicholson carry on the story:—

RANDOLPH TO NICHOLSON

"BIZARRE, 25 *March,* 1807. . . . I fully intended to have written to you the day before my departure from Washington, but was prevented by an accident which had nearly demolished me. Being very unwell on Monday night, the 2d, and no carriage to be procured, I accepted the offer of one of his horses from Dr. Bibb (successor to Spalding), and we set out together for Georgetown. Not very far beyond our old establishment (Sally Dashiell's), the only girth there was to the saddle gave way, and as it fitted the horse very badly it came with his rider at once to the ground. Figure to yourself a man almost bruised to death, on a dark, cold night, in the heart of the capital of the United States, out of sight or hearing of a human habitation, and you will have a tolerably exact idea of my situation, premising that I was previously knocked up by our legislative orgies, and some scrapes that our friend Lloyd led me into. With Bibb's assistance, however, I mounted the other horse, and we crept along to Crawford's, where I was seized with a high fever, the effects of which have not yet left me. To end this Canterbury tale, I did not get out of bed until Wednesday afternoon, when I left it to begin a painful journey homewards. Anything, however, was preferable to remaining within the ten-miles-square one day longer than I was obliged. . . . Colonel Burr (*quantum mutatus ab illo!*) passed by my door the day before yesterday, under a strong guard. So I am told, for I did not see him, and nobody hereabouts is acquainted with his person. The soldiers es-

146

corting him, it seems, indulged his aversion to be publicly known, and to guard against inquiry as much as possible he was accoutred in a shabby suit of homespun, with an old white hat flapped over his face, the dress in which he was apprehended. From the description, and indeed the confession of the commanding officer to one of my neighbors, I have no doubt it was Burr himself. His very manner of traveling, although under arrest, was characteristic of the man, enveloped in mystery."

The arrival of Burr at Richmond led to the summons of a grand jury, on which Randolph served. Thus he was brought in contact with a new object of intense aversion, the famous General Wilkinson, who, for twenty years, had played fast and loose with treason, and who, at the last moment, saved Mr. Jefferson's administration from a very serious danger by turning against Burr. Randolph could not think of the man henceforward with ordinary patience, and perhaps his irritation was a little due to the fact that Wilkinson's vices had so much helped to cover what he believed to be Mr. Jefferson's blunders.

RANDOLPH TO NICHOLSON

"RICHMOND, 25 *June*, 1807. . . . Yesterday the grand jury found bills of treason and misdemeanor against Burr and Blennerhassett, *una voce*, and this day presented Jonathan Dayton, ex-senator, John Smith of Ohio, Comfort Tyler, Israel Smith of New York, and Davis Floyd of Indiana, for treason. But the mammoth of iniquity escaped; not that any man pretended to think him innocent, but upon certain wire-drawn distinctions that I will not pester you with. Wilkinson is the only man that I ever saw who was from the bark to the very core a villain. . . . Perhaps you never saw human nature in so degraded a situation as in the person of Wilkinson before the grand jury, and yet this man stands on the very summit and pinnacle of executive favor, whilst James Monroe is denounced. As for such men as the quids you speak of, I should hardly think his Majesty would stoop to such humble quarry, when James Monroe was in view. Tazewell, who is writing on the other side of the table, and whom you surely remember, says that he makes the fifth. The other four you have not mistaken. My friend,

I am standing on the soil of my native country, divested of every right for which our fathers bled. Politics have usurped the place of law, and the scenes of 1798 are again revived. Men now see and hear, and feel and think, *politically*. Maxims are now advanced and advocated, which would almost have staggered the effrontery of Bayard or the cooler impudence of Chauncy Goodrich, when we were first acquainted. But enough of this! It will not be long, I presume, before I shall see you again. The news of the capture of the Chesapeake arrived this morning, and I suppose the President will convene Congress, of course. I have been looking for something of this sort ever since the change of ministry and rejection of the treaty was announced. I have tried to avert from my country a war which I foresaw must succeed the follies of 1805—6, but I shall not be the less disposed to withdraw her from it or carry her through with honor."

The President did not immediately convene Congress. With great wisdom and forbearance, accepting the British minister's disavowal of the Chesapeake outrage, he waited to hear from England, only issuing a proclamation to exclude the British ships of war from our harbors. Congress was called together for October 26, and Randolph then appeared at Washington in a temper bad even for him. The northern democrats controlled everything. Macon was obliged to decline being a candidate for the speakership; Varnum of Massachusetts was put in the chair, and his first act was to appoint George W. Campbell of Tennessee, "that prince of prigs and puppies," chairman of the Ways and Means Committee. Randolph showed his temper on the very first day by bringing a charge against Nicholas B. Vanzandt, the regular candidate for clerk of the House, too suddenly and positively for contradiction, which caused Vanzandt to be defeated and disgraced. The man happened to be a *protégé* of Mrs. Madison. That Randolph should have been beside himself with rage and mortification is natural enough, for he could no longer doubt the odium in which he had involved himself and even his friend Macon, who, dazzled by his wit and overawed by his will, found himself isolated and shunned, dropped from the speakership, and at cross-purposes with his party. The spell was now at an end, and Macon, although retaining friendly relations with Randolph, hastened at this session to draw away from him in politics, and gave an almost unqualified support to the administration. Mr. Jefferson, with his usual dexterity, had already reduced Randolph's influence in the House by providing his ally, Nicholson, with a seat on the bench, and Nicholson probably welcomed this means of escape from a position which Randolph had made so uncomfortable. Within a few weeks more Randolph succeeded in making himself a mere laughing stock for his enemies. Even Macon and Nicholson were obliged to agree that recovery of his influence was scarcely possible. The story of this last and fatal eccentricity, hardly mentioned by his biographers, merits a place here as further evidence of that irrationality which made his opinions worthless, and his political course for ten years to come little more than a series of wayward impulses.

He had been vehement in regard to the Chesapeake outrage, and considered Mr. Jefferson's cautious measures very insufficient. Nicholson had called his attention to Lord Chatham's Falkland Island speech, and he wrote from Bizarre, in reply, as follows, July 21, 1807:

RANDOLPH TO NICHOLSON.

"I have indulged myself in reading once more the speech to which you allude. It is the inspiration of divine wisdom, and as such I have ever adored it. But, my good friend, I cannot with you carry my zeal so far as to turn missionary and teach the gospel of politics to the heathens of Washington. More easily might a camel pass through a needle's eye than one particle of the spirit of Chatham be driven into that 'trembling council,' to whom the destinies of this degraded country are unhappily confided. . . . But great God! what can you expect from men who take *Wilkinson* to their bosoms, and at the same time are undermining the characters of Monroe and Macon, and plotting their downfall! There is but one sentiment here, as far as I can learn, on the subject of the late outrage: that, as soon as the fact was ascertained, Congress should have been convened, a strict embargo laid, Erskine [the British minister] sent home, our Ministers recalled, and then we might begin to deliberate on the means of enforcing our rights and extorting reparation. The Proclamation (or, as I term it, the *apology*)

is received rather coldly among us. Many persons express
themselves much mortified at it. Every one I see asks what
government means to do, and I might answer, 'What they
have always done; nothing!' . . . I should not be surprised,
however, if the Drone or Humble Bee (the Wasp has sailed
already) should be dispatched with two millions (this is
our standing first bid) to purchase Nova Scotia, and then we
might go to war in peace and quiet to ascertain its boundaries."

So soon as Congress met, Randolph hastened to
proclaim these sentiments, with additions of startling im-
port, rivaling Mr. Crowninshield's projected triumphs.
Not only should Congress have been immediately convened, and our ministers in London, Pinkney and Monroe, recalled, after requiring full measures of redress,
which were to be sent over by a special envoy; not
only should the nation have been put into a posture
of defense; but, "redress being refused, instant retaliation should have been taken on the offending party. I
would have invaded Canada and Nova Scotia, and made
a descent on Jamaica. I would have seized upon Canada and Nova Scotia as pledges to be retained against
a future pacification, until we had obtained ample redress for our wrongs." This was soaring on the wings
of Chatham, and indeed it would have been necessary
to soar on some wings if Randolph meant to attack
Nova Scotia and Jamaica. Redress was refused; for, although the British government disavowed the attack on
the Chesapeake, the men were not returned, but either
hanged or kept in jail for the next four years. Randolph,
however, instead of continuing to demand redress, or
seizing upon Canada and Nova Scotia, declared that he
would not, without great reluctance, vote money for the
maintenance of "our degraded and disgraced navy."

A few weeks after this tirade, news arrived of fresh
aggressions from England and France; the Berlin Decree
was to be enforced, and the Orders in Council were to
be issued without delay. The next day the President
sent down a confidential message asking for an embargo, and the House went at once into secret session.
What passed there is only partially known, but it was
asserted by Mr. Fisk of Vermont, in a speech made
later in the session, that there had been a scramble

between Randolph and Crowninshield as to who should have the honor first to propose the measure, and Randolph urged expedition, as he had a bill ready prepared. Certain it is that Randolph got the better of Crowninshield, and his resolution ordering an embargo stands on the secret journal of the House. A bill for the same purpose just then came down from the Senate, and Randolph, after supporting it on December 18 as the only measure which could promote the national interests, rose on December 19 to oppose it as partial, unconstitutional, a new invention, and he alleged as his strongest objection that it was expressly aimed at Great Britain. He voted against it.

This last somersault was more than even Macon and Nicholson could understand. Nicholson wrote, in astonishment, to ask what it meant, and Randolph's reply and defense are worth reading:—

RANDOLPH TO NICHOLSON.

"*December* 24, 1807.... Come here, I beseech you. I will then show you how impossible it was for me to have voted for the embargo. The circumstances under which it presented itself were peculiar and compelled me to oppose it, although otherwise a favorite measure with me, as you well know. It was, in fact, to crouch to the insolent mandate of Bonaparte, 'that there should be no neutrals;' to subscribe to that act of perfidy and violence, his decree, at the moment when every consideration prompted us to resist and resent it. Non-importation and non-exportation,—what more can he require? Ought we to have suffered ourselves to be driven by him out of the course which, whether right or wrong, our government had thought proper to pursue towards England? to be dragooned into measures that in all human calculation must lead to immediate war? Put no trust in the newspaper statements. They will mislead you. But come and view the ground, and I will abide the issue of your judgment."

To Nicholson, then, Randolph did not plead the unconstitutionality of the embargo, or its bad influence as a stretch of centralized power. To announce such a discovery to Nicholson would have been ridiculous, after both of them had for two years insisted on an embargo as the wisest of possible measures. Only the immediate circumstances excused the vote, the wish not to act partially against England, the very power which had just declared war on our commerce, after having committed that outrage, disavowed but not yet redressed, which had caused Randolph, only a few weeks before, to urge an attack upon Canada.

Such a combination of contradictions and inconsistencies was enough to destroy the weight of Pitt or Peel; no reputation, least of all one so indifferent as Randolph's, could stagger under it. He still hoped to retrieve his fortunes by securing the defeat of Mr. Madison, but to do so he was now obliged to keep himself in the background, for fear of hurting Monroe's chances by coupling them with his own unpopularity. Just at this moment Monroe reached America, and Randolph was reduced to see him by stealth. The same day on which he wrote to Nicholson to excuse his course about the embargo he wrote also to Monroe, asking an interview:—

RANDOLPH TO MONROE.

"*December* 24, 1807. My dear Sir,—In abstaining so long from a personal interview with you, I leave you to judge what violence I have committed upon my private feelings. Before your arrival, however, I had determined on the course which I ought to pursue, and had resolved that no personal gratification should induce me to hazard your future advancement, and with it the good of my country, by any attempt to blend the fate of a proscribed individual with the destiny which, I trust, awaits you. It is, nevertheless, of the first consequence to us both that I should have a speedy opportunity of communing fully with you. This, perhaps, can be best effected at my own lodgings, where we shall not be exposed to observation or interruption. I shall, however, acquiesce with pleasure in any other arrangement which may appear more eligible to you.

"Yrs. unalterably."

This coquetry between Monroe and Randolph continued all winter, while Randolph's friends were making ready to nominate Monroe for the presidency. To prevent the nomination of Madison was no longer possible; all that could be done was to make independent nominations of Monroe in Virginia, and of George Clinton in New York, on the chance of defeating Mr. Madison, and substituting the stronger of his two rivals in his place. The Secretary, however, overbore all opposition. Giles and W. C. Nicholas managed his canvass in Virginia, and on January 21, 1808, a large caucus of the Virginia legislature nominated him for the presidency. Two days later, at a congressional caucus called by Senator Bradley of Vermont, eighty-three senators and members confirmed the action of Virginia. Macon, Randolph, and all the "old republicans" held themselves aloof from both caucuses, but all they could do for Monroe was to give him a weak independent nomination.

How far Mr. Monroe made himself a party to this transaction is not quite clear. There is, however, no doubt that he was in full sympathy with the old republicans against Mr. Madison, and Randolph's letters imply that his sympathy was more than passive.

RANDOLPH TO MONROE.

"GEORGETOWN, *March* 9, 1808.... A consciousness of the misconstruction (to your prejudice) which would be put upon any correspondence between us has hitherto deterred me from writing. You will have no difficulty in conceiving my motives in putting this violence upon my feelings, especially after the explanation which I gave of them whilst you were here. The prospect before us is daily brightening. I mean of the future, which until of late has been extremely gloomy. As to the present state of things, it is far beyond my powers to give an adequate description of it. Mr. W. C. N. begins of late to make open advances to the federalists, fearing, no doubt that the bait of hypocrisy has been seen through by others. I must again refer you to Mr. Leigh for full information of what is going on here. The indiscretion of some of the weaker brethren, whose intentions, I have no doubt, were good, as you will have perceived, has given the enemy great advantage over us."

"GEORGETOWN, *March* 26, 1808.... Among the events of my public life, and especially those which have grown out of the last two years, no circumstance has inspired such keen regret as that which has begotten the necessity of the reserve between us to which you allude; not that I have been insensible to the cogent motives to such a demeanor on both sides; far from it. I must have been blind not to have perceived them. They suggested themselves at a very early period to my mind, and my conduct was accordingly regulated by them. But there are occasions in life, and this, with me, was one of them, in which necessity serves but to embitter instead of resigning our feelings to her rigid dispensations. I leave you then to judge with what avidity I shall seize the opportunity of renewing our intercourse when the causes which have given birth to its suspension shall have ceased to exist, since amongst the enjoyments which life has afforded me there are few, very few, which I value in comparison with the possession of your friendship. In a little while I shall quit the political theatre, probably forever, and I shall carry with me into retirement none of the surprise and not much of the regret excited by the blasting effects of ministerial artifice and power upon my public character, should I find, as I fear I shall, that they have been enabled to reach even your own."

The worst trait of these insidious attempts to poison Monroe's mind was not their insinuations, but their transparent character of revenge. Monroe was one tool, and Clinton another; both equally used by Randolph, not to forward his own views of public good, but to pull down Mr. Madison. If there was nothing in Monroe's character or career which could lead any sensible man to believe him truer than Madison to the forgotten traditions of his party, there was everything in George Clinton's history to prove that he was a blind agent of the northern democracy. His late career as Governor of New York had been notoriously and scandalously controlled by his nephew De Witt, and the selfishness of De Witt Clinton was such that to trust in his hands the fortunes of "old republicanism" would have been one degree more ridiculous than to trust them, as Randolph did twenty years afterwards, to the tender sympathies of Andrew Jackson. Not patriotism, but revenge, inspired Randolph's passion; the impulse to strike down those whom he chose to hate. As he worked on Monroe's wounded pride to make of it a weapon against Madison, so he incited and urged the friends of Monroe in other States to devote themselves to the interests of

Clinton. Thus he wrote to Nicholson to stir up Maryland.

RANDOLPH TO NICHOLSON.

"*February* 20, 1808. . . . Our friend gains ground very fast at home. Sullivan, the Governor of Massachusetts, has declared against M[adiso]n. The republicans of that great State are divided on the question, and if Clay be not deceived, who says that Pennsylvania, Duane non obstante, will be decidedly for the V[ice] P[resident], the S[ecretary] of S[tate] has no chance of being elected. Impress this, I pray you, on our friends. If the V. P.'s interest should be best, our electors (in case we succeed) will not hazard everything by a division. If the election comes to the House of Representatives M[adiso]n is the man."

"*March* 24, 1808. . . . Lloyd says that the opponents of Madison in Maryland and in Baltimore particularly are unnerved; that they are timed, and that unless the V[ice] P[resident]'s friends exert themselves all is lost in your State; that if yourself were to go to Queen Anne's and make known your support of C[linton] it would decide the Eastern Shore. This I am certain you will do, as well as everything else in your power to promote the cause. It is necessary to *speak* and to *speak out*; especially those who justly possess the public confidence, which you do in a most eminent degree."

At the same time he was consumed by a feverish impulse to thrust himself forward in the House. Thus he lost prestige with every day that passed. As the session drew to its close, and his obstructive temper became more and more evident, Macon wrote to Nicholson bewailing it, but confessing the impossibility of controlling him:—

"I am really afraid that our friend R. will injure himself with the nation in this way. An attempt is now making, and will, I think, be continued, to impress on the minds of the people that he speaks with a view to waste time. If this opinion should prevail, it will, I fear, injure not only him, but the nation also, because what injures him in public estimation will injure the people also. His talents and honesty cannot be lost without a loss equal to them both, and they cannot be ascertained. But you know him as well as I do."

This was written on April 14, 1808; the session closed on the 25th, and on June 1 Macon wrote again:—

"Madison, I still think, will be the next President. If the New Yorkers mean to run Clinton in good earnest, as we country people say, it is time they had begun. The Madisonians will not lose anything by neglect or indolence. They may overact their part, and, in their zeal to keep Randolph down, may make some lukewarm about Madison. If R. had stuck to the embargo, he would have been up in spite of them."

All the efforts of Randolph and his friends to defeat Mr. Madison vanished in thin smoke. When November arrived, there was little or no opposition; Virginia was solid in his support, and he received 122 out of 175 electoral votes, the full strength of his party, except six votes for Clinton in New York. His first act as President justified in Randolph's eyes the worst that had ever been said of him. Allowing himself to be dragooned by Giles and General Smith into abandoning Mr. Gallatin, his first choice for Secretary of State, President Madison nominated for that office Robert Smith, whose administration of the navy had been a scandal not only to Randolph, but to Gallatin. Thus at the outset the new administration was thrown into the hands of a selfish faction, which proclaimed their contempt for old republican principles to every one who would listen. Gallatin alone, without courage or hope, tried to persevere in the old path.

To pursue Randolph's course farther through the meanderings of his opposition would be waste of time. He at last convinced himself that his own party was not less extravagant and dangerous than those federalists whose doctrines he had begun by so furiously denouncing. To discover that one has made so vast a blunder is fatal to elevation of purpose; under the reaction of such disappointment, no man can keep a steady course. The iron entered Randolph's soul. Now for the first time his habits became bad, and at intervals, until his death, he drank to excess. After days or weeks of indulgence, during which the liquor served only to give him more vivacity, he seemed suddenly to sink under it, and remained in a state of prostration until his system reacted from the abuse. Probably in consequence of this license his mind showed signs of breaking down. He was at times distinctly irrational, though never quite incapable of self-control. His health began to give way; his lungs became affected; his digestive organs were ruined; erratic gout, as the doctors called it, ran through his system. Nevertheless, he returned every autumn to Washington, and, although isolated and powerless, he found a sort of dismal pleasure in watching the evils he could no longer prevent or cure.

In abandoning Jefferson, Madison, Giles, W. C. Nicholas, and the whole band of his old coadjutors, Randolph had still shown some degree of shrewdness in trying to retain the respect and support of Monroe. So long as Monroe, Tazewell, John Taylor of Caroline, and a few more respectable Virginians, stood apart from the administration and professed old republican principles, Randolph was not quite deserted. There was always a chance that he and his friends might come back to power, and there is a certain historical interest in the quarrel which at last separated him even from Monroe, and left him hopeless and desperate.

Mr. Madison's cabinet was from the first a failure. Gallatin, the Secretary of the Treasury, stood alone as the representative of old republicanism, although only on its economical side, and Gallatin's struggle to prevent the Treasury from being plundered by factions under the Smiths and Giles was patient and prolonged. Two years passed, during which it was easy to see that Mr. Madison grew steadily weaker, while Duane, Giles, General Smith, old Vice-President Clinton, and a score of other personal enemies were straining every nerve to break him down by driving Gallatin from the Treasury. In the event of Gallatin's defeat, as in that of his victory, Randolph might expect to find himself once more acting with a large party, and with good hopes of reasonable success. To wait the crisis and to use it was an easy task, for he had but to hold his tongue and to support his friends. Unfortunately he could do neither.

Some extracts from his letters to Nicholson, to whom, as a connection of Gallatin's by marriage, he wrote strongly as the crisis approached, will best show how deep an interest felt in the result.

RANDOLPH TO NICHOLSON.

"GEORGETOWN, *February* 14, 1811. . . . For some days past I have been attending the debates in the Senate. Giles made this morning the most unintelligible speech on the subject of the Bank of the U. S. that I ever heard. He spoke upwards of two hours, seemed never to understand himself (except upon one commonplace topic, of British influence), and consequently excited in his hearers no other sentiment but pity or disgust. But I shall not be surprised to see him puffed in all the newspapers of a certain faction. The Senate have rejected the nomination of Alex. Wolcott to the bench of the Supreme Court,—24 to 9. The President is said to have felt great mortification at this result. The truth seems to be that he is President *de jure* only. Who exercises the office *de facto* I know not, but it seems agreed on all hands that there is something behind the throne greater than the throne itself. I cannot help differing with you respecting [Gallatin's] resignation. If his principal will not support him by his influence against the cabal in the ministry itself as well as out of it, a sense of self-respect, it would seem to me, ought to impel him to retire from a situation where, with a tremendous responsibility, he is utterly destitute of power. Our cabinet presents a novel spectacle in the political world; divided against itself, and the most deadly animosity raging between its principal members, what can come of it but confusion, mischief, and ruin! Macon is quite out of heart. I am almost indifferent to any possible result. Is this wisdom or apathy? I fear the latter."

"Since I wrote to you to-night, Stanford has shown me the last 'Aurora,' a paper that I never read; but I could not refrain, at his instance, from casting my eyes over some paragraphs relating to the Secretary of the Treasury. Surely under such circumstances Mr. G[allatin] can no longer hesitate how to act. It appears to me that only one course is left to him,—to go immediately to the President, and to demand either the dismissal of Mr. S[mith] or his own. No man can doubt by whom this machinery is put in motion. There is no longer room to feign ignorance, or to temporize. It is unnecessary to say to you that I am not through you addressing myself to another. My knowledge of the interest which you take, not merely in the welfare of Mr. G., but in that of the State, induces me to express myself to you on this subject. I wish you would come up here. There are more things in this world of intrigue than you wot of, and I would like to commune with you upon some of them."

"Georgetown, *February* 17, 1811. . . . I am not convinced by your representations respecting [Gallatin], although they are not without weight. Surely it would not be difficult to point out to the President the impossibility of conducting the affairs of the government with such a counteraction in the very Cabinet itself, without assuming anything like a disposition to dictate. Things as they are cannot go on much longer. The administration are now, in fact, aground, at the pitch of high tide, and a spring tide, too. Nothing remains but to lighten the ship, which a dead calm has hitherto kept from going to pieces. If the cabal succeed in their present projects, and I see nothing but promptitude and decision that can prevent it, the nation is undone. The state of affairs for some time past has been highly favorable to their views, which at this very moment are more flattering than ever. I am satisfied that Mr. G. by a timely resistance to their schemes might have defeated them, and rendered the whole cabal as impotent as nature would seem to have intended them to be; for in point of ability (capacity for intrigue excepted) they are utterly contemptible and insignificant. I do assure you, my friend, that I cannot contemplate the present condition of the country without the gloomiest presages. The signs of the times are of the most direful omen. The system cannot continue, if system it may be called, and we seem rushing into one general dissolution of law and morals. Some Didius, I fear, is soon to become the purchaser of our empire; but, in whatever manner it be effected, everything appears to announce the coming of a *master*. Thank God, I have no children; but I have those who are yet dear to me, and the thoughts of their being hewers of wood and drawers of water, or, what is worse, sycophants and time-servers to the venal and corrupt wretches that are to be the future masters of this once free and happy land, fill me with the bitterest indignation. Would it not almost seem that man cannot be kept free; that his ignorance, his cupidity, and his baseness will countervail the effects of the wisest institutions that disinterested patriotism can plan for his security and happiness?"

"Richmond, *March* 10, 1811. . . . I could not learn, as I passed through Washington, how matters stood respecting G[allatin] and S[mith]. The general impression there was that S[mith] would go out, and that the Department of State would be offered to Monroe. I do, however, doubt whether Madison will be able to meet the shock of the 'Aurora,' 'Whig,' 'Enquirer,' 'Boston Patriot,' etc., etc.; and it is highly probable that, beaten in detail by the superior activity and vigor of the Smiths, he may sink ultimately into their arms, and unquestionably will, in that case, receive the law from them. I know not why I should think so much on this subject, but it engrosses my waking and sleeping thoughts."

Now came the long-looked-for revolution which should have restored Randolph's influence. Whether or not Gallatin was affected by these appeals, certain it is that early in the month of March he resigned his office; that Mr. Madison declined to accept the resignation, and worked up his courage to the point of dismissing Robert Smith, and defying the senatorial cabal of Giles, Leib, Samuel Smith, and Vice-President Clinton. On March 20, 1811, the President wrote to Monroe, offering him the Department of State, and with it, of course, the prospect of succession to the throne itself. On the 23rd, Monroe accepted the offer. The "old republicans" once more saw the Executive wholly in their hands.

This critical moment, when everything depended upon harmony, was chosen by Randolph as the time to quarrel with Monroe, as he had already quarreled with Madison and Jefferson. That the fault was altogether his own is not to be said, for in truth the immediate fault was Monroe's. Two years had now elapsed since Monroe's return home in a sort of disgrace; he was poor; he was, in real truth, no more fanatical about his old principles than Madison himself, and at least it was not he who had drawn up the Virginia resolutions of 1798; he wanted to get back into office; his connection with Randolph stood in his way, and it is probable that he allowed himself to repudiate this influence somewhat too openly. In the month of January, 1811, Randolph was at Richmond, and heard stories to this effect. A little more tact or less pride would have made him patient while Monroe was climbing again up the ladder of office; but patience was not Randolph's best trait. He immediately wrote the following letter to the man for whose character he had all through life felt so profound reverence and such affectionate respect:—

RANDOLPH TO MONROE

BELL TAVERN, Monday Night
Jan. 14, 1811.

DEAR SIR, — The habits of intimacy which have existed between us make it, as I conceive, my duty to inform you that reports are industriously circulated in this city to your disadvantage. They are to this effect: That in order to promote your election to the Chief Magistracy of the Commonwealth you have descended to unbecoming compliances with the members of the Assembly, not excepting your bitterest personal enemies; that you have volunteered explanations to them of the differences heretofore subsisting between yourself and administration which amount to a dereliction of the ground which you took after your return from England, and even of your warmest personal friends. Upon this, although it is unnecessary for me to pass a comment, yet it would be disingenuous to conceal that it has created unpleasant sensations not in me only, but in others whom I know you justly ranked as among those most strongly attached to you. I wished for an opportunity of mentioning this subject to you, but none offered itself, and I would not seek one, because, when I cannot afford assistance to my friends, I will never consent to become an incumbrance on them. I write in haste, and therefore abruptly. I keep no copy, and have only to enjoin on you that this communication is in the strictest sense of the term *confidential,* solely for your own eye. Yours,

JOHN RANDOLPH OF ROANOKE.

To this characteristic assault Mr. Monroe responded as best as he could. He sent his son-in-law, George Hay, to Randolph, and Randolph refused to talk with him. He wrote to John Taylor of Caroline, and to Randolph himself. Randolph's final reply was sent from Washington precisely at the time of the cabinet crisis, when Monroe's appointment as Secretary of State was becoming daily more certain.

RANDOLPH TO MONROE

GEORGETOWN, *March* 2, 1811

DEAR SIR,—I have purposely delayed answering your letters because you seem to have taken up the idea that I labored under some excitement (of an angry nature it is to be presumed from the expressions employed in your communication to Colonel Taylor, as well as in that to myself), and I was desirous that my reply should in appearance as well as in fact proceed from the calmest and most deliberate exercise of my judgment.

How my letters in Richmond could excite an unpleasant feeling in your bosom *towards me* I am wholly at a loss to comprehend. Let me beg you to review them, to reflect for a moment on the circumstances of the case, and then ask yourself whether I could or ought to have done otherwise than as I did in apprising you of the reports injurious to your honor that were in the mouth of every man of every description in Richmond. I certainly held no intercourse with those who were hostile to your election, but it surely required no power of inspiration to divine that, when such language was held by your own supporters, those to whom you were peculiarly obnoxious would hardly omit to make a handle of it to injure you. You may well feel assured that no man would venture to approach *me* with observations directly derogating from your character.

Those who spoke to me on the subject generally mentioned it as a source of real regret and sorrow; a few sounded to see how far they might go, and, receiving no encouragement, drew off. But it was impossible for me to shut my ears or eyes to the passing scene, and in my hearing the most injurious statements were made, with which, as well as with the general impression of all with whom I conversed in relation to them, I deemed it my duty to acquaint you; *mutatis mutandis,* I should have expected a similar act of friendship on your part.

Ask yourself again, my dear sir, whether your cautious avoidance, and that of every one near you, of every sort of communication with me, and of every mark of accustomed respect and friendship, was not in itself a change in the relation between us, which nothing on my part could have given the least occasion for; and whether I was not authorized to infer, as well as the public,— in short, whether it was not intended that the public *should* infer,—not only that all political connection, but that all communication, was at an end between us.

Under these circumstances, is it *my* conduct or your own that is likely to put a stop to our old intercourse; and is it *you* or *I* that have that right to complain of the abandonment of the old ground of relation that existed between us? Let me add that a passage in your letter to Col. Taylor (I mean that which was in circulation at Richmond) respecting the motives of the minority (with whom you had just disavowed all political connection whatever) has been deemed by many of the most intelligent among them as a just cause of complaint, as furnishing to their persecutors a colorable pretext for renewing and persevering in the most unpopular and odious of all the charges that have been brought against them. We cannot doubt the sincerity of your impression, but know it to be erroneous, and feel it to be injurious to us.

And now let me declare to you, which I do with the utmost sincerity of heart, that during the period to which you refer I never felt one angry emotion towards you. Concern for your honor and character was uppermost in my thoughts. A determination to adhere to the course of conduct which my own sense of propriety and duty to myself pointed out had almost dwindled into a secondary consideration.

Accept my earnest wishes for your prosperity and happiness. I have long since abandoned all thoughts of politics except so far as is strictly necessary to the execution of my legislative duty.

Again I offer you my best wishes.

JOHN RANDOLPH OF ROANOKE.

Thus Randolph bade farewell to another President that was to be. Three weeks after this letter was written, Monroe was Secretary of State, and in a short time it appeared that, had Randolph not abandoned him, he had certainly been quite earnest in his intention to abandon Randolph. No more was heard of "old republican" principles from Monroe until many years had elapsed; but within a short time it appeared that he was ready to accept, if not to welcome, what Randolph most opposed—a war with England, loans, navies, armies, and even a military conscription.

During all these troubles and through all manner of party feuds, personal quarrels, and hostile intrigues, in spite of the fact that he now habitually voted with the federalists, Randolph succeeded in keeping control of his district and in securing his reëlection both in 1809 and 1811, when John W. Eppes took up his residence there with the avowed purpose of breaking Randolph down. In 1813, however, his opposition to the war with England proved too heavy a weight to carry, and Mr. Eppes, after a sharp contest, defeated him, while the "Richmond Enquirer" denounced him as "a nuisance and a curse."

⊰[X]⊱

Eccentricities

IF DISAPPOINTMENT and sorrow could soften a human heart, Randolph had enough to make him tender as the gentlest. From the first, some private trouble weighed on his mind, and since he chose to make a mystery of its cause a biographer is bound to respect his wish. The following letter to his friend Nicholson, written probably in the year 1805, shows his feeling on this point:—

RANDOLPH TO NICHOLSON.

"Monday, 4 March. Dear Nicholson.—By *you* I would be understood; whether the herd of mankind comprehend me or not, I care not. Yourself, the Speaker, and Bryan are, of all the world, alone acquainted with my real situation. On that subject I have only to ask that you will preserve the same reserve that I have done. Do not misunderstand me, my good friend. I do not doubt your honor or discretion. Far from it. But on this subject I am, perhaps, foolishly fastidious. God bless you, my noble fellow. I shall ever hold you most dear to my heart.

From such expressions not much can be safely inferred. Doubtless he imagined his character and career to be greatly influenced by one event or another in his life, but in reality both he and his brother Richard seem to have had from the first the same vehement, ill-regulated minds, and the imagination counted for more with them than the reality, whatever it was. His was a nature that would have made for itself a hell even though fate had put a heaven about it. Quarreling with his brother's widow, he left Bizarre to bury himself in a poor corner among his overseers and slaves at Roanoke.

165

"I might be now living at Bizarre," he wrote afterwards, "if the reunion of his [Richard's] widow with the
[traducers?] of her husband had not driven me to Roanoke;" "a savage solitude," he called it, "into which I
have been driven to seek shelter." This was in 1810. He
had already quarreled with his stepfather, Judge Tucker,
as kindhearted a man as ever lived, and of this one-sided
quarrel we have an account which, even if untrue, is
curious. It seems that Randolph had been talking violently against the justice and policy of the law which
passed estates, in failure of direct heirs, to brothers of
half-blood; whereupon Judge Tucker made the indis-
creet remark: "Why, Jack, you ought not to be against
that law, for you know if you were to die without issue
you would wish your half-brothers to have your estate."
"I'll be damned, sir, if I do know it," said Randolph,
according to the story, and from that day broke off
relations with his stepfather. In 1810 he was only with
the utmost difficulty dissuaded by his counsel from
bringing suit against Judge Tucker for fraudulent management of his estate during that guardianship which
had ended more than fifteen years before. He knew
that the charge was false, but he was possessed with it.
Two passions, besides that for drink, were growing on
him with age,—avarice and family pride; taken together, three furies worse than the cruelest disease or the
most crushing disasters. Yet disaster, too, was not wanting. His nephew St. George, Richard's eldest son, deaf
and dumb from his birth, became quite irrational in
1813, and closed his days in an asylum. The younger
nephew, Tudor, whom he had loved as much as it was
in his nature to love any one, and who was to be the
representative of his race, fell into a hopeless consumption the next year, and, being sent abroad, died at
Cheltenham in 1815. Thus Randolph, after falling out
with his stepfather and half-brothers, after quitting Bizarre and quarreling with his brother's widow, lost his
nephews, failed in public life, and was driven from his
seat in Congress. Had he been an Italian he would have
passed for one possessed of the evil eye, one who
brought destruction on all he loved, and every peasant
would have secretly made the sign of the cross on meeting him. His defeat by Eppes in the spring of 1813
disgusted him with politics, and he visited his mortifica-

tion on his old friends. Macon wrote to Nicholson
February 1, 1815:—

"Jonathan did not love David more than I have Randolph, and I still have that same feeling towards him, but
somehow or other I am constrained from saying [anything]
about it or him, unless now and then to defend him against
false accusations, or what I believe to be such. There is
hardly any evil that afflicts one more than the loss of a
friend, especially when not conscious of having given any
cause for it. I cannot account for the coldness with which
you say he treated you, or his not staying at your house
while in Baltimore. Stanford now and then comes to where
I sit in the House, and shows me a letter from R. to him,
which is all I see from him. He has not wrote to me since
he left Congress [in March, 1813], nor I but once to him,
which was to inclose him a book of his that I found in the
city when I came to the next session. I have said thus much
in answer to your letter, and it is more than has been said
or written to any other person."

The sudden and happy close of the war in January,
1815, brought about a curious revolution in the world
of politics. Everything that had happened before that
convulsion seemed now wiped from memory. Men once
famous and powerful were forgotten; men whose political sins had been dark and manifold were forgiven and
received back into the fold. Among the rest was Randolph. He recovered his seat in the spring of 1815, and
returned to Congress with a great reputation for bold
and sarcastic oratory. He came back to a new world,
to a government which had been strengthened and na-
tionalized by foreign war beyond the utmost hopes of
Washington or John Adams. Mr. Jefferson's party was
still in power, but not a thread was left of the principles
with which Mr. Jefferson had started on his career in
1801. The country had a debt compared with which
that of the federalist administrations was light; it had a
navy which was now more popular than ever Mr. Jefferson had been in his palmiest days, and an army which
Randolph dared no longer call "ragamuffin;" the people
had faced the awful idea of conscription, at the bidding
of James Madison and James Monroe, two men who
had nearly broken up the Union, in 1798, at the mere

suggestion of raising half a dozen regiments; at the same command the national bank was to be reëstablished;—in every direction states' rights were trampled on;—and all this had been done by Randolph's old friends and his own party. During his absence, Congress, like schoolboys whose monitor has left the room, had passed the bill for the Yazoo compromise. This was not the whole. Chief Justice Marshall and the Supreme Court were at work. Their decisions were rapidly riveting these results into something more than mere political precedents or statute law. State sovereignty was crumbling under their assaults, and the nation was already too powerful for the safety of Virginia.

Mr. Jefferson, in his old age, took the alarm, and began to preach a new crusade against the Supreme Court and the heresies of federal principles. He rallied about him the "old republicans" of 1798. Mr. Madison and Mr. Monroe, Mr. Gallatin and the northern democrats, were little disposed to betake themselves again to that uncomfortable boat which they had gladly abandoned for the broader and stancher deck of the national ship of state; but William B. Giles was ready to answer any bugle-call that could summon him back to the Senate, or give him another chance for that cabinet office which had been the ambition of his life; and John Randolph was at all times ready to clap on again his helmet of Mambrino and have a new tilt at the windmill which had once already demolished him. If Virginia hesitated, South Carolina might be made strong in the faith, and Georgia was undaunted by the Yazoo experience. If the northern democrats no longer knew what states' rights meant, the slave power, which had grown with the national growth, could be organized to teach them.

Into this movement Randolph flung himself headlong, and in such a party he was a formidable ally. Doubtless there was much about him that seemed ridiculous to bystanders, and still more that not only seemed, but was, irrational. Neither his oratory nor his wit would have been tolerated in a northern State. To the cold-blooded New Englander who did not love extravagance or eccentricity, and had no fancy for plantation manners, Randolph was an obnoxious being. Those traits of character and person of which he was proud, as evi-

dence of his Pocahontas and Powhatan ancestry they instinctively attributed to an ancestral type of a different
kind. It was not the Indian whom they saw in this lean,
forked figure, with its elongated arms and long, bony fore-
finger, pointing at the objects of his aversion as with a
stick; it was not an Indian countenance they recognized in
this parchment face, prematurely old and seamed with a
thousand small wrinkles; in that bright, sharply sparkling
eye; in the flattering, caressing tone and manner, which
suddenly, with or without provocation, changed into wan-
ton brutality. The Indian owns no such person or such
temperament, which, if derived from any ancestry, belongs
to an order of animated beings still nearer than the Indian to the jealous and predaceous instincts of dawning
intelligence.

There is no question that such an antagonist was
formidable. The mode of political warfare at first
adopted by instinct, he had now by long experience
developed into a science. Terror was the favorite resource of his art, and he had so practiced as to have
reached a high degree of success in using it. He began
by completely mastering his congressional district. At
best, it is not easy for remote, sparsely settled com-
munities to shake off a political leader who has no
prominent rival in his own party, and no strong outside
opposition, but when that leader has Randolph's advantages it becomes impossible to contest the field. His
constituents revolted once, but never again. His peculiarities were too well known and too much in the natural
order of things to excite surprise or scandal among
them. They liked his long stump speeches and sharp,
epigrammatic phrases, desultory style and melodramatic
affectations of manner, and they were used to coarseness that would have sickened a Connecticut peddler.
They liked to be flattered by him, for flattery was one
of the instruments he used with most lavishness. "In
conversing with old men in Charlotte County," says a
native of the spot, writing in 1878, "they will talk a
long time about how Mr. Randolph flattered this one to
carry his point; how he drove men clean out of the
country who offended him; how ridiculous he sometimes
made his acquaintances appear: they will entertain you a
long time in this way before they will mention one word
about his friendship for anybody or anybody's for him."

He was simple enough in his methods, and, as they were all intended to lead up to terror in the end, there was every reason for simplifying them to suit the cases.

"How do you do, Mr. L? I am a candidate for Congress, and should be pleased to have your vote."

"Unfortunately, I have no vote, Mr. Randolph."

"Good-morning, Mr. L."

He never forgave a vote given to his opponent, and he worked his district over to root out the influences which defeated him in 1813. One example of his method is told in regard to a Mr. S., a plain farmer, who had carried his precinct almost unanimously for Eppes. Randolph is said to have sought him out one court day in the most public place he could find, and, addressing him with great courtesy, presently put to him a rather abstruse question of politics. Passing from one puzzling and confusing inquiry to another, raising his voice, attracting a crowd by every artifice in his power, he drew the unfortunate man farther and farther into the most awkward embarrassment, continually repeating his expressions of astonishment at the ignorance to which his victim confessed. The scene exposed the man to ridicule and contempt, and is said to have destroyed his influence. He sometimes acted a generous, sometimes a brutal part; the one, perhaps, not less sincere than the other while it lasted, but neither of them in any sense simple expressions of emotion. Although he professed vindictiveness as a part of his Powhatan inheritance, and although he proclaimed himself to be one who never forsook a friend or forgave a foe, it is evident that his vindictiveness was often assumed merely in order to terrify; there was usually a method and a motive in his madness, noble at first in the dawn of young hope, but far from noble at last in the gloom of disappointment and despair. "He did things," says Mr. Henry Carrington, "which nobody else could do, and made others do things which they never did before, and of which they repented all the days of their lives; and on some occasions he was totally regardless of private rights, and not held amenable to the laws of the land."

This trait of his character gave rise to a mass of local stories, many of which have found their way into print, but which are for the most part so distorted in passing through the mouths of overseers and neighbors

as to be quite worthless for biography. Another mass
of legend has collected itself about his life in Washington and his travels. The less credit we give to the more
extravagant of these stories, the nearer we shall come
to the true man. At times he was violent or outrageous
from the mere effect of drink, but, to do him justice,
his brutality was commonly directed against what he
supposed, or chose to think, presumption, ignorance, dis-
honesty, cant, or some other trait of a low and groveling
mind. He rarely insulted any man whom he believed
to be respectable, and he was always kind and affectionate to those he loved; but although he controlled himself
thus far in society, he carried terrorism in politics to
an extreme. He could be gentle when he pleased, but
he often preferred to be arrogant. Only a few months
before his death, in February, 1833, he forced some
states'-rights resolutions through a meeting of the county of Charlotte. A certain Captain Watkins, who was at
the meeting, declined to follow him, and avowed himself a supporter of President Jackson. Randolph, while
his resolutions were under discussion, addressed himself
to Captain Watkins, saying that he did not expect "an
old Yazoo speculator" to approve of them. Captain Watkins rose and denied the charge. At this, Randolph
looked him steadily in the face, and pointing his finger
at him said,—

"You are a Yazoo man, Mr. Watkins."

Mr. Watkins, much agitated and embarrassed, rose
again and made an explanation. Randolph, with the
same deliberation, simply repeated,—

"You are a Yazoo man, Mr. Watkins."

A third time Mr. Watkins rose, and was met again
by the same cold assertion, "You are a Yazoo man;"
until at last he left the room, completely broken down.

Mr. Watkins had, in fact, once owned some of the
Yazoo land warrants. He was, of course, no admirer of
Randolph, who rode rough-shod over him in return. If it
be asked why a man who treated his neighbors thus was
not fifty times shot down where he stood by exasperated
victims, the answer is that he knew those with whom he
was dealing. He never pressed a quarrel to the end,
or resented an insult further than was necessary to repel it. He was notorious for threatening to use his weapons on every occasion of a tavern quarrel, but at such

times he was probably excited by drink; when quite himself he never used them if it was possible to avoid it. In 1807 he even refused to fight General Wilkinson, and allowed the general to post him as a coward; and he did this on the ground that the general had no right to hold him accountable for his expressions: "I cannot descend to your level." Indeed, with all Randolph's quarrelsome temper and vindictive spirit, he had but one duel during his public life. His insulting language and manner came not from the heart, but from the head: they were part of his system, a method of controlling society as he controlled his negroes. His object was to rule, not to revenge, and it would have been folly to let himself be shot unless his situation required it. Randolph had an ugly temper and a strong will; but he had no passions that disturbed his head.

In what is called polite society these tactics were usually unnecessary, and then bad manners were a mere habit, controllable at will. In such society therefore, Randolph was seen at his best. The cultivated Virginian, with wit and memory, varied experience, audacious temper, and above all a genuine flavor of his native soil; the Virginian, in his extremest form, such as any one might well be curious once to see,—this was the attraction in Randolph which led strangers to endure and even to seek his acquaintance. Thus, as extremes meet, Massachusetts men were apt to be favorites with this Ishmaelite; they were so thoroughly hostile to all his favorite prejudices that they could make a tacit agreement to disagree in peace. Josiah Quincy was one of his friends; Elijah Mills, the Massachusetts senator, another. In a letter dated January 19, 1816, Mr. Mills thus describes him:—

"He is really a most singular and interesting man; regardless entirely of form and ceremony in some things, and punctilious to an extreme in others. He, yesterday, dined with us. He was dressed in a rough, coarse, short hunting-coat, with small-clothes and boots, and over his boots a pair of coarse cotton leggings, tied with strings round his legs. He engrossed almost the whole conversation, and was exceedingly amusing as well as eloquent and instructive."

Again on January 14, 1822:—

"Our Massachusetts people, and I among the number, have grown great favorites with Mr. Randolph. He has invited me to dine with him twice, and he has dined with us as often. He is now what he used to be in his best days, in good spirits, with fine manners and the most fascinating conversation. . . . For the last two years he has been in a state of great perturbation, and has indulged himself in the ebullitions of littleness and acerbity, in which he exceeds almost any man living. He is now in better humor, and is capable of making himself exceedingly interesting and agreeable. How long this state of things may continue may depend upon accident or caprice. He is, therefore, not a desirable inmate or a safe friend, but under proper restrictions a most entertaining and instructive companion."

In 1826 Mr. Mills was ill, and Randolph insisted on acting as his doctor.

"He now lives within a few doors of me, and has called almost every evening and morning to see me. This has been very kind of him, but is no earnest of continued friendship. In his likings and dislikings, as in everything else, he is the most eccentric being upon the face of the earth, and is as likely to abuse friend as foe. Hence, among all those with whom he has been associated during the last thirty years, there is scarcely an individual whom he can call his friend. At times he is the most entertaining and amusing man alive, with manners the most pleasant and agreeable; and at other times he is sour, morose, crabbed, ill-natured, and sarcastic, rude in manners, and repulsive to everybody. Indeed, I think he is partially deranged, and seldom in the full possession of his reason."

The respectable senator from Massachusetts, "poor little Mills," as Randolph calls him, seems to have snatched but a fearful joy in this ill-assorted friendship.

The system of terrorism, which was so effective in the politics of Charlotte, was not equally well suited to the politics of Washington; to overawe a congressional district was possible, but when Randolph tried to crush Mr. Jefferson and Mr. Madison by these tactics, the experiment not only failed, but reacted so violently as to drive him out of public life. Nevertheless, within the walls of the House of Representatives his success was

considerable; he inspired terror, and to oppose him required no little nerve, and, perhaps, a brutality as
reckless as his own. He made it his business to break in
young members as he would break a colt, bearing down
on them with superciliousness and sarcasm. In later life
he had a way of entering the House, booted and
spurred, with whip in hand, after the business had begun, and loudly saluting his friends to attract attention;
but if any one whom he disliked was speaking, he
would abruptly turn on his heel and go out. Mr. S. G.
Goodrich describes him in 1820, during the Missouri
debate, as rising and crying out in a shrill voice, which
pierced every nook and corner of the hall, "Mr. Speaker, I have but one word to say,—one word, sir; and that
is to state a fact. The measure to which the gentleman
has just alluded originated in a dirty trick." Under some
circumstances he even ventured on physical attacks, but
this was very rare. He had a standing feud with Willis
Alston of North Carolina, and they insulted each other
without serious consequences for many years. Once, in
1811, as the members were leaving the House, Alston,
in his hearing, made some offensive remark about a
puppy. Randolph described the scene to Nicholson in a
letter dated January 28, 1811:—

"This poor wretch, after I had prevailed upon the House
to adjourn, uttered *at* me some very offensive language,
which I was not bound to overhear; but he took care to
throw himself in my way on the staircase, and repeat his
foul language to another in my hearing. Whereupon I said,
'Alston, if it were worth while, I would cane you,—and I
believe I will cane you!' and caned him accordingly, with
all the nonchalance of Sir Harry Wildair himself."

The affair, however, got no further than the police
court, and Randolph very justly added in his letter, "For
Macon's sake (although he despises him) I regret it,
and for my own, for in such cases victory is defeat."
He called himself an Ishmael: his hand was against
everybody, and everybody's hand was against him. His
political career had now long ended, so far as party
promotion was concerned, and there remained only an
overpowering egotism, a consuming rage for notoriety,

contemptible even in his own eyes, but overmastering him like the passion for money or drink.

Of all his eccentricities, the most pitiful and yet the most absurd were not those which sprang from his lower but from his higher instincts. The better part of his nature made a spasmodic struggle against the passions and appetites that degraded it. Half his rudeness and savagery was due to pride which would allow no one to see the full extent of his weakness. At times he turned violently on himself. So in the spring of 1815 he snatched at religion, and for an instant felt a serious hope that through the church he might purify his nature; yet even in his most tender moments there was something almost humorous in his childlike incapacity to practice for two consecutive instants the habit of self-control or the simplest instincts of Christianity. "I am no disciple of Calvin or Wesley," he wrote in one of these moods, "but I feel the necessity of a changed nature; of a new life; of an altered heart. I feel my stubborn and rebellious nature to be softened, and that it is essential to my comfort here, as well as to my future welfare, to cultivate and cherish feelings of good-will towards all mankind; to strive against envy, malice, and all uncharitableness. I think I have succeeded in forgiving all my enemies. There is not a human being that I would hurt if it were in my power; not even Bonaparte."

If in his moments of utmost Christian exaltation he could only think he had forgiven his enemies and would hurt no human being if he had the power, what must have been his passion for inflicting pain when the devil within his breast held unchecked dominion!

⊰[XI]⊱

Blifil and Black George

So LONG as Mr. Monroe was in office, although his administration, aided by the Supreme Court, paid less regard to states' rights and leaned more strongly to centralization than either the administrations of Madison or Jefferson, Randolph did not venture again upon systematic opposition. He had learned a lesson: he would have no more personal quarrels with Virginian Presidents, and restrained his temper marvelously well, but not because he liked Monroe's rule better than that of Monroe's predecessors; far from it! "The spirit of profession and devotion to the court has increased beyond my most sanguine anticipations," said he in 1819; "the Emperor [Monroe] is master of the Senate, and through that body commands the life and property of every man in the republic. The person who fills the office seems to be without a friend. Not so the office itself." In 1820 one of the President's friends made, on his behalf, an advance to Randolph. "I said," writes Randolph, February 26, 1820, "that he had invited Garnett, as it were, out of my own apartment, that year [1812], to dine with General Moreau, Lewis, and Stanford, the only M. C.'s that lodged there besides myself, and omitted to ask me, who had a great desire to see Moreau; that I lacqueyed the heels of no great man; that I had a very good dinner at home." Although fully warranted in feeling hatred for Monroe, Randolph remained in harmony with the administration until he was going to Europe, in March, 1822, and issued, from "on board the steamboat Nautilus, under weigh to the Amity" packet, a letter to his constituents, expressing his intention to stand again for Congress in 1823:—

176

"I have an especial desire to be in that Congress, which will decide (probably by indirection) the character of the executive government of the confederation for at least four years, — perhaps forever; since now, for the first time since the institution of this government, we have presented to the people the army candidate for the presidency in the person of him [Calhoun] who, judging from present appearance, will receive the support of the Bank of the United States also. This is an union of the sword and purse with a vengeance, — one which even the sagacity of Patrick Henry never anticipated, in this shape at least. Let the people look to it, or they are lost forever.... To this state of things we are rapidly approaching, under an administration the head of which sits an *incubus* upon the state, while the lieutenants of the new Mayor of the Palace are already contending for the succession."

Had Randolph's knowledge of history been more accurate or his memory quicker than it was, he would not here have fallen into the blunder of insulting the President by a compliment. To speak of the *incubus* Monroe as a "new Mayor of the Palace" was nonsense, for, of all men that ever lived, the Mayors of the Palace were the most efficient rulers. What Randolph doubtless meant was to brand Monroe as "this new *roi fainéant,*" this do-nothing king Childerich, whose lieutenants, Calhoun, Crawford, Adams, were contending for the succession.

Against Monroe Randolph did not care to break his lance, even though Monroe was the worst of all the Virginian traitors to states' rights, and the most ungrateful for support and encouragement in his days of disgrace. Not Monroe, but Monroe's lieutenants were to be denounced in advance. Randolph liked none of them, but especially hated Calhoun and Clay, then representatives of the ardent nationality engendered by the war of 1812. Mr. Clay was Speaker, and, with a temper as domineering and a manner as dictatorial as that of Randolph himself, he could not fail to rouse every jealous and ugly demon in Randolph's nature, and draw out all the exhaustless vituperation of his tongue. The inevitable quarrel began during the debate on the Missouri Compromise, when Randolph made a determined effort to drive Clay from its support. They

are said to have met for consultation in a private interview, after which they held no further relations even of
civility, and it is easy to imagine that the language exchanged in such a dialogue may have been such as
neither might care to repeat. In any case it is true that
Clay, as Speaker, rode ruthlessly over Randolph's opposition, and jockeyed him out of his right to move a
reconsideration of the bill. The war between them was
henceforth as bitter as either party could make it, and
came within a hair's breadth of costing Randolph his life.

Personal antipathies, jealousy, prejudice, and the long
train of Randolph's many vices had, therefore, something
to do with the certain hostility towards Monroe's successor for which he was now preparing; but between
his opposition in 1825 and that in 1806 there was this
difference: in 1806 his quarrel was with old friends,
whom, on a mere divergence of opinion in regard to
details of policy, he had no right to betray; in 1825,
his quarrel was legitimate and his policy sound, from
his point of view. This fact partially rehabilitated his
reputation, and made him again, to no small extent,
an important historical character. John Randolph stands
in history as the legitimate and natural precursor of
Calhoun. Randolph sketched out and partly filled in the
outlines of that political scheme over which Calhoun
labored so long, and against which Clay strove success-
fully while he lived,—the identification of slavery with
states' rights. All that was ablest and most masterly, all
except what was mere metaphysical rubbish, in Calhoun's statesmanship had been suggested by Randolph
years before Calhoun began his states'-rights career.

Between the slave power and states' rights there was
no necessary connection. The slave power, when in
control, was a centralizing influence, and all the most
considerable encroachments on states' rights were its
acts. The acquisition and admission of Louisiana; the
embargo; the war of 1812; the annexation of Texas
"by joint resolution;" the war with Mexico, declared by
the mere announcement of President Polk; the Fugitive
Slave Law; the Dred Scott decision,—all triumphs of the
slave power,—did far more than either tariffs or internal
improvements, which in their origin were also southern
measures, to destroy the very memory of states' rights
as they existed in 1789. Whenever a question arose of

extending or protecting slavery, the slaveholders became friends of centralized power, and used that dangerous weapon with a kind of frenzy. Slavery in fact required centralization in order to maintain and protect itself, but it required to control the centralized machine; it needed despotic principles of government, but it needed them exclusively for its own use. Thus, in truth, states' rights were the protection of the free States, and as a matter of fact, during the domination of the slave power, Massachusetts appealed to this protecting principle as often and almost as loudly as South Carolina.

The doctrine of states' rights was in itself a sound and true doctrine; as a starting point of American history and constitutional law, there is no other which will bear a moment's examination; it was as dear to New England as to Virginia, and its prostitution to the base uses of the slave power was one of those unfortunate entanglements which so often perturb and mislead history. This prostitution, begun by Randolph, and only at a later time consummated by Calhoun, was the task of a man who loudly and pathetically declared himself a victim to slavery, a hater of the detestable institution, an *ami des noirs;* who asserted that all the misfortunes of his life—and they had been neither few nor inconsiderable—were light in the balance when compared with the single misfortune of having been born the master of slaves. It was begun in the Missouri debate in 1819 and 1820, but unfortunately Randolph's speeches in these sessions, although long and frequent, are not reported, and his drift is evident only from later expressions. His speech on internal improvements, January 31, 1824, set forth with admirable clearness the nature of this new fusion of terrorism with lust for power,—the birth-marks of all Randolph's brood. Struck out like a spark by sharp contact with Clay's nobler genius, this speech of Randolph's flashes through the dull atmosphere of the time, until it leaps at last across a gap of forty years and seems to linger for a moment on the distant horizon, as though consciously to reveal the dark cloud of smoke and night in which slavery was to be suffocated.

"We are told that, along with the regulation of foreign commerce, the States have yielded to the general govern-

ment in as broad terms the regulation of domestic commerce,—I mean the commerce among the several States,—
and that the same power is possessed by Congress over the
one as over the other. It is rather unfortunate for this argument that, *if it applies to the extent to which the power to
regulate foreign commerce has been carried by Congress,
they may prohibit altogether this domestic commerce,* as
they have heretofore, under the other power, prohibited foreign commerce. But why put extreme cases? This government cannot go on one day without a mutual understanding
and deference between the state and general governments.
This government is the breath of the nostrils of the States.
Gentlemen may say what they please of the preamble to
the Constitution; but this Constitution is not the work of the
amalgamated population of the then existing confederacy,
but the offspring of the States; and however high we may
carry our heads and strut and fret our hour, 'dressed in a
little brief authority,' *it is in the power of the States to
extinguish this government at a blow. They have only to
refuse to send members to the other branch of the legislature,* or to appoint electors of President and Vice-President,
and the thing is done. . . . I said that this government, if put
to the test—a test it is by no means calculated to endure—
as a government for the management of the internal concerns of this country, is one of the worst that can be conceived, which is determined by the fact that it is a government not having a common feeling and common interest
with the governed. I know that we are told—and it is the
first time the doctrine has been openly avowed—that upon
the responsibility of this House to the people, by means of
the elective franchise, depends all the security of the people
of the United States against the abuse of the powers of
this government. But, sir, how shall a man from Mackinaw
or the Yellowstone River respond to the sentiments of the
people who live in New Hampshire? It is as great a mockery,—a greater mockery than to talk to these colonies about
their virtual representation in the British Parliament. I have
no hesitation in saying that the liberties of the colonies
were safer in the custody of the British Parliament than they
will be in any portion of this country, if all the powers of
the States as well as of the general government are devolved
on this House. . . . We did believe there were some parchment barriers,—ño! what is worth all the parchment barriers
in the world, that there was in the powers of the States

some counterpoise to the power of this body; but if this bill passes, we can believe so no longer.

"There is one other power which may be exercised in case the power now contended for be conceded, to which I ask the attention of every gentleman who happens to stand in the same unfortunate predicament with myself,—of every man who has the misfortune to be and to have been born a slaveholder. If Congress possess the power to do what is proposed by this bill, they may not only enact a sedition law,—for there is precedent,—but *they may emancipate every slave in the United States,* and with stronger color of reason than they can exercise the power now contended for. And where will they find the power? They may follow the example of the gentlemen who have preceded me, and hook the power on to the first loop they find in the Constitution. *They might take the preamble, perhaps the warmaking power*; or they might take a greater sweep, and say, with some gentlemen, that it is not to be found in this or that of the granted powers, but results from all of them, which is not only a dangerous but *the most* dangerous doctrine. Is it not demonstrable that slave labor is the dearest in the world, and that the existence of a large body of slaves is a source of danger? Suppose we are at war with a foreign power, and freedom should be offered them by Congress as an inducement to them to take a part in it; or suppose the country not at war, at every turn of this federal machine, at every successive census, that interest will find itself governed by another and increasing power, which is bound to it neither by any common tie of interest or feeling. And if ever the time shall arrive, as assuredly it has arrived elsewhere, and in all probability may arrive here, that a coalition of knavery and fanaticism shall for any purpose be got up on this floor, *I ask gentlemen who stand in the same predicament as I do to look well to what they are now doing, to the colossal power with which they are now arming this government. The power to do what I allude to is, I aver, more honestly inferable from the warmaking power than the power we are now about to exercise. Let them look forward to the time when such a question shall arise, and tremble with me at the thought that that question is to be decided by a majority of the votes of this House, of whom not one possesses the slightest tie of common interest or of common feeling with us.*"

On the whole, subject to the chance of overlooking some less famous effort, this speech, with its companions at this session, may be fairly taken as Randolph's masterpiece, and warrants placing him in very high rank as a political leader. Grant that it is wicked and mischievous beyond all precedent even in his own mischievous career; that its effect must be to create the dangers which it foretold, and to bring the slave power into the peril which it helped to create: grant that it was in flagrant contradiction to his speeches on the Louisiana Purchase, his St. Domingo vote, and his outcry for an embargo; that it was inspired by hatred of Clay; that it related to a scheme of internal improvement which Mr. Jefferson himself had invented, and upon which he had once looked as upon the flower, the crown, the hope, and aspiration of his whole political system; that it was a deliberate, cold-blooded attempt to pervert the old and honorable principle of states' rights into a mere tool for the protection of negro slavery, which Randolph professed to think the worst of all earthly misfortunes; that it assumed, with an arrogance beyond belief, the settled purpose of the slave power to strain the Constitution in its own interests, and to block the government at its own will,—grant all this and whatever more may be required, still this speech is wonderfully striking. It startles, not merely by its own brightness, although this is intense, but by the very darkness which it makes visible.

Not content with laying down his new political principle for the union of slaveholders behind the barrier of state sovereignty, Randolph repeatedly returned to it, as was his custom when trying to impress a fear on men's minds. His speeches on the tariff at this session of 1824, considered as a mere extension of the speech on internal improvements, are full of astonishingly clever touches.

"We [of the South] are the eel that is being flayed, while the cookmaid pats us on the head and cries, with the clown in King Lear, 'Down, wantons, down!' " "If, under a power to regulate trade, you prevent exportation; if, with the most approved spring lancets, you draw the last drop of blood from our veins; if, *secundum artem*, you draw the last shilling from our pockets, what are the checks of the Constitution to us? A fig for the Constitution! When the scorpion's sting is probing us to the quick, shall we stop to chop logic? Shall we get some learned and cunning clerk to say whether the power to do this is to be found in the Constitution, and then, if he, from whatever motive, shall maintain the affirmative, shall we, like the animal whose fleece forms so material a portion of this bill, quietly lie down and be shorn?" "If, from the language I have used, any gentleman shall believe I am not as much attached to this Union as any one on this floor, he will labor under great mistake. But there is no magic in this word *union*. I value it as the means of preserving the liberty and happiness of the people. Marriage itself is a good thing, but the marriages of Mezentius were not so esteemed. The marriage of Sinbad the Sailor with the corpse of his deceased wife was an *union*; and just such an union will this be, if, by a bare majority in both Houses, this bill shall become a law."

This is very clever, keen, terse, vivacious; put in admirably simple and well-chosen English; and the discursions and digressions of the speaker were rather an advantage than a drawback in these running debates. Much of Randolph's best wit was in parentheses; many of his boldest suggestions were scattered in short, occasional comments. On the question of taxing coarse woolens, such as negroes wear, he thrust a little speech into the debate that was like a dagger in the very bowels of the South:—

"It is notorious that the profits of slave labor have been for a long time on the decrease, and that on a fair average it scarcely reimburses the expense of the slave, including the helpless ones, whether from infancy or age. The words of Patrick Henry in the Convention of Virginia still ring in my ears: 'They may liberate every one of your slaves. The Congress possess the power, and will exercise it.' Now, sir, the first step towards this consummation so devoutly wished by many is to pass such laws as may yet still further diminish the pittance which their labor yields to their unfortunate masters, to produce such a state of things as will insure, in case the slave shall not elope from his master, that his master will run away from him. Sir, the blindness, as it appears to me,—I hope gentlemen will pardon my expression,—with which a certain portion of this country—I allude particularly to the seaboard of South Carolina and Georgia—has lent its aid to increase the powers of the general government on points, to say the least, of doubtful construction, fills me with astonishment and dismay. And I look forward almost without a ray of hope to the time which the next census, or that which succeeds it, will assuredly bring forth, when this work of destruction and devastation is to commence in the abused name of humanity and religion, and when the imploring eyes of some will be, as now, turned towards another body, in the vain hope that it may arrest the evil and stay the plague."

On another occasion he is reported as saying of the people of the North, "We do not govern them by our black slaves, but by their own white slaves;" and again, with an amount of drastic effrontery which at that early day was peculiar to himself, "We know what we are doing. We of the South are united from the Ohio to Florida, and we can always unite; but you of the North are beginning to divide, and you will divide. We have conquered you once, and we can and will conquer you again. Ay, sir, we will drive you to the wall, and when we have you there once more we mean to keep you there, and will nail you down like base money."

What could be more effective than these alternate appeals to the pride and the terrors of a slave-owning oligarchy? Where among the most venemous whispers of Iago can be found an appeal to jealousy more infernal than some of those which Randolph made to his southern colleagues in the Senate?

"I know that there are gentlemen not only from the northern but from the southern States who think that this unhappy question—for such it is—of negro slavery, which the Constitution has vainly attempted to blink by not using the term, should never be brought into public notice, more especially into that of Congress, and most especially here. Sir, with every due respect for the gentlemen who think so, I differ from them *toto cœlo*. Sir, it is a thing which cannot be hid; it is not a dry rot, which you can cover with the carpet until the house tumbles about your ears; you might as well try to hide a volcano in full eruption; it cannot be hid; it is a cancer in your face."

After twisting this barb into the vitals of his slave-owning friends, he went on to say:—

"I do not put this question to you, sir; I know what your answer will be. I know what will be the answer of every husband, son, and brother throughout the southern States. I know that on this depends the honor of every matron and maiden,—of every matron, wife or widow, between the Ohio and the Gulf of Mexico. I know that upon it depends the life's blood of the little ones which are lying in their cradles in happy ignorance of what is passing around them; and not the white ones only,—for shall not we, too, kill?"

No man knew better how to play upon what he called the "chord which, when touched, even by the most delicate hand, vibrates to the heart of every man in our country." He jarred it till it ached. The southern people, far away from the scene of his extravagances, felt the hand so roughly striking their most sensitive nerve, and responded by the admiration that a tortured animal still shows for its master. They remembered his bold prophecies and startling warnings, his strong figures of speech, his homely and terse language. Many now learned to love him. His naturally irrepressible powers for mischief-making were never so admirably developed. He had at last got hold of a deep principle, and invented a far-reaching scheme of political action.

Circumstances favored him. The presidential election of 1824 ended in the House of Representatives. Mr. Clay controlled the result; he preferred J. Q. Adams to General Jackson; he caused Mr. Adams's election, and then, like the man of honor and courage that he was, he stood by the President he had made. Those readers who care for the details of this affair can find them in Mr. Parton's entertaining life of Andrew Jackson; here need only be said that Randolph saw his opportunity, and repeated against Clay and Adams the tactics he had used against Madison and Jefferson, but which he now used with infinitely more reason and better prospects of success. Randolph's opposition to both the Adamses was legitimate; if he hated this "American house of Stuart," as he called it, he had good grounds for doing so; if he despised J. Q. Adams, and consid-

ered him as mean a man for a Yankee as Mr. Madison
was for a Virginian, it was not for an instant imagined
or imaginable that either of the Yankee Presidents ever
entertained any other feeling than contempt for him;
they had no possible intellectual relation with such a
mind, but were fully prepared for his enmity, expected
it, and were in accord with Mr. Jefferson's opinion, in
1806, that it would be unfortunate to be embarrassed
with such a *soi-disant* friend. The warfare which Randolph at once declared against the administration of
J. Q. Adams was not only inevitable; it was, from many
points of view, praiseworthy, for it cannot be expected
that any one who has sympathy with Mr. Jefferson's
theories of government in 1801, unfashionable though
they are now, will applaud the theories of J. Q. Adams
in 1825. The two doctrines were, in outward appearance, diametrically opposite; and although that of Mr.
Adams, in sound accord with the practice if not with
the theories of Mr. Jefferson, seems to have won the
day, and though the powers of the general government
have been expanded beyond his utmost views, it is not
the business of a historian to deny that there was, and
still is, great force in the opposite argument.

Mr. Adams, however, stood somewhat too remote for
serious injury, and his position was, at best, too weak
to warrant much alarm on the part of Randolph and his
friends. Not Adams, but Clay, divided the South and
broke, by his immense popularity, the solid ranks of the
slaveholding, states'-rights democracy which Randolph
wished to organize. It was against Clay that the bitterest
effusions of Randolph's gall were directed, and to crush
the Kentuckian was the object of all his tactics. Mr.
Clay was Secretary of State, and could not reply to
the attacks made upon him in Congress, but he retali-
ated as he best could, and sustained a losing fight with
courage and credit.

Meanwhile Randolph, soured by what he considered
the neglect of his State, had not shown that attention to
his duties which is usually expected of members. He was
late in attending Congress, made long absences, and
even declined to serve at all from 1817 to 1819. Suddenly, on December 17, 1825, he was elected to the
Senate to fill a vacancy caused by the appointment of

James Barbour as Secretary of War to Mr. Adams. This election was a curious accident, for the true choice of the Virginian legislature was undoubtedly Henry St. George Tucker, Randolph's half-brother, and it was only his forbearance that gave Randolph a chance of success. The first vote stood: Tucker, 65; Randolph, 63; Giles, 58; Floyd, 40. According to the rule of the House, Floyd was then dropped, and the second ballot stood: Tucker, 87; Randolph, 79; Giles, 60. At each ballot 226 votes were cast. Mr. Tucker had, however, instructed his friends in no event to allow his name to come in direct competition with Randolph's, and accordingly when, on the third ballot, the contest was narrowed down to Tucker and Randolph, not only was the former name withdrawn, but 42 members abstained from voting at all. Randolph got 104 votes, not even a majority of the legislature, although Mr. Tucker's determination to withdraw, not announced till after the votes were deposited, was well known, and made the choice inevitable.

He took his seat immediately. Almost at the same moment President J. Q. Adams sent to the Senate nominations of two envoys to the proposed Congress of American nations at Panama. To this scheme of a great American alliance Mr. Clay was enthusiastically attached, but on its announcement every loose element of opposition in the Senate drew together into a new party, and Randolph once more found himself, as in 1800, hand in hand with that northern democracy which he had so many years reviled. In the place of Aaron Burr, New York was now led by Martin Van Buren, whose gentle touch moulded into one shape elements as discordant as Andrew Jackson and John C. Calhoun, Nathaniel Macon and Thomas H. Benton, John Randolph, James Buchanan, and William B. Giles.

On January 15, 1826, Mr. Van Buren began his campaign by moving to debate the President's confidential message in public. Randolph opposed the motion out of respect for the Prseident. He went back to the old stage tricks of his opposition to Madison. He was again descending to comedy. The scene was arranged beforehand, and he affected respect only in order that he might give more energy to his vehemence of contempt. Mr. Clay defied Van Buren's attack, and Randolph then gave rein to all his bitterness. On February 27, 1826, he wrote in delight at his success:—

"As to Van Buren and myself, we have been a little cool . . . He has done our cause disservice by delay in the hope of getting first Gaillard, then Tazewell . . . I was for action, knowing that delay would only give time for the poison of patronage to do its office. . . . But if he has not, others have poured 'the leprous distilment into the porches of mine ears.' The V. P. [Calhoun] has actually made love to me; and my old friend Mr. Macon reminds me daily of the old major who verily believed that I was a nonesuch of living men. In short, Friday's affair has been praised on all hands in a style that might have gorged the appetite of Cicero himself."

Intoxicated by the sense of old power returning to his grasp, Randolph now lashed on his own passions, until at length, in a speech which exhausted the unrivaled resources of his vocabulary in abusing the President and Secretary, after attributing to them every form of political meanness, he said, "I was defeated, horse, foot, and dragoons,—cup up and clean broke down by the coalition of Blifil and Black George,—by the combination, unheard of till then, of the Puritan with the blackleg." Not content with this, it is said that he went on to call Mr. Clay's progenitors to account for bringing into the world "this being, so brilliant yet so corrupt, which, like a rotten mackerel by moonlight, shined and stunk."

Not for this background abuse, but for certain insinuations against his truth, Mr. Clay called him out. Randolph had not meant to fight; his object was to break Clays' influence, not to kill him; his hatred was of the head, not of the heart;—but he could not refuse. Virginians would not have tolerated this course even in him. He had said to General Wilkinson in 1807, "I cannot descend to your level;" but he could not repeat it to Henry Clay without losing caste. On April 8, 1826, they exchanged shots, and Clay's second bullet pierced the folds of the white flannel wrapper which Randolph, with his usual eccentricity, wore on the field. Randolph threw away his second fire, and thereupon offered his hand, which Clay could not refuse to accept.

As for the President, his only revenge was one which went more directly to its aim than Mr. Clay's bullet, and fairly repaid the allusion to Blifil and Black George borrowed from Lord Chatham. Mr. Adams applied to Randolph the lines in which Ovid drew the picture of Envy:—

> "Pallor in ore sedet; macies in corpore toto;
> Pectora felle virent; lingua est suffusa veneno."

> His face is livid; gaunt his whole body;
> His breast is green with gall; his tongue drips poison.

With equal justice he might have applied more of Ovid's verses:—

> "Videt ingratos, intabescitque videndo,
> Successus hominum; carpitque et carpitur una;
> Suppliciumque suum est."

> He sees with pain men's good fortune,
> And pines in seeing; he taunts and is mocked at once;
> And is his own torture.

Thus Randolph organized the South. Calhoun himself learned his lesson from the speeches of this man, "who," said Mr. Vance of Ohio, in the House of Representatives, on January 29, 1828, "is entitled to more credit, if it is right that this administration should go down, for his efficiency in effecting that object than any three men in this nation." "From the moment he took his seat in the other branch of the legislature, he became the great rallying officer of the South." To array the whole slaveholding influence behind the banner of states' rights, and use centralization as the instrument of slavery; alternately to take the aggressive and the defensive, as circumstances should require, without seeming to quit the fortress of defense to throw loaded dice at every cast, and call, "Heads I win, tails you lose," at every toss,—this was what Randolph aimed at, and what he actually accomplished so far as his means would allow. The administration of Adams, a Puritan and an old federalist, who had the strongest love for American nationality, was precisely the influence needed to consolidate the slaveholding interest. Randolph converted Calhoun; after this conversion Clay alone divided the slave power, and Clay was to be crushed by fair means or foul. The campaign succeeded. Clay was crushed, and the slave power ruled supreme.

-⊰[XII]⊱-

"Faculties Misemployed"

RANDOLPH CERTAINLY became more sagacious with age, but he did not improve in political sagacity, alone. That his moral sense was lost may be true, for his mind had been dragged through one degradation after another, until its finer essence was destroyed; but in return it had gained from its very degradation a quality which at first it wanted. Randolph was a worse man than in his youth, but a better rhetorician. No longer heroic even in his own eyes, he could more coolly play the hero. His epigrammatic effects were occasionally very striking, especially on paper. He rose to what in a man of true character would have been great elevation of tone in his retort on Mr. McLane of Delaware. That member had said with perfect justice that he would not take Randolph's head if he were obliged to take his heart along with it.

"How easy, sir, would it be for me to reverse the gentleman's proposition, and to retort upon him that I would not, in return, take that gentleman's heart, however good it may be, if obliged to take such a head into the bargain! But, sir, I do not think this,—I never thought it,—and therefore I cannot be so ungenerous as to say it; for, Mr. Speaker, who made me a searcher of hearts? ... And, sir, if I should ever be so unfortunate, through inadvertence or the heat of debate, as to fall into such an error [as that which Mr. McLane had made in his argument], I should, so far from being offended, feel myself under obligation to any gentleman who would expose its fallacy even by ridicule,—as fair a weapon as any in the whole parliamentary armory. I shall not go so far as to maintain, with Lord Shaftesbury, that it is the un-

191

erring test of truth, whatever it may be of temper; but if it
be proscribed as a weapon as unfair as it confessedly is
powerful, what shall we say, I put it, sir, to you and to the
House, to the poisoned arrow? to the tomahawk and the
scalping-knife? Would the most unsparing use of ridicule
justify a resort to these weapons? Was this a reason that the
gentleman should sit in judgment on my heart? yes, sir, *my
heart!*—which the gentleman, whatever he may say in his
haert, believes to be a frank heart, as I trust it is a brave
heart! Sir, I dismiss the gentleman to his self-complacency,
—let him go,—yes, sir, let him go and thank his God that
he is not as *this* publican!"

This was the best of all Randolph's retorts, and remarkable for expression and temper. Unhappily for its
effect, it wanted an element which alone gives weight
to such a style of rhetoric. It was melodramatic, but
untrue. One may imagine with what quiet amusement
Mr. Jefferson, Mr. Madison, Mr. Monroe, Mr. Clay, not
to speak of a score of smaller victims like Gideon Granger, the poor clerk Vanzandt, and many an old member, must have smiled on reading this announcement
that Randolph's frank, brave heart repudiated the use
of the poisoned arrow, the tomahawk, and the scalping
knife. He was happier, because truer to himself, in the
more brutal forms of personal attack, as in turning on
Mr. Beecher of Ohio, who persisted in breaking his
long pauses by motions for the previous question: "Mr.
Speaker, in the Netherlands a man of small capacity,
with bits of wood and leather, will in a few moments
construct a toy that, with the pressure of the finger and
the thumb, will cry, 'Cuckoo! Cockoo!' With less of
ingenuity and inferior materials the people of Ohio have
made a toy that will, without much pressure, cry, 'Previous question, Mr. Speaker! Previous question, Mr.
Speaker!' " This must have been very effective as spoken with his shrill voice, and accented by his pointing
finger, but it may be doubted whether Randolph ever
produced much serious effect in the elevated style. His
most famous bit of self-exaltation was in the speech on
retrenchment and reform in 1828:—

"I shall retire upon my resources; I will go back to the
bosom of my constituents,—to such constituents as man

never had before, and never will have again; and I shall receive from them the only reward I ever looked for, but the highest that man can receive,—the universal expression of their approbation, of their thanks. I shall read it in their beaming faces, I shall feel it in their gratulating hands. The very children will climb around my knees to welcome me. And shall I give up them and this? And for what? For the heartless amusements and vapid pleasures and tarnished honors of this abode of splendid misery, of shabby splendor; for a clerkship in the war office, or a foreign mission, to dance attendance abroad instead of at home, or even for a department itself?"

If the criticism already made be just, that the reply to McLane was melodramatic but untrue, the same criticism applies with treble force to this famous appeal to his constituents. Without inquiring too deeply what the children in Charlotte County would have said to a suggestion of climbing Randolph's knee, or whether conflicting emotions could not be read on the beaming faces of his constituents, it is enough to add that there can be little doubt of Randolph's actual aberration of mind at this time. He talked quite wildly, and his acts had no relation with his language. This patriot would accept no tawdry honors from a corrupt and corrupting national government! He would not take a seat in the Cabinet, like Clay, to help trample on the rights of Virginia! He would not take a foreign mission, to pocket the people's money without equivalent! He owed everything to his constituents, and from them alone he would receive his reward! This speech was made in February, 1828. In September, 1829, he was offered and accepted a special mission to Russia; he sailed in June, 1830; remained ten days at his post; then passed near a year in England; and returning home in October, 1831, drew $21,407 from the government, with which he paid off his old British debt. This act of Roman virtue, worthy of the satire of Juvenal, still stands as the most flagrant bit of diplomatic jobbery in the annals of the United States government.

Had Randolph, at this period of his life, shown any respect for his own dignity, or had he even respected the dignity of Congress, he would have been a very formidable man, but he sacrificed his influence to an

irrational vanity. His best friends excused him on the
ground that he was partially insane; his enemies declared that this insanity was due only to drink; and perhaps a charitable explanation will agree with his own
belief that all his peculiarities had their source in an
ungovernable temper, which he had indulged until it led
him to the verge of madness. Be this as it may, certain
it is that his flashes of inspiration were obtained only
at a painful cost of time and power. During these last
years Randolph was like a jockey, thrown early out of
the race, who rides on, with antics and gesticulations,
amid the jeers and wonder of the crowd, towards that
winning-post which his old rivals have long since passed.
He despised the gaping clowns who applauded him, even
while he enjoyed amusing them. He despised himself,
perhaps, more than all the rest. Not once or twice only,
but day after day, and especially during his short senatorial term, he would take the floor, and, leaning or
lolling against the railing which in the old senate chamber surrounded the outer row of desks, he would talk
two or three hours at a time, with no perceptible reference to the business in hand, while Mr. Calhoun sat
like a statue in the Vice-President's chair, until the
senators one by one retired, leaving the Senate to adjourn without a quorum, a thing till then unknown to
its courteous habits; and the gallery looked down with
titters or open laughter at this exhibition of a half-
insane, half-intoxicated man, talking a dreary monologue,
broken at long intervals by passages beautiful in their
construction, direct in their purpose, and not the less
amusing from their occasional virulence. These long
speeches, if speeches they could be called, were never
reported. The reporters broke down in attempting to
cope with the rapid utterance, the discursiveness and in-
terminable length, the innumerable "Yes, sirs," and
"No, sirs," of these harangues. Mr. Niles printed in his
Register for 1826 one specimen verbatim report, merely
to show why no more was attempted. In the same volume, Mr. Niles gave an account of a visit he made to
the senate gallery on May 2, 1826, when Randolph was
talking. Lolling against the rail, stopping occasionally to
rest himself and think what next to talk about, he
rambled on with careless ease in conversational tones,
while the senate chamber was nearly empty, and the

imperturbable Calhoun patiently listened from his throne. Mr. Niles did not know the subject of debate, but when he entered the gallery Randolph was giving out a plan to make a bank:—

"Well, sir, we agree to make a bank. You subscribe $10,000, you $10,000, and you $10,000 or $20,000; then we borrow some rags, or make up the capital out of our own promissory notes. Next we buy an iron chest—for safety against fire and against thieves—but the latter was wholly unnecessary—who would steal our paper, sir? All being ready, we issue bills—I wish I had one of them [hunting his pockets as though he expected to find one]— like the Owl Creek bank, or Washington and Warren, black or red—I think, sir, they begin with 'I promise to pay'— yes, *promise* to pay, sir—promise to pay."

He dwelt upon this making of a bank for about five minutes, and then said something concerning Unitarians in religion and politics, making a dash at the administration, and bringing in Sir Robert Walpole. Then he spoke of the Bible, and expressed his disgust at what are called "family Bibles," though he thought no family safe without a Bible—but not an American edition. Those published by the Stationers Company of London ought only or chiefly to have authority, except those from the presses of the Universities of Oxford and Cambridge. He described these corporations briefly; they would be fined £10,000 sterling if they should leave the word *not* out of the seventh commandment, however convenient it might be to some or agreeable to others (looking directly at certain members, and half turning himself round to the ladies). He never bought an American edition of any book; he had no faith in their accuracy. He wished all his books to have Cadell's imprint,—Cadell, of the Strand, London. But people were liable to be cheated. He bought a copy of Aristotle's Ethics to present to a lady—to a lady, sir, who could understand them—yes, sir—and he found it full of errors, though it had Cadell's imprint—which he gave to be understood was a forgery. From the Bible he passed to Shakespeare, drubbing some one soundly for publishing a "family Shakespeare." He next jumped to the American "Protestant Episcopal Church," and disavowed all connection with it, declaring that he belonged to the Church of Old England; he had been baptized by a man regularly authorized by the bishop of London, who had laid his hands upon him (laying his own hands on the head of the gentleman next to him), and he spoke warmly of the bishop and of the priest. Then he quoted from the service, "Them that," as bad grammar. Suddenly he spoke about wine—it was often mentioned in the Bible, and he approved of drinking it—if in a gentlemanly way—at the table—not in the closet—not in the closet; but as to whiskey, he demanded that any one should show him the word in the Bible—it was not there—no, sir you can't find it in the whole book. Then he spoke of his land at Roanoke, saying that he held it by a *royal* grant. In a minute or two he was talking of the "men of Kent," saying that Kent had never been conquered by William the Norman, but had made terms with him. He spoke of a song on the men of Kent which he would give a thousand pounds to have written. All these subjects were discussed within the space of thirty-five minutes.

These illustrations of the almost incredible capacity for attitudinizing which belonged to Randolph's later career do not affect the fact that he discovered and mapped out from beginning to end a chart of the whole course on which the slave power was to sail to its destruction. He did no legislative work, sat on no committees, and was not remotely connected with any useful measure or idea; but he organized the slave power on strong and well-chosen ground; he taught it discipline, gave it popular cohesion, pointed out to it that it must break down Henry Clay, and, having taught his followers what to do, helped them to do it.

In this campaign, Randolph and his friends made but one strategical mistake, and it was one of which they were conscious. In order to pull down Adams and Clay, they were forced to set up Andrew Jackson, a man whom they knew to be unmanageable, despotic in temper and military in discipline. Meanwhile Randolph was defeated in his candidacy for reëlection to the Senate. Virginia could not tolerate his extravagances, and sent John Tyler to take his place. Deeply wounded, he was still consoled by the devotion of his district, which immediately returned him to his old seat in the House.

He was also a member of the constitutional convention of Virginia in 1829, and of course took the conservative side on the great questions it was called to consider. Broken to pieces by disease, and in the last stages of consumption, when President Jackson, amid the jeers of the entire country, offered him the mission to Russia, he accepted it, in order to remain in England about eighteen months. Of this journey, as of his other journeys, it is better to say as little as possible; they have no bearing on his political opinions or influence, and exhibit him otherwise in an unfavorable light. A warm admirer of everything English, nothing delighted him so much as attentions from English noblemen. He was impressed by the atmosphere of a court, and plumped down on his knees before the Empress of Russia, who was greatly amused, as well she might be, at his eccentric ideas of republican etiquette. Criticism infuriated him. "The barking of the curs against me in Congress," he wrote from London on February 19, 1831, "I utterly despise. I think I can see how some of them, if I were present, would tuck their tails between their hind legs, and slink—ay, and stink too!"

On his return home, in October, 1831, he hastened to Charlotte to make a speech in defense of his conduct as minister; but the subject which chiefly occupied his thoughts was the poverty, the dirt, the pride, and the degeneracy of Virginia, until he was roused to new life by the nullification excitement which his own doctrines, now represented by Mr. Calhoun, were stirring up in South Carolina and Georgia.

Jackson's administration had displeased him from the start, but so long as he wore its livery his tongue had been tied. Now, however, when South Carolina raised the standard of resistance, and refused obedience to an act of Congress, Randolph was hot in his applause. He felt that the days of 1798 had returned. He wanted to fight with her armies in case of war. When the President's famous proclamation, "the ferocious and bloodthirsty proclamation of our Djezzar," appeared, he was beside himself with rage. "The apathy of our people is most alarming," he wrote. "If they do not rouse themselves to a sense of our condition and put down this wretched old man, the country is irretrievably ruined. The mercenary troops who have embarked for Charleston have not disappointed me. They are working in their vocation, poor devils! *I trust that no quarter will be given to them.*" Weak and dying as he was, he set out to rouse Virginia, and spoke in several counties against Jackson, as he had spoken against John Adams. Nullification, he said, was nonsense. He was no nullifier, but he would not desert those whose interests were identical with his own. One of the touches in these harangues is very characteristic of the taste and temper of this *ami des noirs*:—

"There is a meeting-house in this village, built by a respectable denomination. I never was in it, though, like myself, it is mouldering away. The pulpit of that meeting-house was polluted by permitting a black African to preach in it. If I had been there, I would have taken the uncircumcised dog by the throat, led him before a magistrate, and committed him to jail. I told the ladies, they, sweet souls, who dressed their beds with the whitest sheets and uncorked for him their best wine, were not far from having negro children."

He forced a set of states'-rights resolutions down the throat of his country, driving poor Captain Watkins and the other malcontents out of his presence. Nevertheless, the President's proclamation remained and the force bill stood on the statute book,—first-fruits of Randolph's attempt to maintain the slave power by a union of slaveholders behind the bulwark of states' rights; while the next was the elevation of Henry Clay to a position more powerful than ever, as arbiter between the South and the North.

Anxious to get back to England, where he hoped, by aid of climate, to prolong his existence, Randolph started again for Europe; but, seized by a last and fatal attack on his lungs, he died in Philadelphia, May 24, 1833. Of his deathbed, it is as well not to attempt a description. It was grotesque—like his life. During the few days of his last illness his mind was never quite itself, and there can be no pleasure or profit in describing the expiring irrational wanderings of a brain never too steady in its processes. His remains were taken to Virginia, and buried at Roanoke. His will was the subject of a contest in the courts, which produced a vast quantity of curious evidence in regard to his character, and at last a verdict from the jury that in the later years of his life he was not of sane mind. It is, perhaps, difficult to draw any precise line between eccentricity and insanity, but it is still more difficult to understand how the jury could possibly have held the will of 1821, which emancipated his slaves, to be a saner document than that of 1832, which did not.

The question of his sanity has greatly troubled his biographers. He himself called his "unprosperous life the fruit of an ungovernable temper." So far as his public speeches are concerned, there is no apparent proof that he was less sane in 1831 than in 1806, except that he was weakened by age, excesses, and disease. Nevertheless, it seems to be certain that, on several occasions, he was distinctly irresponsible; his truest friends, the Tuckers, thought so, and the evidence supports them; but whether this condition of mind was anything more than the excitement due to over-indulgence of temper and appetite is a question for experts to decide. Neither sickness nor suffering, however, is an excuse for habitual want of self-restraint. Myriads of other men have suffered as much without showing it in brutality or bitterness, and he himself never in his candid moments pretended to defend his errors: "Time misspent, and faculties misemployed, and senses jaded by labor or impaired by excesses, cannot be recalled."

Notes on the Text

The following are matters of minor errors or questions of interpretation of interest chiefly to specialists in the field. The numbers refer to pages in the text.

Page 19. Bacon's Rebellion occurred in 1676, not 1675. Perhaps this is a typographical error that slipped by the proof-
readers.

Page 21. Adams has confused Benedict Arnold's incursion
into Virginia with the more serious invasion by Lord Cornwallis in 1781, from which Banastre Tarleton was detailed to catch
Governor Jefferson. One will rarely find historians who com-
pare Jefferson to a "tired fox."

Page 52. "The still greater absurdities of leading federalists" is
vague in the extreme. Here Adams seems to suggest his entire
agreement with the Jeffersonian propaganda against the Federalists as crypto-monarchists, a view that is hardly sustained
throughout his writings.

Pages 68–70. It may be worth mentioning here that the idea
that initially worried President Jefferson, that the Louisiana
Purchase had no warrant in the Constitution, may itself be
absurd; most of Jefferson's closest friends urged him not to
worry about the matter. One can hardly guess how seriously to
take Henry Adams's solemn treatment of the idea; if Jefferson
had advanced a constitutional amendment as he had originally
proposed, he would have declared to the world that he had
sinned against the Constitution, and, perhaps worse, run up
against something quite explicit in the Constitution: laws cannot be enforced *ex post facto.* Would that not also apply to
amendments?

Page 96. The Federalist Party, "whose leaders were . . . preparing for the dissolution of the Union": again, Henry Adams is wonderfully vague. A few New Englanders and New Yorkers did talk about secession in the wake of the Louisiana Purchase; they actually caused less stir than several honest southerners who talked about secession in 1798–99. In any case it is important to note that, first, in the early years of the United States, various parts of the Union considered the advantages of breaking away from time to time; and second, any informed list of the major leaders of the Federalist Party in 1804 would find only one man, and he not in the first rank, suggesting disunion—Timothy Pickering of Massachusetts. Alexander Hamilton, Charles C. Pinckney, John Marshall, William Pinkney, and even George Cabot of Massachusetts—to name a few—were still devoted to the Union, though not to Mr. Jefferson. Adams is here engaging in the familiar ploy of identifying a whole party by one extremist wing.

Page 100. Here, untypically, Adams relaxes his usual caution on behalf of his family, and praises his ancestor in a particularly unpleasant way as one "whose capacity for expressing contempt was exceeded only by his right to feel it."

Page 105. The Supreme Court was never impregnable, and John Marshall lived to see one of his judgments—in *Worcester v. Georgia*—ignored by a defiant state and a hostile President Jackson.

Page 141. "The treaty was indeed a very bad one." In fact, very few histories of the early United States say anything about the contents of the treaty James Monroe and William Pinkney of Maryland had forged in 1806 with the only British ministry inclined toward friendship with the United States during Jefferson's terms. In one very important respect—the indirect carrying trade to Europe—the Monroe-Pinkney Treaty was better than Jay's Treaty, which John and John Quincy Adams had supported in the 1790s, and whose terms were respected by President Jefferson until their expiration in 1805, much to the profit of the United States. See Donald R. Hickey, "The Monroe-Pinkney Treaty: A Reappraisal," *William and Mary Quarterly*, 3rd ser., 44 (January 1987): 65–88. What was arguably most remarkable about Monroe and Pinkney's treaty project was that President Jefferson declined to send it to or discuss it with the Senate. It is surely untrue that the treaty had much to do with the fortunes of the Old Republicans as distinct from all other Americans, but its rejection in the brave hope of a much better one certainly carried the United States closer to war.

Pages 190 and 198. It is impossible to believe both that Henry Clay was "crushed" in 1828 and then was in "a position more powerful than ever" in 1832–33. His fortunes were nowhere near so low in the first instance, nor so high in the second. It was, after all, John Quincy Adams who lost the presidential election of 1828, clearing the way for Clay's candidacy four years later. If Henry Clay served the Union in helping to compromise over the tariff and avoid armed conflict during the Nullification Crisis, he was doing so only after losing a presidential contest which he had entertained strong hopes of winning.

Finally, one should note an action of John Randolph's that Henry Adams should have mentioned but did not. In 1803 Randolph wrote a committee report rejecting a petition from the Indiana territorial legislature asking for a suspension of Article Six of the Northwest Ordinance for a few years; in other words, they wished to introduce slavery into the territory. Obviously at that time Randolph believed that the provision of the Northwest Ordinance prohibiting slavery was both constitutional and sound policy; he urged the citizens of Indiana Territory (which then included the Illinois country), to count the absence of slavery as a positive blessing, and predicted, truly as it turned out, that the area would achieve population and prosperity more quickly with a free labor system. Indiana Territory used the subterfuge of an indentured servant law to introduce slavery anyway, but within a few years Indiana and then Illinois voted slavery out, whether explicit or in disguise.

Related Documents

1

From Randolph's speech in the House of Representatives, opposing a report recommending that the regular army be increased by ten thousand men, along with other preparations for war, November 1811. Henry Adams was not the only historian or biographer to note that Randolph, in his last years, often strayed far from the topics before the House and Senate in his long, rambling, and impromptu speeches. But in the following passages one finds an immense fund of allusion and reference, astonishing if altogether spontaneous and unprepared, and, if one has the patience to follow, quite relevant to the broad subject of preparing the United States for war.

On what ground, I have been, and still am, unable to see, [the Select Committee on Foreign Relations] have felt themselves authorized (when the subject was before another committee) to recommend the raising of standing armies, with a view (as has been declared) of immediate war—a war not of defence, but of conquest, of aggrandizement, of ambition—a war foreign to the interests of this country, to the interests of humanity itself.

I know not how gentlemen, calling themselves republicans, can advocate such a war. What was their doctrine in 1798–9, when the command of the army, that highest of all possible trusts in any government, be the form what it may, was reposed in the bosom of the Father of his country! the sanctuary of a nation's love!, the only hope that never came in vain? When other worthies of the revolution, Hamilton, Pinckney, and the younger Washington, men of tried patriotism, of approved conduct and valor, of untarnished honor, held subordinate command under him? Republicans were then unwilling to trust a standing army even to his hands who had given proof that he was above all human temptation. Where now is the revolutionary hero to whom you are about to confide this sacred trust? To whom will you confide the charge of leading the flower of our youth to the heights of Abraham [Quebec]? Will you find him in the person of an acquitted felon [General James Wilkinson]? What! *Then* you were unwilling to vote an army, when such men as have been named held high command! when Washington himself was at the head. Did you *then* show such reluctance, feel such scruples? and are you now nothing loth, fearless of every consequence? Will you say that your provocations were less then than now, when your direct commerce was interdicted, your ambassadors hooted with derision from the French court, tribute demanded, actual war waged upon you? Those who opposed the army then, were, indeed, denounced as the partisans of France, as the same men, some of them at least, are now held up as the advocates of England; those firm and undeviating republicans, who then dared, and now dare, to cling to the ark of the Constitution, to defend it even at the expense of their fame rather than surrender themselves to the wild projects of mad ambition! There is a fatality, Sir, attending plenitude of power. Soon or late, some mania seizes upon its possessors; they fall from the dizzy height, through the giddiness of their own heads. Like a vast estate, heaped up by the labor and industry of one man which seldom survives the third generation, power gained by patient assiduity, by a faithful and regular discharge of its attendant duties, soon gets above its own origin. Intoxicated with their own greatness, the federal party fell. Will not the same causes produce the same effects now as then? Sir, you may raise this army, you may build up this vast structure of patronage, this mighty apparatus of favoritism; but "lay not the flattering unction to your souls"; you will never live to enjoy the succession; you sign your political death warrant. . . .

I am not surprised at the war-spirit which is manifesting itself in gentlemen from the South. In the year 1805–6, in a struggle for the carrying-trade of belligerent colonial produce, this country was most unwisely brought into collision with the great powers of Europe. By a series of most impolitic and ruinous measures, utterly incomprehensible to every rational, sober-minded man, the Southern planters, by their own votes, succeeded in knocking down the price of cotton to seven cents, and of tobacco (a few choice crops excepted) to nothing, and in raising the price of blankets (of which a few would not be amiss in a Canadian campaign), coarse woollens, and every article of first necessity, three or four hundred per cent. And, now that by our own acts we have brought ourselves into this unprecedented condition, we must get out of it in any way but by an acknowledgment of our own want of wisdom and forecast. But is war the true remedy? Who will profit by it? Speculators; a few lucky merchants who draw prizes in the lottery; commissaries and contractors. Who must suffer by it? The people. It is their blood, their taxes, that must flow to support it. . . .

I am gratified to find gentlemen acknowledging the demoralizing and destructive consequences of the non-importation law; confessing the truth of all that its opponents foretold when it was enacted; and will you plunge yourselves in war because you have passed a foolish and ruinous law, and are ashamed to repeal it? "But our good friend, the French Emperor, stands in the way of its repeal," and, as we cannot go too far in making sacrifices to him, who has given such demonstration of his *love for the Americans,* we must, in point of fact, become parties to his war. "Who can be so cruel as to refuse him this favor?" My imagination shrinks from the miseries of such a connection. I call upon the House to reflect whether they are not about to abandon all reclamation for the unparalleled outrages, "insults and injuries" of the French Government; to give up our claim for plundered millions, and ask what reparation or atonement we can expect to obtain in hours of future dalliance, after we shall have made a tender of our person to this great deflowerer of the virginity of republics. We have, by our own wise (I will not say *wiseacre*) measures, so increased the trade and wealth of Montreal and Quebec that, at last, we begin to cast a wistful eye at Canada. Having done so much towards its improvement, by the exercise of our "restrictive energies," we begin to think the laborer worthy of his hire, and to put in claim for our portion. Suppose it ours, are we any nearer our point? As his minister said to the King of Epirus, "May we not as well take our bottle of wine before as after this exploit?" Go! march to Canada! Leave the broad bosom of the Chesapeake, and her hundred tributary rivers, the whole line of sea-coast, from Machias to St. Mary's, unprotected! You have taken Quebec—have you *conquered England?* Will you seek for the deep foundations of her power in the frozen deserts of Labrador?

> "Her march is on the mountain wave,
> Her home is on the deep!"

Will you call upon her to leave your ports and harbors untouched, only just till you can return from Canada to defend them? The coast is to be left defenceless, whilst men of the interior are revelling in conquest and spoil. But grant for a moment, for mere argument's sake, that in Canada you would touch the sinews of her strength, instead of removing a clog upon her resources—an incumbrance, but one, which, from a spirit of honor, she will vigorously defend. In what situation would you then place some of the best men of the nation? As Chatham [William Pitt the Elder] and [Edmund] Burke, and the whole band of her patriots prayed for [Britain's] defeat in 1776, so must some of the truest friends to the country deprecate the success of our arms against the only power that holds in check the arch enemy of mankind. . . .

What, Sir, is the situation of the slaveholding States? During the war of the Revolution, so fixed were their habits of subordination, that when the whole Southern country was overrun by the enemy, who invited them to desert, no fear was ever entertained of an insurrection of the slaves. During the war of seven years, with our country in possession of the enemy, no such danger was ever apprehended. But should we therefore be unobservant spectators of the progress of society within the last twenty years? Of the silent but powerful change wrought by time and chance upon its composition and temper? When the fountains of the great deep of abomination were broken up, even the poor slaves did not escape the general deluge. The French revolution polluted even them. Nay, there were not wanting men in that House—witness their legislative Legendre, the butcher who once held a seat there, to preach upon that floor these imprescriptible rights to a crowded audience of blacks in the galleries; teaching them that they were equal to their masters; in other words, advising them to cut their throats. Similar doctrines are disseminated by peddlers from New England and elsewhere throughout the Southern country, and masters have been found so infatuated as by their lives and conversation, by a general contempt of order, morality, and religion, unthinkingly to cherish those seeds of self-destruction to them and their families. What is the consequence? Within the last ten years, repeated alarms of insurrection among the slaves, some of them awful indeed. From the spreading of this infernal doctrine, the whole Southern country has been thrown into a state of insecurity. Men, dead to the operation of moral causes, have taken away from the poor slave his habits of loyalty and obedience to his master, which lightened his servitude by a double operation; beguiling his own cares, and disarming his master's suspicions and severity; and now, like true empirics in politics, you are called upon to trust to the mere physical strength of the fetter which holds him in bondage. You have deprived him of all moral restraint; you have tempted him to eat of the tree of knowledge; just enough to perfect him in wickedness; you have opened his eyes to his nakedness; you have armed his nature against the hand that has fed, that has clothed, him; that has cherished him in sickness; that hand which, before he became a pupil of your school, he had been accustomed to press with respectful affection. You have done all this, and then show him the gibbet and the wheel, as incentives to a sullen, repugnant obedience. God forbid, Sir, that the Southern States should ever see an enemy on their shores, with these infernal principles of French fraternity in the van. While talking of taking Canada, some of us are shuddering for our own safety at home. I speak from facts when I say that the night-bell never tolls for fire in Richmond that the mother does not hug the infant more closely to her bosom. I have been a witness of some of the alarms in the capital of Virginia. . . . [Randolph was in Richmond in 1800 when the conspiracy of Gabriel was discovered and its supposed ringleaders arrested, shortly before a wholesale massacre was to begin.]

[From William Cabell Bruce, *John Randolph of Roanoke* (New York: Putnam's, 1922), vol. 1, pp. 372–77.]

2

From Randolph's speech in the Virginia Constitutional Convention of 1829, opposing the disfranchisement of certain freeholders. Here, near the end of his life, Randolph was perhaps as lucid and cogent as ever in his career. The issue before the convention elicited his conservatism in that he was once again opposing change, but he was also defending a class of men quite different from his own.

I believe that I shall hardly be contradicted, when I state that the great moving cause, which led to this Convention, has been the regulation of the Right of Suffrage. After all the out-cry that has been raised on the subject, judge my surprise, when I found that a proposition coming from the Legislative Committee, and which extends the Right of Suffrage almost *ad infinitum,* to many classes of persons within the Commonwealth, contained a blow at the elective franchise of the freeholder, the present sovereign of this land. We are met to extend the Right of Suffrage; nobody can tell how far under the out-cry that it is *too much* restricted, and the very first step we take, is to restrict it *still further, quoad* the freeholder. Do gentlemen suppose the freeholders will be blind to this? What becomes of all the considerations of philanthropy of which we have heard so much? What becomes of all the gentlemen's abstractions? Sir, the only good I ever knew these abstractions to do, is to abstract money out of the pockets of one great division of the country, to put it into the pockets of another, a species of abstraction the least of all others to my taste.

Sir, I demand, as a freeholder, in behalf of the freeholders, on what plea you are to put them, and them only, to the ban of this Convention. Other and larger classes of persons are selected to be drawn within the range of the elective privilege, while the poorer classes of the freeholders are to be disfranchised. So, after all, this great and illustrious Assembly are met to make war on the poorer classes of the freeholders of the Commonwealth. You are not only to extend rights, but you are to take away the rights, the vested rights, of a large and respectable, however they may be a poor, class of your fellow-citizens. Sir, I will never consent to deprive the freeholder of his rights, however trivial in the view of assessors or patricians, his humble shed may appear. I saw this measure in the Legislative Committee, and I thought I saw, what I think I see now, (here Mr. R. pointed with his finger), a snake in the grass. I will never consent to be the agent in taking away from any man the Right of Suffrage he now enjoys.

[From Russell Kirk, *John Randolph of Roanoke* (Indianapolis, IN: Liberty Press, 1978), pp. 534–35.]

3

One of John Randolph's many letters to young relatives. Here Randolph proves his thorough knowledge of and sympathies with the classical virtues which mature men and women labored to instill in children and youths from classical antiquity up to the nineteenth century.

Indeed, this independence, which is so much vaunted, and which young people think consists in doing what they please, when they grow up to man's estate (with as much justice as the poor negro thinks liberty consists in being supported in idleness by other people's labour)—this independence is but a name. Place us where you will; along with our rights there must co-exist correlative duties, and the more exalted the station, the more arduous are these last. Indeed, as the duty is precisely correspondent to the power, it follows that the richer, the wiser, the more powerful a man is, the greater is the obligation upon him to employ his gifts in lessening the sum of human misery; and this employment constitutes happiness, which the weak and wicked vainly imagine to consist in wealth, finery, or sensual gratification. Who so miserable as the bad Emperor of Rome? Who more happy than Trajan and Antoninus? Look at the fretful, peevish, rich man, whose senses are as much jaded by attempting to embrace too much gratification as the limbs of the poor post-horse are by incessant labor. . . . Habit is truly called "second nature." To form good habits is almost as easy as to fall into bad. What is the difference between an industrious, sober man and an idle drunken one, but their respective habits? . . . Remember that *labour is necessary to excellence.* This is an eternal truth, although vanity cannot be brought to believe, or indolence to heed it. I am deeply interested in seeing you turn out a respectable man, in every point of view; and, as far as I could, have endeavoured to furnish you with the means of acquiring knowledge and correct principles, and manners, at the same time. Self-conceit, and indifference are unfriendly, in an equal degree, to the attainment of knowledge, or the forming of an amiable character. The first is more offensive, but does not more completely mar all excellence than the last; and it is truly deplorable that both flourish in Virginia, as if it were their native soil. A petulant arrogance, or supine, listless indifference, marks the character of too many of our young men. They early assume airs of manhood; and these premature men remain children for the rest of their lives. Upon the credit of a smattering of Latin, drinking grog, and chewing tobacco, these striplings set up for legislators and statesmen; and seem to deem it derogatory from their manhood to treat age and experience with any degree of deference. They are loud, boisterous, over-bearing, and dictatorial: profane in speech, low and obscene in their pleasures. In the tavern, the stable, or the gaming-house, they are at home; but, placed in the society of *real* gentlemen and men of letters, they are awkward and uneasy; in all situations, they are contemptible. . . . The blind pursuit of wealth, for the sake of hoarding, is a species of insanity. There are spirits, and not the least worthy, who, content with an humble mediocrity, leave the field of wealth and ambition open to more active, perhaps more guilty, competitors. Nothing can be more respectable than the independence that grows out of self-denial. The man who, by abridging his wants, can find time to devote to the cultivation of his mind, or the aid of his fellow-creatures, is a being far above the plodding sons of industry and gain. His is a spirit of the noblest order.

[From Bruce, *John Randolph,* vol. 2, pp. 478–82.]

Index

213

About the Editor

Robert McColley is Professor of History at the University of Illinois. He is coeditor (with Barbara M. Posadas) of *Refracting America*, vol. 1: *Gender, Race, Ethnicity, and Environment in American History to 1877* (1993); editor of *Federalists, Republicans, and Foreign Entanglements* (1969); and author of *Slavery and Jeffersonian Virginia* (1964; rev. ed., 1973). He is currently on the editorial board of *The Virginia Magazine of History and Biography,* and regularly reviews classical compact discs for *Fanfare: The Magazine for Serious Record Collectors.*